T0366993

STAGING CHEKHOV: CHERRY ORCHARD

A tribute to Yuri Zavadski

Actor and Director
for Stanislavski

by
John D. Mitchell

Foreword
by
Norris Houghton

Cover photo by Frederick Rolf

Published by
Institute for Advanced Studies in the Theatre Arts
Press
in association with
Florida Keys Community College

First Edition

Copyright 1991 by Institute for Advanced Studies
in the Theatre Arts (IASTA)

All rights reserved, including the right of reproduction, in whole or in
part, in any form or by any means, electronic or mechanical, including
photocopying, recording, or by any information storage and retrieval
system, without permission in writing from the publisher. Inquiries
should be addressed to IASTA, 12 West End Avenue, Suite 304, New
York, NY 10023.

LCN 91-073015

Printed in the United States of America

All rights reserved. This play may not be acted, read aloud to an
audience, broadacast, televised, performed or presented in any way, as
a whole or in part without permission. Inquiries should be addressed
to IASTA, 12 West End Avenue, Suite 304, New York, NY 10023.

"The goal of art is most profound . . . the director must know how to embody all the actor's experiences in the living artistic image, using the play's material and the actor's professional qualities. Also, for a fine artist knowledge of the system is not enough. It is not enough to know how to live your role on the stage. You must have a strong, well-trained voice of pleasant - or, in any case - expressive timbre, perfect diction, a plasticity of movement - without being a *poseur* - a face that is beautiful and mobile, a good figure, and expressive hands."[1]

— Constantin Stanislavski

1   Gorchakov, Nikolai M. **Stanislavski Directs**. Foreword by Norris Houghton, translation by Miriam Goldina. New York: Limelight Edition, 1985.

DEDICATION

To

Gala Ebin, as one of the founders of IASTA

and

**Mrs. Alexis Afan, my teacher for Conversational
Russian at the Berlitz School of Languages,
New York City.**

TABLE OF CONTENTS

FOREWORD

by

Norris Houghton

As every student of world literature knows, Anton Chekhov's first major play, **Seagull**, was virtually laughed off the stage at its first presentation in 1896 in St. Petersburg. Today, that trio of his works which followed — **Uncle Vanya**, **Three Sisters**, **Cherry Orchard** — together with a reappraisal of **Seagull**, lifted him through the subsequent half-century from being a laughing stock to a position alongside George Bernard Shaw as the greatest dramatist of the age.

The name of Konstantin Stanislavski became simultaneously almost equally well-known as the supreme interpreter of Chekhov's works at the Moscow Art Theatre, which produced them all under Stanislavski's direction. Indeed, the director created a "system" of acting technique especially devised to reveal Chekhov's unique and subtle brand of realism, with its "subtext" that, in turn, led to truth.

Along the way, the Moscow Art Theatre developed a series of offshoots, the second and probably the most significant of which (after the one headed by the playwright's nephew Michael) was the Studio of Yevgenny Vakhtangov, created in the early 1900's. Vakhtangov led his group of young actors slightly away from the Stanislavski system in the direction of fusing psychological truth with heightened artistic stylization.

One of this group of young actors, whose early grounding was in Stanislavski's Art Theatre, and who became a founding member of the Vakhtangov Theatre, was Yuri Zavadski. After the untimely death of his mentor, Zavadski drew some of the actors from the Vakhtangov group into a theatre of his own, which he called the Mossoviet.

Zavadski came to New York in 1960 under the State Department's reciprocal exchange program, at the invitation of John D. Mitchell, to work on a production of **Cherry Orchard** at the Institute for Advanced Studies in the Theatre Arts (IASTA); I went to Moscow shortly thereafter in the same reciprocal program.

Before I went, however, it was my privilege to watch Zavadski at work with young American artists on Chekhov's great play and to listen to him deliver lectures at 11 pm, after the theatre, to a public largely composed of American performers eager to hear, if not actively to participate in rehearsals, with the great successor to Stanislavski and Vakhtangov. It was, then, a rich gift that IASTA made to American theatre folk, one which now is carried forward in the ensuing pages.

*Gala Ebin, IASTA founder and Russian translator, with Yuri Zavadski during rehearsals of **Cherry Orchard** .*

ACKNOWLEDGMENTS

I wish to express a very real sense of indebtedness to Gala Ebin, one of the initial five founders of the Institute for Advanced Studies in the Theatre Arts. As close associate to Yuri Zavadski, she passionately and faithfully interpreted his directions to his American cast for **Cherry Orchard**. Likewise, she painstakingly translated his lectures and his interviews. I choose to quote from her - the verbatim quotations are accurate insofar as these were the actual words heard and understood by the cast. The ideas expressed are complete and pure Zavadski. The English wording may reflect the pressure of fast, oral simultaneous translation, rather than Mr. Zavadski's own flowing style." Gala was ever modest, for her command of her first language, Russian, as well as English, was ever impressive.

I cannot resist adding that at first Gala resisted our Chekhov production being **Cherry Orchard**. Staff meetings became stormy as Gala fought for Chekhov's **Uncle Vanya** as our third Institute production. She saw in that play roles for the older actresses who had been so committed to the Institute. Correspondence with Yuri Zavadski tipped the scales for **Cherry Orchard**. From that moment Gala's loyalty and commitment to the production of **Cherry Orchard** was total.

As will be seen later in the introduction, it would be solely the very questionable value of hindsight to say that **Cherry Orchard** was the better choice over **Uncle Vanya** since Zavadski firmly legislated that he would work with one cast only, and that a cast of relatively young professional American actors.

In many ways the New York cast of actors in Yuri Zavadski's **Cherry Orchard** contributed to the realization of this book. They were: Bill Berger, Stephen A. Daley, Joy Dillingham, Margaret Draper, Annette Hunt, Graham Jarvis, Elena Karam, Niels Miller, Patricia Peardon, Frederick Rolf, Robert Stattel, and Eugene Wood.

Many thanks to George Drew, who designed the stage sets for the New York production of **Cherry Orchard**. It is appropriate as well to list for thanks those who made the technical aspects of the rehearsals and the performances run smoothly: Jacques Chwat, Cece Drew, George Drew, Christine Edwards, Albert L. Gibson, Morgan James, Walt Sonnenburg, Patricia Tunder, and Svetlana Vasily.

Happily, I had meetings in London, England, 1964 when Yuri Zavadski had been invited to England as part of the worldwide celebration of the four-hundredth birthday celebration for William Shakespeare. These conversations prompted a revival in 1965 of Yuri Zavadski's **Cherry Orchard** as part of the International Classic Theatre Festival in Denver, Colorado. I quote from the program:

"Dr. Mitchell's production of **Cherry Orchard** is inspired by Yuri Zavadski's work at IASTA in 1960 on Acts I and IV. For the total *mise-en-scene*, he is indebted to his observations of rehearsals at the Moscow Art Theatre under Victor Stanitsyn, currently the director for the MXAT production of **Cherry Orchard**. This past February, at the time the Moscow Art Theatre performed in New York, Mr. Stanitsyn visited IASTA, and he and

Dr. Mitchell continued their discussions regarding this current production of **Cherry Orchard**."

The Denver cast of actors for **Cherry Orchard** were: Peter Blaxill, Armand Coullet, Stephen Daley, Michael Durrell, Jack Eddleman, Deborah Gordon, Muriel Higgins, Tom Keo, Bill Martin, Miriam Mitchell, Roger Stewart Newman, Miriam Porter, Eric Tavares, William Whedbee, and Elaine Winters.

It is difficult to single out any one member of the Institute for Advanced Studies in the Theatre Arts' professional actors for praise and acknowledgment. An impressive number of actors repeatedly sought a *stretch* in the Institute productions. However, Eric Tavares, singularly, would seem to have set a record by being in more than 18 of IASTA's New York and Festival productions. His strength at first seemed uniquely comedic, and then, with the challenging role of Bosola in John Webster's **The Duchess of Malfi**, he demonstrated a versatility which has been on show ever since in his acting career.

I wish to acknowledge certain friends, family and colleagues who have contributed to this book. Some distantly in time were involved in making Yuri Zavadski's production of **Cherry Orchard** a reality; some very recently provided encouragement that this be a book, a tribute to him. Among them are Michel Saint-Denis; Cultural Officer Nathan Tuch of the American Embassy, Moscow; Robert Epstein; Robert Whitehead and Robert Dowling; Russell and Mimi Porter of the University of Denver; my assistant for the Denver Festival production Tom Keo; William A. Seeker, President, and Nelson Reed, Business Manager, both of the Florida Keys Community College; the late C. George Willard; Dr. Mary W. John; Pegge Abrams of Duke University; Mary Jean Parsons; Christine Edwards, my wife Mimi and my children John Daniel, Lorenzo, and Barbarina, as well as their spouses.

Special thanks are due to Alan Upchurch for his collaboration on our translation of Chekhov's **Cherry Orchard**. Special thanks as well to Frederick Rolf and to Margaret Draper for providing photographs of Yuri Zavadski's **Cherry Orchard**. Frederick Rolf as well, caught the charisma of Mr. Zavadski as he directed his American actors at the Institute, and thanks as well to George Drew for his assistance with the mise-en-scene drawings for this book.

Francine Douwes, who designed and typeset **Staging Chekhov: Cherry Orchard** using the latest computer technology, and Gil Forman of IASTA have been steadfast in their collaborative efforts with me and with their unfailing enthusiasm for the book. I wish to especially thank Paula Downey for her enthusiasm and for her excellent work in preparing this manuscript as well as previous ones, and thanks are also due to Elena Baranova for typing the Russian portion of the book as well as for additional translation.

Thanks are due to the Blue Hill, Maine Public Library and to the Monroe County Public Library in Key West, Florida for their cheerfully enabling me to use their facilities.

It seems appropriate for me to close acknowledgments with thanks to all the theatre professionals who sought insights at **Cherry Orchard** rehearsals and from watching, at work, a master director such as Yuri Zavadski who acted with and directed for Constantin Stanislavski.

INTRODUCTION

Yuri Zavadski directing a rehearsal of Act One, with Bill Berger as **Lopakhin** *and Robert Stattel as* **Trofimov.**

INTRODUCTION

by

John D. Mitchell

MOSCOW: 1959

A rapping at the door of our room at the National Hotel prompted me to ask myself, "Who could that be? No one has courage to come above the lobby floor to visit a foreigner!" I opened the door. There stood a tall, fur-hatted Russian. It was February, and it had been snowing heavily. He removed his *shapka* (Russian for this type of hat) and revealed a well-shaped bald head.

"*Allo*, John Mitchell," said the man unknown to me, his bright eyes twinkling. "*Merci pour vos lettres.*" It dawned on me here was Yuri Zavadski; as Michel Saint-Denis had advised, we'd corresponded these past months in French. I ushered him in at once.

Within moments of that first meeting I was struck by the charisma of that aristocratic gentleman, Mr. Z, as our American actors later came to refer to him.

In French he urged we stick to French. "*J'ai oublié l'anglais que je parlais autrefois.*" He explained that he'd forgotten speaking English through lack of use during World War II. "Shakespeare," he went on to say, "is one of my passions. I can still read English."

Thereafter, our meetings were frequent in our hotel rooms or in company with other stage directors of Moscow as arranged by the Ministry of Culture of the USSR.

FIRST AWARENESS OF YURI ZAVADSKI

1958 had been a germinal year. The Institute for Advanced Studies in the Theatre Arts had been founded. At the invitation of the Rockefeller Foundation, Michel Saint-Denis had come to the United States. As an early mentor for the Institute (IASTA), Michel told me of his meeting the Russian stage director Yuri Zavadski in Paris. Zavadski had come there for conferences of the International Theatre Institute (UNESCO). Michel and Yuri formed a spontaneous and warm friendship. They had the French language in common, and they talked of theatre.

On the second day of their acquaintance, Zavadski said precipitously to Saint-Denis, "*Chèr ami, je voudrais aller au cinema. Il n'importe pas le film. Un film français.*" He pressed Saint-Denis that they go at once.

Michel Saint-Denis was puzzled, but agreed, and took Zavadski by the arm, steering him to the nearest movie house on the Boulevard des Capucines.

Once in the darkened auditorium, Zavadski was now guiding Saint-Denis; he headed immediately for an exit at the far end of the cinema. Once out in the street to the rear of the theatre, he winked at his French colleague saying, in French, that now they could talk freely.

As related to us by Saint-Denis, it dawned at once upon him that Zavadski was fully aware of the fact that, at all times while abroad, he had been under the surveyance of the KGB. Saint-Denis admired greatly Zavadski's courage and spirit of independence.

Michel Saint-Denis' talk of Yuri Zavadski as a director to be invited to the Institute for Chekhov caused me to remember Edna Youngquist, my Rockford Senior High School drama teacher, who had told me of her seeing a production of **Cherry Orchard** as performed by the Moscow Art Theatre. Stanislavski had played Gayev. This was at a time when MXAT was on tour in the United States in the 1920's. It must have been a memorable performance, the fact that years later I remembered her talk of that production. In my university days, the plays of Chekhov heightened my interest in Russian theatre and had stimulated an interest in all facets of theatre production in Moscow. I became aware of Yuri Zavadski from reading Norris Houghton's **Moscow Rehearsals**.

Norris Houghton had this to report of his observation of Zavadski: "The two [Studio Theatres] which seemed to be most important at this time are the studios of Zavadski and of Simonov. Both of them were pupils of Vakhtangov, both are actors of excellence themselves and both are trying to combine the Stanislavsky and Meierhold ideas of theatre in line with Vakhtangov's approach, but sifted through their own personal temperaments . . . Zavadski's theatre has added to soundness of psychological portrayal a heightening of style . . . brilliantly theatrical. Zavadski works toward the irony which Vakhtangov loved so well, but it is gentler than Meierhold's . . . He uses the grotesque and caricature to fine advantage — in this he has learned a lesson from Meierhold. He has also learned the use of dynamic movement. Everything about his stage seems in action. . . Zavadski, besides being managing director of his own studio theatre, also acts occasionally at the Moscow Art Theatre and sometimes directs plays for the Red Army Theatre.[2]

Houghton notes that it was not uncommon for a stage director to be rehearsing three different productions in three different places, and that his work day would run often from ten in the morning until eleven at night. [3]

As advised by Michel Saint-Denis, I wrote letters of invitation to Zavadski in French. I wrote as well to a director of the Moscow Art Theatre, Victor Stanitsyn (later, in Moscow, Stanitsyn invited me to attend rehearsals he was conducting the following week).

I.T.I. (UNESCO) facilitated my getting in communication by letter with Yuri Zavadski. It had never been an easy matter getting responses from persons of the USSR nor is it easy, even today, with *glasnost*.

Early in 1959, after my having written many letters in the previous months, three of the five Founders of IASTA arrived in Moscow in mid-winter.

---

2   Houghton, Norris **Moscow Rehearsals**. New York: Harcourt, Brace and Company, 1936.

3   Ibid.

I had a meeting with a Mr. Kamenev of the Ministry of Culture, and Zavadski came to see us often at the National Hotel.

The very first meeting with Kamenev had been completely in Russian. I used what I had learned at the Berlitz School of Languages and was assisted throughout by the Intourist interpreter.

The second contact I had with Mr. Kamenev was a telephone call early in the morning at the National Hotel. I was puzzled at first as to who it might be on the other end of the phone, for this gentleman was speaking English with scarcely an accent. When I asked who he was, he explained smoothly that we had just met the day before and that he was Mr. Kamenev. He urged me to go at once to see the Minister in the Ministry of Culture.

On one occasion, when Intourist seemingly turned a deaf ear to our request for tickets for a production of Mayakovsky's **Klop (Bedbug)** at the Theatre of Satire, we cabled Zavadski for help in getting tickets. We got the tickets, fortunately, and thus we were able to compare the Russian production with one we'd seen in Paris earlier that year. The Russian production was more disciplined and it had more appeal for me.

We left Moscow optimistic that Yuri Zavadski would be able to have the permission he needed to come to America. Nathan Tuck of the American Embassy had assured us that under the new treaty of cultural exchange between the United States and the Soviet Union we could be optimistic. Norris Houghton had already agreed to be the American counterpart in the exchange with Yuri Zavadski. He was to go later to the Soviet Union to write a sequel to his book **Moscow Rehearsals**. Norris' book, **Return Engagement** was the result.

A few months after the IASTA research and scouting trip around the world, at which time we had our meetings in Moscow with Yuri Zavadski, most unexpectedly both Robert Whitehead, the Broadway producer, and Robert Dowling of the City Investing Corporation which owned a number of Broadway theatres, came to my office at the Institute.

"Zavadski is coming here?," asked Bob Whitehead.

"Yes," I replied.

"I've just seen Zavadski's production of Shakespeare's **The Merry Wives of Windsor** at his Mossoviet Theatre, Moscow," continued Whitehead, brimming with admiration for Zavadski's artistry. Nodding in agreement, Mr. Dowling added, "We've such admiration for his work that we hope that Zavadski will come to direct for the Lincoln Center Repertory Theatre."

I showed to them both a recent publication of I.T.I. (UNESCO), in which I had underlined sentences of a speech of Zavadski's:

"I consider myself to be a faithful and consequent disciple of Stanislavsky and of Vakhtangov, but I interpret my position as a disciple, my fidelity, quite freely; I adopt certain 'internal' principles and not their external procedures; in practice I never cease to renovate the method, while facing the tasks imposed upon me by current existence."[4]

It seemed that neither Whitehead nor Dowling were admirers of the Actor's Studio or of Lee Strasberg, and they voiced that they liked what they read of Yuri Zavadski's point-of-view.

---

4 **World Premieres**, *Mondiales*, February 1960, No. 5., I.T.I. UNESCO.

ZAVADSKI ARRIVES

Spring of 1960 arrived and, with mixed feelings of trepidation and enthusiasm, we awaited confirmation that soon Zavadski would be on his way to the USA. As letters and telegrams no longer allayed our anxieties, telephone calls ensued. Gala Ebin was invaluable since she was in full command of the Russian language. The most troublesome phrase coming from Zavadski, when translated in English, was that the day of his arrival in New York would be set 'in some days.' It was frustrating; all enrolled in the Institute were keyed up feverishly for his arrival: a Russian director who had acted with Stanislavski! He was to be the very first ever to come to America to direct professional American actors.

We were not disappointed. Initial reassurance came with a telephone call from him from the Copenhagen, Denmark, airport where he changed planes for New York.

As Robert Epstein, Gala Ebin, and I drove to the New York airport to meet Yuri Zavadski, I was thinking of how difficult the last year had been effecting this arrival of a Soviet director to come and direct American professional at the Institute for Advanced Studies in the Theatre Arts.

On the drive back to Manhattan from the airport, our Soviet director, Yuri Zavadski, was being welcomed with small talk by us, his hosts. "The Algonquin Hotel, where you will stay while you are in New York, has made available to you the suite known as Laurence Olivier's." There was no response from Mr. Zavadski. "Is it possible Zavadski has never heard of Olivier?" I thought. [We learned much later, of course, he knew very well who Laurence Olivier was.]

On Zavadski's first evening in New York, I wished to duplicate in some manner, the hospitality each of us of IASTA had received in Moscow. Our press agent had suggested that we take Zavadski to the Four Seasons Restaurant, a handsome and much admired restaurant. One of the striking things about the luxurious restaurant was, to represent a change of season, fully-grown trees were placed in tubs around the restaurant. Since it was Spring, there were cherry trees in blossom, a most appealing sight.

Throughout the meal, Yuri Zavadski was as genial as he had been with us in Moscow. He picked at his food making no comment, nor did he respond or comment on the beauty and the opulence of the restaurant. We were puzzled. Had dining out in Moscow dulled his palate? (In 1956, and again in 1959, I had never succeeded in getting a satisfactory meal in Moscow; waiter service had also been deplorable.)

Over dinner, Zavadski, with Gala Ebin interpreting, told us, "My first wife was Ulanova." Each of us being aware that she was the legendary ballerina, we replied to his confidence, "Ulanova is spoken of with awe in the West."

Later by consensus, we, who had been made aware of his first marriage, agreed, "We'll not repeat this," Bob had said, "I daresay Zavadski desires privacy about his life."

Au contraire! At every party during the next few weeks, Yuri Zavadski's opening conversational gambit was likely to be, "You know, Ulanova was my first wife."

A year or so later we learned, to our amusement, that Zavadski would inform Americans visiting him in Moscow, "You know, I stayed in Laurence Olivier's suite at the hotel in New York, and I also dined at the Four Seasons restaurant." These anecdotes, I believe, reveal the charming pixie side to Mr. Z.

The day following his arrival, Zavadski informed Bob Epstein, "I want to see a tailor." This indeed he did. His auditioning American actors came later in the day!

Various stars of the New York stage had made known to the Institute their interest in being directed by Mr. Zavadski in **Cherry Orchard**. Younger actors who had been directed earlier at IASTA by Willi Schmidt and Jacques Charon were hopeful that with two casts they, too, would be in **Cherry Orchard**.

In the executive office at the Institute, the first clap of thunder delivered by Yuri Zavadski was, "I will only direct Act I and Act II. I would need six months, not six weeks, to do the full play."

Following his unusual and fascinating approach to auditioning the actors — he just chatted with each actor in turn — he informed me that he would direct but only one cast — consisting of young actors, no stars.

He did not verbalize what had prompted that decision. We had no choice; we acceded. We could only speculate as to his decisions. Quite possibly he feared that stars would not be as malleable as younger actors. Undoubtedly he had known stars who had set their characterizations before any rehearsal. Moreover, as he well knew, older actors in control of the Moscow Art Theatre resisted giving up to younger actors roles they had created. Even the greatly aged Stanislavski continued to play Vershinen in Chekhov's **Three Sisters**, despite the fact that Stanislavski was far older than the character of Vershinen which he had created in the lifetime of Chekhov.

MR. Z. AT IASTA

Before commencing rehearsals of **Cherry Orchard**, Yuri Zavadski said to his cast of American actors:

*My task has been to acquaint the **Cherry Orchard** cast and the Institute's observing members with Stanislavski's method as I see it in its present development.*

The reason I have the courage to undertake this assignment is because for twelve years, from 1924 to 1936, under Stanislavski I was an actor at the Moscow Art Theatre, and I appeared in his productions.

*I came to Stanislavski as an actor and a director of some experience. Before going over to the Moscow Art Theatre, I had spent the previous seven years with Vakhtangov playing . . . Prince Kalaf in Vakhtangov's production of **Princess Turandot** by the Italian playwright Carlo Gozzi.*

A reporter from The New York Times who had attended Mr. Zavadski's first day of rehearsal wrote, "Thirty American actors sat spellbound yesterday as a Soviet director discoursed for five hours on the first twelve words of a play he was putting into rehearsal. Through an interpreter, he spoke on love, religion, the masculinity of American women's hands and the lateness of trains in pre-revolutionary Russia. At the close of the first rehearsal of Chekhov's **Cherry Orchard**, Mr. Zavadski said, 'Chekhov was the best author to work with in the United States."

Almost all previous and later directors from abroad who came to the Institute had not very much liked being observed, even by theatre professionals, as they directed.

Brecht, when he was directing his Berliner Ensemble Company in East Berlin, was quite vocal of his wanting to have open rehearsals where there could be qualified observers. By contrast the American director Elia Kazan, on one of the occasions he came to observe a rehearsal of Zavadski's at the Institute, told me that he, under no circumstances, would ever allow there to be open rehearsals with observers when he was directing. Yuri Zavadski did adjust to the open rehearsal policy of the Institute.

However, he said, "Institute members are to arrive well in advance of the start of the rehearsal . . . They may absent themselves from a rehearsal only when I announce a break in the rehearsal." To an astonishing degree, observing professionals cooperated fully, including not only Elia Kazan, but Robert Lewis, Harold Clurman, Stella Adler and many others.

New York's directors, producers, actors, all fell under the charismatic spell of Mr. Z. (as he had come affectionately to be called by his cast).

Although months had passed, construction continued beneath the IASTA Studio Theatre on the Maidman Theatre. The building on 42nd Street had formerly been a bank and there was much jack-hammering of the vaults in order to remove them.

"That noise," Mr. Z. said, "will disturb the essential concentration of the actors." "It must stop!" Bob Epstein ran interference with the workmen below. He was unusually successful in getting them to respect our rehearsals on the floor above.

Our research in Moscow had enlightened us as to sets and costumes for 19th Century Russian plays and for the plays of Chekhov. The stereotype of Russians as lugubrious and heavy frequently permeates stage design elsewhere than in Russia. Heavy and ornate Victorian or Biedermeir furniture is counter to Russian taste in furnishings in the 19th Century. Empire furniture was the catalyst for tables, chairs, and cupboards in Russia. Fan lights are to be seen everywhere in Russian mansions of the period.

A French influence is essential for costuming of **Cherry Orchard**, particularly for the clothes of Mme. Ranyevsky. They would be in contrast to the Russian apparel for Varya and Dunyasha. Zavadski commented on Mme. Ranyevsky's liking for coffee as a French affectation. This was a key to the actress for her characterization for Mme. Ranyevsky.

Quite by chance I had come upon a passage in **Stanislavski Directs** in which the young Yuri Zavadski was taking directions from Stanislavski in **Woe From Wisdom** by Griboyedov. It was like coming upon a old snapshot: an unexpected find of one who I had come to admire, know and hold in affection. At once in my mind's eye I saw a young, handsome Zavadski with a full head of blond hair.

"In 1924 Stanislavski and Nemirovich-Danchenko decided to do a new production of Griboyedov's **Woe From Wisdom**. The decision was to use young actors in leading parts. Zavadski, then a member of the Moscow Art Theatre troupe was given the role of Chatsky, a role for which Stanislavski was famous.

"One day at rehearsal, Stanislavski interrupted the actors because he said to them that they were intellectualizing, not acting. He invited them and even encouraged them to overact.

"Stanislavski suddenly started attacking Zavadski with the same force [as he had attacked the actress Stepanova]. His voice thundered through the theatre as it always did when he spoke to someone who made him lose his temper.

"But Zavadski understood Stanislavski's intention and did not let him finish Famusov's [the character of the play which Stanislavski was now playing] monologue from the fourth act.

"In the same tone, he [Zavadski] answered with Chatsky's monologue. Zavadski spoke the monologue with much bitterness and passion. Then on his last phrase he spontaneously jumped from his seat and left the auditorium.

"'He's really off his head!' Stanislavski addressed Lisa [a character of the play] seriously . . .

"Zavadski quietly returned and sat down. Stanislavski drank some tea, which was always there at the director's table for him. 'Well,' he said, 'we all overacted to the hilt. In order to keep in line with you, I was forced to shout. But now we've learned how far our characters would go if they were not restrained by the conditions of time, by the surroundings, by the line within which the character grows, and by an artistic sense of proportion. At all times you had sincere notes . . . you, Zavadski, . . . the entire monologue sounded strong, sincere, and convincing. Try to remember what thoughts urged you to speak these lines and what your state of being was . . . we were overplaying . . . we learned what are the limits of our own feelings, how far you, [Zavadski,] can go in bitterness and disillusion [as the character of Chatsky.]"[5]

ZAVADSKI ON VAKHTANGOV

"Zavadski turned to speak of Vakhtangov and the production that proved to be Vakhtangov's most remarkable and inventive production, **Princess Turandot**. It started with a prologue and a song which all the actors sang.

"Music opens the play. The lights die down, the whole company come before the curtain and sing to you. They look most odd, for the women still wear the fashions of 1922. To the haunting waltz tune they tell you what you are about to see and as the curtain goes up they step back and proceed to deck themselves with the colored rags that lie on the stage. They troop off and their place is taken by the scene shifters — young men and girls in dark blue kimono suits with colored caps. Still moving in time to the waltz rhythm they set the stage before our eyes. Most of the scenery is very light and what is flown in the flies is counterweighted with gaily colored little sandbags. The colored weights soar into the air and doors and windows, pillars and arches sail gracefully on to the stage. Everything is done with a

---

5   Zavadski Gorchakov, Nikolai M. **Stanislavski Directs**. New York: Limelight Editions, 1985.]

sense of smooth expertness — no seeming hurry and yet no delay — and all the the time this soft insidious waltz time moves like a strong undercurrent. When the stage is set they make their bow - exit - and the play begins". [6]

All actors were in front of the curtain: men in tails, women in evening gowns. Once one of the actors of the show had introduced each character to the audience, the actors with slight changes and additions in their costumes changed themselves into Gozzi's characters in front of the audience. [7]

". . . The form of **Turandot** was dictated by the condition of the times. In 1922 Russia was exhausted; famine and civil war had taken their tragic toll and the life of the country was at the low ebb. In the theatre there was little or no scenery — it had all been chopped up and used for firewood . . . costumes for the theatre were quite unattainable. These were the conditions which faced Vakhtangov and which he turned to his own ends. No costumes? Right - let us use what we can lay our hands on, bits of rags, odd scarves and lengths of stuff patched and worn and used in previous plays — this French towel for a long white beard, this black wool for the raven tresses of the princess — a cloak for the prince thrown over his ordinary evening dress — fantastic masks' of painted paper for the clown and pantaloon. Will they look like real costumes to the audience? No hope of that. But what if we let them into our secret — let them see us dress up in our rags and oddments — let us make a point of pretending that these rags are glittering satin and rich velvet, that this tinsel paper in the Caliph's jeweled turban? It will be a charade in which the audience takes part. By hiding nothing from them we are asking them to see far more than we can show. No scenery? So — the fantasy shall have dream scenery: a twisted pole and a curving arch for the palace, a semicircle of muslin rising behind the couch strewn with brilliant cushions is the boudoir of her [Princess Turandot's] environment". [8]

Rhythm is the keynote of the acting in Turandot: the figures seem to dance along to the gay lilting tunes, making bright patterns of sound and movement.

At the end of the play the actors sang the same song in a different rhythm, saying good-bye to the audience.

"There is a surprising piece of fooling half way through the play which was introduced at the original production by the actor Zavadski. It is in the form of an interlude played by the scene shifters. Five or six of them come out and perform a mime burlesque of the whole play, imitating the gestures and mannerisms of the various characters with shattering accuracy. All to music. It is a brilliant idea to satirize a satire and a dangerously difficult thing to do, but the audience received this interlude with sustained applause at every performance. It is one of the high spots in the play. [9]

Vakhtangov staged the last scene when he himself was already near death and conscious that he was dying. As he was finishing rehearsals, his temperature was 104 degrees and he was too ill to attend the dress rehearsal. For

---

6   Gyseghen, André van. **The Theatre in Soviet Russia**. London:

7   Italics, in this case, are Yuri Zavadski speaking directly.

8   Gyseghen, André van., op.cit.

9   Ibid.

Vakhtangov this production was a farewell to life, a testament to the beauty of life".

Vakhtangov was a close and faithful disciple, but he was not an orthodox follower of Stanislavski. Vakhtangov proved in this production that Stanislavski method, deeply understood, can be applicable to any theatrical problem.

ZAVADSKI ON STANISLAVSKI

Chekhov is Stanislavski's first author, and Stanislavski theory on acting was born and developed through Chekhov's works. Stanislavski method is not only a way of working, but it is a key to understanding Chekhov, to reaching Chekhov.

Now, Stanislavski method has basically two sides. That does not mean that the totality and richness of the way to acting is limited to these two sides. However, I would like to stress two particular aspects of his method of acting.

Stanislavski appreciated the laws of creativity, at the heart of his system. Laws govern creativity. Americans, Russians, the French have to breathe, eat, drink, sleep to survive; likewise there are certain general laws of creativity which exist for all branches of art, for all directions in art.

The second side of the Method is the direction of the art to which Stanislavski devoted most of his life and which he considered the most precious and most important in art. It probably came to him, primarily, through his work on the plays of Chekhov. But, also for creating his Method, he was prepared by all the preceding Russian literature, and the best Russian theatre artists before him.

Those who have read Stanislavski have probably noticed that giving examples of the right kind of playing, he uses, not himself and his colleagues, but artists of the past, or artists contemporary to him from different countries: Salvini, Duse. These people did not know the Method as we understand it, but through their creative genius had it in them and used it in their acting. In a certain measure, Stanislavski wanted to channel the forces of genius and intuition into conscious awareness. I am quite sure that all of you know this, because this is the Stanislavski formula: conscious awareness to reach the subconscious creativity.

It is very important to understand it in totality, because in the understanding of the Method, there is sometimes a leaning to one side or to the other. Some make the Method into a cold and dry calculation. They say, 'You've just got to play; what do you mean by a Method?' Others consider the Method, Stanislavski art and the Moscow Art Theatre, as the art of feeling and experiencing, leaving calculations and awareness aside, putting it in the second place.

The great Russian poet, Pushkin, was a symbol of great creativity and flights of imagination; but he was also a very wise man, and he said, 'Don't confuse rapture with inspiration, because rapture does not account for the power of the mind to place all the separate parts in their relationship to the whole.' According to Pushkin, talent has to be wise, and wisdom has to be inspired.

To bring up an artist; to give him the unity of thought and feeling, was the task that Stanislavski put before himself — to teach a man to penetrate deep into the world of experience and events, and to create the life of the human spirit.

Chekhov is the author who offers this opportunity to the actors to an enormous degree; rather, more correctly, he demands it of the actor. You cannot play Chekhov in a superficial manner. Chekhov shows life in its inter-relationships and interpolations of events.

Actually, according to Stanislavski and according to Chekhov, you should not play the characters, but rather, what happens between people in their interrelationships. To create this third dimension, what happens between them, creates the world of human relationships - Chekhov's world - which is unrepeatable and unique. Stanislavski was tied up with Chekhov. Stanislavski suggested to everybody to create a method of his own. He used to say that it is pointless to accept the Method abstractly as the medicine to cure all diseases. It is the same as imagining a cupboard full of medicines for various illnesses, and deciding in advance, in order never to be ill, to drink and eat all the medicines.

All you need is the creative discipline, and the Method must be under-stood first of all as a regime of self-discipline. This applies first of all to actors, but also to the directors. I recall that one of the great actors of the Moscow Art Theatre, Leonidov, and actor of enormous temperament, used to say that Stanislavski was very sly — that he invented the Method for himself; that he was fighting his shortcomings. But as Stanislavski's shortcomings happened to coincide with the shortcomings of most of the others, his Method proved generally usable. In reality we know that an actor gets bored with playing. This shortcoming of an actor, Stanislavski studied very carefully, as it was his own. Stanislavski studied how not to portray a character, but how to become a character.

This is also a footnote or correction on how to understand the Method. American theatre generally chooses actors for a play as they are chosen for a movie-type casting. Most of the time the actors really play themselves. There is a Stanislavski expression: to play from yourself. It is from yourself, but not yourself. This means that in each new part, you recreate yourself and that is the uniqueness of the Method.

Stanislavski said, 'The art of the Moscow Art Theatre is such that it requires constant renewal, constant persistent work on itself. It is built on reproducing and conveying true, organic life. It cannot tolerate the stagna-tion of traditions even in beautiful forms. It is alive; like all living things, it is forever unfolding in movement. What was good yesterday is no longer valid today. Today's performance is not what yesterday's performance was. For this type of art, a special technique is necessary — not the study of fixed theatrical forms, but a technique of mastery over the laws of the creative nature of man, a capacity to affect that nature, to govern it, the ability to develop one's intuitiveness, one's creative possibilities in every perfor-mance.'

These words are directed at people who transform Stanislavski Method into a false dogma.

Stanislavski put major emphasis on the voice. He had started as an opera singer, and all his life he worked on his voice. I remember once when he came to rehearsals — he was almost seventy then — he said, 'Finally, I have placed my voice.'

I will never forget my last impression of him as an actor. He was playing Uncle Vanya. A day before opening night I met him in the hallways and he was very old; his shoelaces had become untied, and he could not even bend down to tie them. I was very perturbed about what would happen: 'Is he going to put rouge on his cheeks to look like a young man?' But, when he walked on stage it was a miracle: he was young. He had on no makeup, but he was young with his whole being. That was the miracle of real art.

My meetings with the actors here with whom I have worked, and with the observers, confirm for me a similarity between American and Russian acting, not only because Stanislavski books appeared here a long time ago and because many of his pupils have and are still continuing to teach here, but because I think American actors are very talented. Stanislavski used to say that his Method was good only for talented people. That's another mistake. Some people think that with Stanislavski Method, you can turn anybody into an actor. The first requirement for appreciating and under- standing the Method is talent. Then, with the help of this Method you can develop talent. This feeling of common traits of character between the two nations absolutely astonished me during rehearsals of **Cherry Orchard**. At times I wondered why my American actors didn't speak Russian, because their creative character is quite the same as the Russian actor's.

But American actors are used to playing only one play. Therefore, they are brought up accordingly, and the problem of creating a different charac- terization each day is a challenge which still faces the American theatre tomorrow. Actors in Russia play many part in the course of a year; they will create two, three, four new roles. Therefore, they have developed a slightly different technique. It is probably difficult for American actors to play a different part every day. For Russian actors it is unthinkable to play the same part every day.

Discipline must be learned. This is a very complicated theme. This is a problem which also worries the Russian actors in connection with the Method; it worried Stanislavski himself. Stanislavski was always very upset because theatre are was so amateurish We cannot, for instance, imagine a pianist sitting down and playing Beethoven immediately. But, in the theatre, we take someone from the street and give him a major part! If we are to approach theatre art seriously, fully, the problem is to create an artist who is a master craftsman permeated with his craft.

Acting requires constant renewal, constant, persistent work, built on reproducing and conveying the true organic life. It may not be the stagnation of tradition even in beautiful forms. What was good yesterday is no longer valid today. It is like all living things, forever unfolding in movement. Today's performance is not what yesterday's was. For this type of art a special technique is necessary, not the study of fixed theatrical forms but a technique to effect that needs acting.

Stanislavski was interested in the expressiveness of the spoken word and in the laws of speech. At one time he was disinterested in any externals, but in his concept of the physical and psychological. However all rules of music helped in this study; the elemental categories from stillness to infinite speed; from absolute quiet to the greatest volume; from smooth rhythmic movement to staccato. Tempo, pitch, and rhythm all were means at the actors command. The realization of the use of these laws is mastery for the actor."

I would like to settle the question of Stanislavski and Vakhtangov by saying that they are individual and different. But, in the basic concept, their understanding of theatre art is one.

WHY 'STAGING CHEKHOV: CHERRY ORCHARD'?

The interviews with the actors who had been directed by Yuri Zavadski almost three decades ago, stimulated my own recall of the man, as friend and as master stage director.

Robert Stattel, Patricia Peardon, Frederick Rolf, Annette Hunt, Steve Daley, Margaret Draper — each had a remarkable and vivid recall of the rehearsals and their performing in Chekhov's **Cherry Orchard**.

Zavadski's directing made the play so real. It's never happened to me before. By the time we had finally given performance before audiences, **Cherry Orchard** had become so real for me that there was no acting involved in it. We actors just talked, which is really, for me, the ultimate in acting: one doesn't have to perform, acting just happens.

I remember one performance. I had made my entrance, and I was talking, as Trofimov. Suddenly, there was loud music coming from a neighboring building; I was so thrown by that that I, as the character Trofimov, just didn't understand how that could be happening for I was so involved in the world of Chekhov's 19th century play that that music was not a part of my world. That was an extraordinary acting experience for me which I've never forgotten.[10]

I also learned that each actor felt an indebtedness to Chekhov and to Mr. Zavadski for a precious contribution to their careers. "I always use approaches to acting learned under Yuri Zavadski in my own work today, regardless of the type of play or the style of the play." [11] Being directed by Yuri Zavadski in Chekhov at the Institute had given them singular acting experiences.

The experiences of Jack Eddleman and of Peter Blaxill as related in the book **Actors Talk: About Styles of Acting** for the revival of Yuri Zavadski's production of **Cherry Orchard** in Denver, Colorado, as part of the International Classic Theatre Festival, reinforced my awareness of the provocative impact that Chekhov alone had upon talented actors.

Small wonder these actors' recall sparked my desire to do a book as a tribute to Yuri Zavadski. Yuri Zavadski was more than an inspired and inspiring master director. Nay even more, he was simply a great human being and all who came in contact, even fleetingly with him were changed.

---

10 Mitchell, John D. **Actors Talk: About Styles of Acting**, interview with Robert Stattel. Midland, Michigan: Northwood Institute Press, 1988, p. 41.

11 Ibid, page 41

Moreover, my hope is that this tribute to Chekhov as well may make a contribution to all who wish to stage these seemingly enigmatic and challenging comedies of Chekhov.

"Chekhov deals in the little things, the particulars that go to make up general experience; he leads us to the greater experience step by step by touching us with a thousand insights . . . it is, moreover, his immense particularity which makes him so stage worthy and such a joy to act."[12]

Stage worthy and a joy to act! It was self-evident to each of us as founders of the Institute for Advanced Studies in the Theatre Arts that a play of Chekhov's was a must. For me, Chekhov had come to mean something very special.

"In 1922 Granville Barker . . . recalled his pleasure at seeing **Cherry Orchard** performed by the Moscow Art Theatre. It arose partly, he felt, from the personal magnetism of the individual performers like Olga Knipper (Chekhov's wife), and partly from a close rapport between the actors that was evident even when they were not actively doing anything on stage. American audiences were able to judge these things themselves when the Moscow Art Theatre performed this play as the first of the Chekhov plays in their 1923-24 tour of America . . . with Olga Knipper as Mme. Ranyevsky, Stanislavski as Gayev and Ivan Moskvin as Yepihodov.

"The Moscow Art Theatre was now (1923-24) twenty-five years old and many actors were still performing roles they had played in 1904".[13]

As a university student I was fortunate to see Alfred Lunt and Lynn Fontane in Chekhov's **Seagull**. For me that was a memorable experience.

For the New York Herald-Tribune, Richard Watts wrote of the Lunts' SEAGULL, "beautifully acted by Miss Fontane, Mr. Lunt and an excellent company . . . there is a strange, sly humor about it [the production], too. Part of it is due to the curious *suggestions of whimsical laughter that the Lunts manage to put into it upon occasion.* . . Only the Irish can equal the Russians in leaping back and forth with speed and abandon, between bitterness and gaiety, and Chekhov's [characters] had moments when they *were not unconscious that their excessive concern with tragedies of their souls had its sardonically humorous aspects.*"[14]

How perceptive was Richard Watts as to the comedic intention of Chekhov. Others who reported on the Lunts' production of **Seagull**, as well as some years later Katharine Cornell's production of **Three Sisters**, and much earlier the performances of Chekhov's plays by the Moscow Art Theatre on tour in America, reveal a singular resistance to seeing the plays as comedies.

---

12 Styan, J.L., **Chekhov in Performance**. Cambridge: Cambridge University Press, 1988. p.1

13 Emeljanow, Victor., **Chekhov: The Critical Heritage**. London; Rautledge & Kegan Paul, 1981.

14 Styan, J.L., op.cit. p.244.(Italics added.)

"**Cherry Orchard** was conceived as a comedy, but it's author had difficulty in persuading Stanislavski and his company . . . The truth is the **Cherry Orchard** is a play which treads the tight rope between them [farce and tragedy], and results in the ultimate form of that special dramatic balance we know as Chekhovian Comedy." [15]

Both Granville Barker and Richard Watts gave themselves up to the charismatic power of talented actors playing Chekhov. I have become aware that great actors very, very often arrive intuitively at the intention of the playwright. Their histrionic gifts give them a distinct edge over those who just observe and write about performances in the theatre.

At Northwestern University's School of Speech I assisted in designing the lighting for Alvina Krause's productions of Chekhov's Three Sisters and **Cherry Orchard**. Those many hours of sitting through rehearsals and working on the lighting deepened my admiration for Chekhov as a man of the theatre.

For me, however, the major insight as to what Chekhov meant by his designation of his plays as comedies occurred in the summer of 1956 in the USSR. The Vakhtangov Theatre was on tour in Kiev performing a production of Chekhov's **Seagull**. The actors were not performing farcically or striving even for comedy, but their playing Chekhov's characters before Russian audiences enabled the audience, it seemed, to recognize themselves as Russians up there on the stage. The Russian spectators were amused by seeing themselves depicted as explosive, highly emotional, Russians of a mercurial temperament. For the audience, comedic effect was achieved.

For example, the Vakhtangov Theatre's actress, playing Mme. Arkadina understood that Chekhov's intention was a provincial actress, not a star of the Moscow or St. Petersburg stage. Stage business suggested the actress's vulgarity. Throughout the play she does, [as many Russians do], imbibe from very small shot-like type glasses jiggers of vodka. When Arkadina learns that her lover Trigorin is leaving her, she flings herself to the floor, groveling while clutching his boots. She is intensely Russian and emotional at the thought of parting from her lover. To this the audience reacted with laughter and noticeable amusement.

Years later, in London, the actress Vanessa Redgrave performed the role of Mme. Arkadina in an excellent production of **Seagull**. Had she seen Russian actors perform this play? Her characterization and actions were much akin to the acting of the actress of the Vakhtangov Theatre I had seen. Some of the stage business was the same; e.g. Arkadina's throwing herself at the feet of Trigorin to persuade him not to leave her. Or, as is quite possible, had she as have other great actors, arrived at Chekhov's intention intuitively.

Turn once again to words of Yuri Zavadski to his American cast:

Chekhov is Stanislavski's first author, and Stanislavski's theory of acting was born and developed in Chekhov's works. Stanislavski method is not only a way of working, but it is a key to understanding Chekhov, to reaching Chekhov.

Chekhov is a wonderful link also because he is, today, close to both you and us of Russia. The year 1960 is the hundredth year after his birth; the whole

---

15 Styan, J. L., op.cit. p.245.

world, foremost theatre people everywhere, appreciate anew Chekhov's art and his great influence in the development of world dramatic literature. Chekhov is close to us, especially today, because all his art is permeated with a faith in tomorrow's development of humanity.

That is why we are all so moved by the art of Chekhov which is modest, good, deep. A prophetic art. As Chekhov said, 'Remember that authors whom we call eternal, or good, or who intoxicate us, have one common and very important trait: they are going some place and are beckoning you there. You feel, not with your minds, but with your whole beings that they have some purpose.' Like Hamlet's father's ghost, (who appeared for a purpose,) these authors disturb the imagination.

The best of them are realistic and describe life as it is. Since each line is soaked through, as if with juice, with awareness of purpose, one feels in addition to life as it is, the life that should be. That captures one. He who wants nothing, hopes for nothing, fears nothing cannot be an artist.

NOTES ON THE TRANSLATION AND THE BOOK

My fashioning of a new translation of **Cherry Orchard** with Alan Upchurch revealed that it was not greatly dissimilar from the script used by Zavadski directing American actors in Chekhov's **Cherry Orchard**. There were revelations as I had hoped, for the making of the new translation gave new insights as to the genius of Chekhov as a playwright. Cuts have been restored. Prompted by our wish to be true to Chekhov, sequences of lines in a long speech follow scrupulously the sequence of the original of Chekhov in the Russian. To my satisfaction, in all cases it revealed how great a man of the theatre was Chekhov. He comprehended the art and the technique of acting in depth.

From among the twenty some bound volumes of my log, began in 1947, I was able to easily locate transcribed conversations with both Yuri Zavadski and Stanitsyn at the time I was in Moscow researching professional theatre training, rehearsal practice and performance at Zavadski's Mossoviet Theatre, The Vakhtangov Theatre, and of course MXAT and other Russian Theatres and Schools.

POSTCRIPT

Near the end of the rehearsals of **Cherry Orchard**, Yuri Zavadski became ill. Despite the anxiety that he experienced, he continued to devote full time to the last days of rehearsal.Although he had to return to the USSR for medical treatment before the scheduled opening, he was there for the final dress rehearsal. This was an emotional occasion and all the celebrated actors performing on the stages in New York attended that dress rehearsal. Among those who came to the dress rehearsal was Arthur Miller. After the performance, in my office, he said to me, "**Now** I understand Chekhov."

We at length received, happily, a letter from Mr. Z. in which he reported of his recovery from the illness which had taken him back to Moscow. The letter which we received was most reassuring, "I had decided to undergo a complete overhauling. At the moment I am living in a wonderful governmental sanatorium in a Moscow suburb. I am feeling well and again ready for work. Soon after the vacation, the theatre will assemble and I will begin rehearsals."

Norris Houghton's book **Return Engagement** gave further reassurance that Yuri Zavadski had recovered fully back in the USSR. "The Mossoviet Theatre's popularity is attested to by its completely sold-out houses. Its repertoire is cosmopolitan: alongside Shakespeare, Chekhov, Sardou, and Sarte, there are also productions of Mikhail Lermontov, Carlo Goldoni, Gorki and Ibsen out of the past and at least five contemporary Soviet pieces . . . The Mossoviet is brave to introduce Tennessee Williams into the Soviet capital at all. Zavadski, however, is a devoted promoter of cultural exchange as a means of alleviating international tensions, and this fact undoubtedly entered into his decision to show his countrymen the work of one of America's most popular dramatists."[16]

Yuri Zavadski's invitation to participate, to give lectures on the occasion of the 400th anniversary of the birth of William Shakespeare has been cited already.

Frederick Rolf made a trip to Moscow and had several meetings with Yuri Zavadski. It was an emotional reunion for the Russian director with his American actor who had played the character Gayev.

A year later, Yuri Zavadski returned to the United States and once again there was an emotional and warm reunion with the actors he had directed in **Cherry Orchard** as well as with the many friends he had made during his short stay in New York in 1960.

On that occasion, he and I talked of the conversations that we had had evenings in his hotel room, of my accompanying him to performances of Broadway plays like **West Side Story** and of his visit backstage after a performance of **Five Finger Exercise** with Jessica Tandy. The warmth of friendship that each of us felt for the other gives me complete confidence in preparing this tribute to the great stage director, Yuri Zavadski.

---

16 Houghton, Norris, **Return Engagement**. New York: Holt, Reinhart & Winston, 1962.

Anton Chekhov's

Cherry Orchard

with

stage directions

by

Yuri Zavadski

ВИШНЕВЫЙ САД
Комедия в четырех действиях

ДЕЙСТВУЮЩИЕ ЛИЦА

Раневская Любовь Андреевна, помещица.
Аня, ее дочь, 17 лет.
Варя, ее приемная дочь, 24 года.
Гаев Леонид Андреевич, брат Раневской.
Лопахин Ермолай Алексеевич, купец.
Трофимов Петр Сергеевич, студент.
Симеонов-Пищик Борис Борисович, помещик.
Шарлотта Ивановна, гувернантка.
Епиходов Семен Пантелеевич, конторщик.
Дуняша, горничная.
Фирс, лакей, старик 87 лет.
Яша, молодой лакей.
Прохожий.
Начальник станции.
Почтовый чиновник.
Гости, прислуга.

Действие происходит в имении Л.А.Раневской.

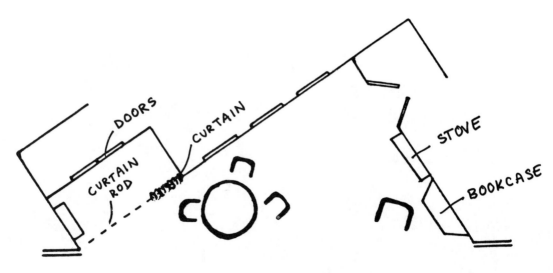

THE CHERRY ORCHARD
A Comedy in Four Acts

LIST OF CHARACTERS

LYUBOV ANDREYEVNA RANYEVSKY, a landowner
ANYA, her daughter, age seventeen
VARYA, her adopted daughter, age twenty-four
LEONID ANDREYEVICH GAYEV, brother of Mrs. Ranyevsky
YERMOLAY ALEXEYEVICH LOPAKHIN, a merchant
PYOTR SERGEYEVICH TROFIMOV, a student
BORIS BORISOVITCH SIMEONOV-PISHCHIK, a landowner
CHARLOTTA IVANOVNA, a governess
SIMYON PANTELEYEVICH YEPIKHODOV, a clerk
DUNYASHA, a maidservant
FIRS, an old manservant, age eighty-seven
YASHA, a young manservant
A PASSER-BY
A STATIONMASTER
A POST OFFICE CIVIL SERVANT
GUESTS and **SERVANTS**

The action takes place on the estate of MRS. RANYEVSKY.

ДЕЙСТВИЕ ПЕРВОЕ

Комната, которая до сих пор называется детскою. Одна из дверей ведет в комнату Ани. Рассвет, скоро взойдет солнце. Уже май, цветут вишневые деревья, но в саду холодно, утренник. Окна в комнате закрыты. Входят Дуняша со свечой и Лопахин с книгой в руке.

ЛОПАХИН

Пришел поезд, слава богу. Который час?

ДУНЯША

Скоро два. (*Тушит свечу*). Уже светло.

ЛОПАХИН

На сколько же опоздал поезд? Часа на два, по крайней мере. (*Зевает и потягивается.*) Я-то хорош, какого чорта свалял! Нарочно приехал сюда, чтобы на станции встретить, и вдруг проспал . . . Сидя уснул. Досада . . . Хоть бы ты меня разбудила.

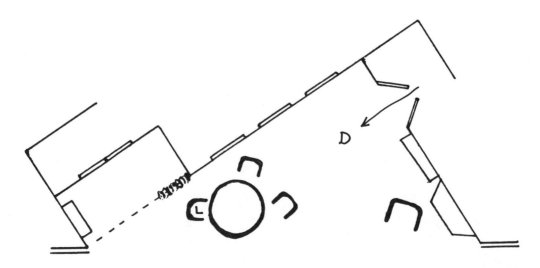

ACT ONE

The setting: A room which has always been called the nursery. One of the doors leads into ANYA's room. Dawn: sunrise during the scene. It is May; the cherry trees are in flower, but it is cold in the garden with the frost of early morning. Windows are shuttered. Enter DUNYASHA with a candle and LOPAK- HIN with a book in his hands.*

LOPAKHIN

The train's in at last, thank God. What time is it?

DUNYASHA

Nearly two. (*She puts out candle. Both notice the dawn.*) It's almost daylight.

LOPAKHIN

That train was late again! Almost two hours at least. Fine fool I am. (*Yawns and stretches.*) Came here on purpose to meet them at the station, sat down in their chair and went right to sleep. How stupid; you might have waked me. . .

* - Differences between Chekhov's original stage directions and Zavadski's staging occur in the text. Both have been included in order to preserve translation accuracy as well as Zavadski's interpretation of the play.

We must stop at every sentence. We have to digest the lines, bearing in mind that Chekhov was writing about a provincial Russian town in 1904, that one got to the railroad station by horse and wagon in those days. Trains were habitually late then. The phrase, 'thank God,' is not used in this context, as a religious sentiment, but is just a custom of speech.

Lopakhin looks as if the family is coming; his thoughts are about the cherry orchard. He is listening for the train.

On Dunyasha's speech, 'it's almost daylight', her thought is: how much have I changed? After Lopakhin's comment 'you might have waked me', Dunyasha can't think of an answer.

ДУНЯША

Я думала, что вы уехали. (*Прислушивается.*) Вот, кажется, уже едут.

ЛОПАХИН

(*прислушивается*). Нет . . . Багаж получить, то да се.. (*пауза*). Любовь Андреевна прожила за границей пять лет, не знаю, какая она теперь стала.. Хороший она человек.

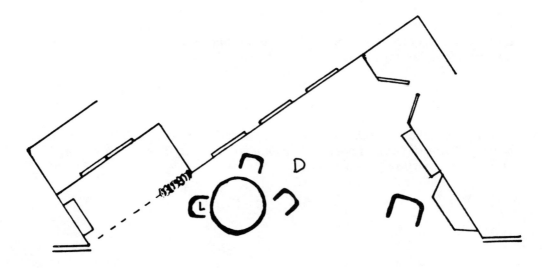

DUNYASHA

I thought you'd gone. (*Listens.*) There! I believe they're coming!

LOPAKHIN

(*Also listening.*) No, in that case the luggage would already have come . . . Lyubov Andreyevna has been abroad five years; I wonder what she's like now . . . she's a splendid woman, a good-natured, simple woman.

On this first speech, Lopakhin notices Dunyasha. On Dunyasha's, 'I thought you'd gone', imitate Mme. Ranyevsky, whose hands are very delicate. On her speech, Dunyasha acts as if she's a lady. She is thinking, 'Lopakhin must have changed. He has missed going to the railroad station to meet the family.' Dunyasha feels superior to Lopakhin; she doesn't truly like him.

Lopakhin as a person is his thoughts, his feelings, his desires; they must be absolutely fresh. Lopakhin, you will walk as if these were your thoughts: Your goal is to find a greater feeling of anticipation. You are wondering at the beginning of the scene what Mme. Ranyevsky will be like. It is a big event that she is coming back after five years. Don't take it casually.

*The actress playing Dunyasha should dig into the text to create the world around the character. Learn how to **become** Dunyasha. What is your thinking for the opening scene? Well, Dunyasha's going to change. Something good is going to happen.*

The first scene the actors must play with anticipation, for the scene's goal is to wait for the arrival of the late train. Actors must listen for and hear the train whistle. The play begins with an air of anticipation and ends with finality.

Acting is a succession of actions to know. It is good for the actor to overdo at first; then, in time, everything becomes clear.

(ЛОПАХИН)

Помню, когда я был мальчонком лет пятнадцати, отец мой покойный - он тогда здесь на деревне в лавке торговал - ударил меня по лицу кулаком, кровь пошла из носу.. мы тогда вместе пришли зачем-то во двор, и он выпивши был. Любовь Андреевна, как сейчас помню, еще молоденькая, такая худенькая, подвела меня к рукомойнику, вот в этой самой комнате, в детской. " Не плачь, говорит, мужичок, до свадьбы заживет..." (*Пауза.*) Мужичок. . . Отец мой, правда, мужик был, а я вот в белой жилетке, желтых башмаках. Со свиным рылом в калашный ряд . . . Только что вот богатый, денег много, а ежели подумать и разобраться то мужик-мужиком... (*Перелистывает книгу.*) Читал вот книгу и ничего не понял. Читал и заснул. (*Пауза.*)

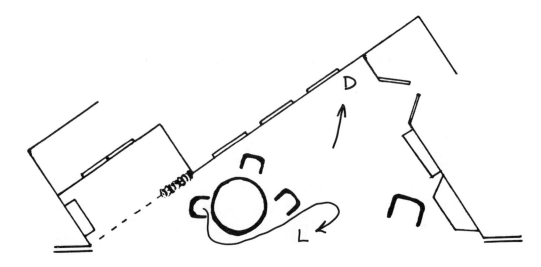

(LOPAKHIN)

I remember when I was a lad of fifteen, my dead father . . . he used to keep a little store here in the village in those days . . . he hit me in the face with his fist and made my nose bleed . . . we were here in the yard, I forget what we'd come about. He'd been drinking. Lyubov Andreyevna, I can see her now . . . she was still very young and so slim . . . led me to the washbowl, here in this very room . . . the nursery. She said, "Don't cry, little peasant, it'll be all right in time for your wedding day" . . . (*Pause.*) . . . Little peasant . . . my father was a peasant, it's true, but here I am in a white waistcoat and yellow shoes, like a pig in the front parlor. I've plenty of money, I'm a rich man . . . but when you come right down to it, a peasant is always a peasant. (*Leafs through book.*) I've been trying to read this book . . . can't understand a word of it . . . fell asleep over it . . . (*Pause.*)

*The staging, the mise-en-scène, is really connected with the manner of human beings' existence. The right mise-en-scène, groupings, relationships, should make the actors aware of some of their inner monologues. The whole meaning of the play is in its contrasts; I have the choice of having the actors do this from **within**. I aim at getting the actors closer to the Russian image, but from within, from their understanding: to awaken a sense of life in them. That is the sense of Chekhov's art.*

Lopakhin, you may clean your boots with your handkerchief if you choose. Lopakhin accepts his limitations; he knows that he is a peasant. Lopakhin has wisdom with all his crudeness. He knows he is a pig in the parlor.

When Lopakhin talks of his father, Chekhov is providing an echo of his own childhood experience; his father beat him frequently; his father also had a store. Dunyasha knows about Lopakhin's father.

Lopakhin makes a long speech; it's not to be taken fast, but with feeling. Pauses are very important. The necessary pauses focus our attention and continue the inner action; other pauses stop the audience's attention. These are the pauses we do not want. Lopakhin's speech about the past may not be a fact, but his feelings about it are revealing. Yes, Lopakhin hated his father, but don't make an angel out of Lopakhin.

ДУНЯША

А собаки всю ночь не спали, чуют, что хозяева
едут.

ЛОПАХИН

Что ты, Дуняша такая . . .

ДУНЯША

Руки трясутся. Я в обморок упаду.

ЛОПАХИН

Очень уж ты нежная, Дуняша. И одеваешься, как
барышня, и прическа тоже. Так нельзя. Надо себя
помнить.

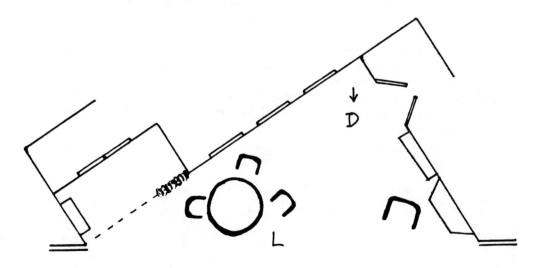

DUNYASHA

The dogs have been barking all night . . . they knew
the masters were coming.

LOPAKHIN

What's wrong with you, Dunyasha . . . why
are you . . .

DUNYASHA

My hands are shaking. I think I'm going to faint.

LOPAKHIN

You're too delicate, Dunyasha. Dressed like a lady
and just look at your hair! That's not right. One
should know one's place.

*Don't speak the line from the character and then shift back into yourself.
Start becoming the character while you sit there: a child-like spontaneity is
needed for the characters we are trying to become; the complete joy in playing.
Play, in a double sense. This is very subtle when a person is playing and
creating. A non-artist will act cerebrally. A true artist will be willing to try
something immediately.*

*I ask all the actors not to learn lines but to know the content. A person
says only part of what he thinks, and each sentence is surrounded by a lot of
unspoken thoughts one can't express. Lopakhin may have a plan or a drawing
of the possibilities of the cherry orchard. His conversation with Dunyasha
should be very casual.*

*Dunyasha thinks, 'He doesn't have to be a peasant if he would just learn
some manners.' On her speech, 'The dogs were barking. . .', Dunyasha
imagines an excited lady and pretends to be like that. This is the key to her
characterization. She sustains this fantasy on Lopakhin's speech, 'What's
wrong with you, Dunyasha? Why are you . . . [so this way?]' (Chekhov let the
actress complete this line in thought.) Dunyasha can't stand the quietness;
she's too excited.*

*Dunyasha is twenty-one years old; this matter of her age is an inner
rhythm. Dunyasha dreams of a big house, beautiful clothes, servants to order
about. Lopakhin considers Dunyasha to be Asiatic and hence low class.*

Входит Епиходов с букетом; он в пиджаке и в ярко вычищенных сапогах, которые сильно скрипят; войдя, он роняет букет.

ЕПИХОДОВ

(*поднимает букет*). Вот садовник прислал, говорит, в столовой поставить. (*Отдает Дуняше букет.*)

ЛОПАХИН

И квасу мне принесешь.

ДУНЯША

Слушаю. (*Уходит.*)

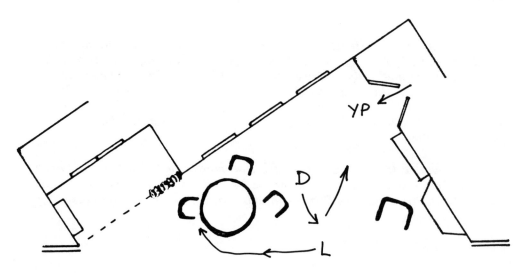

Enter YEPIKHODOV with a nosegay; he wears highly-polished, squeaking top-boots. He drops the nosegay as he comes in.

YEPIKHODOV

(*Picking up the nosegay.*) Here. The gardener sent this, says you are to put them in the dining-room. (*Gives* DUNYASHA *the nosegay.*)

LOPAKHIN

And bring me some kvass.[*]

DUNYASHA

Very well. (*Exits.*)

* — A homemade malt beverage.

Yepikhodov has entered with the flowers the gardener sent. Yepikhodov's direction to Dunyasha characterizes an air of anticipation. Each waits for a happy event: the arrival of Mme. Ranyevsky. Yepikhodov should be waiting for Dunyasha's return. He should try to attract Lopakhin's attention.

Yepikhodov's goal is to communicate with Dunyasha. Yepikhodov gets angry rather than nervous. Some of the nervousness is unnecessary. The more feeling of self-importance Yepikhodov has, the funnier his stumbling becomes.

Dunyasha thinks Yepikhodov is a wonderful man. She's impressed that he seems to love her to distraction. Yepikhodov should ponder more.

Today you can try this inner monologue . . . all I say will sink into your consciousness. With conscious means we are approaching unconscious thoughts and processes to create a performance. Stanislavski worked on this inner monologue in the last years of his life. These words are not yours now but they will become yours when they stop being words and have become thoughts.

The artist's point of view is always important, but the actor must have live feelings to be Chekhovian actors. Tune your soul into Chekhov's world. Actors are to see each new play as a new world.

ЕПИХОДОВ

Сейчас утренник, мороз три градуса, а вишня вся в цвету. Не могу одобрить нашего климата. (*Вздыхает.*) Не могу. Наш климат не может способствовать в самый раз. Вот, Ермолай Алексеич, позвольте вам присовокупить, купил я себе третьего дня сапоги, а они, смею вас уверить, скрипят так, что нет никакой возможности. Чем бы смазать?

ЛОПАХИН

Отстань. Надоел.

ЕПИХОДОВ

Каждый день случается со мной какое-нибудь несчастье. И я не ропщу, привык и даже улыбаюсь.

Дуняша входит, подает Лопахину квас.

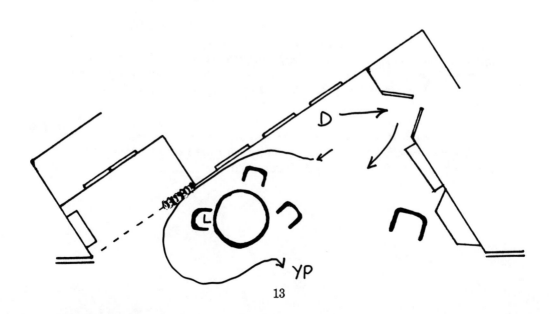

YEPIKHODOV

There's a frost this morning . . . minus three degrees . . . though the cherry trees are all in bloom. I cannot condone our climate. No, I cannot. (*Sighs.*) Our climate is incapable of suitable cooperation. Yermolay Alexeyevitch, permit me to call your attention to a further fact. The day before yesterday I purchased myself a pair of boots, and I dare to assure you, they squeak, so that it's really impossible. What should I grease them with?

LOPAKHIN

Leave me alone! I'm sick of you.

YEPIKHODOV

Every day some misfortune befalls me. I don't complain; I'm used to it; I even take it with a smile.

DUNYASHA comes in. Hands YEPIKHODOV the kvass.

There are a succession of actions for Dunyasha. She can overdo it at first, but what is important is the actress making sure that everything in the house is clean. On Yepikhodov's entrance, Dunyasha covertly reacts to him. She worries about the house; everything must be clean. She feels she is in charge; she is a perfectionist.

Dunyasha lives in the world of imagination; her imagination is the most important thing in her life; she does not know her place as a domestic.

Dunyasha admires Yepikhodov and thinks him a great intellect. She asks herself: 'Would I make him a good wife, or would I be too dumb? Would I ever be able to understand him? Does he think I am intelligent enough? He needs a woman. He's so unlucky; they tease him a lot. Maybe I could change all that for him.'

ЕПИХОДОВ

Я пойду. (*натыкается на стул, который падает.*) Вот... (*Как бы торжествуя.*) Вот видите, извините за выражение, какое обстоятельство, между прочим . . . Это просто даже замечательно! (*Уходит.*)

ДУНЯША

А мне, Ермолай Алексеич, признаться, Епиходов предложение сделал.

ЛОПАХИН

А!

ДУНЯША

Не знаю уж как.. Человек он смирный, а только иной раз, как начнет говорить, ничего не поймешь. И хорошо, и чувствительно, только не поймешь. Мне он как будто и нравится. Он меня любит безумно. Человек он несчастливый, каждый день что-нибудь. Его так и дразнят у нас: двадцать два несчастья . . .

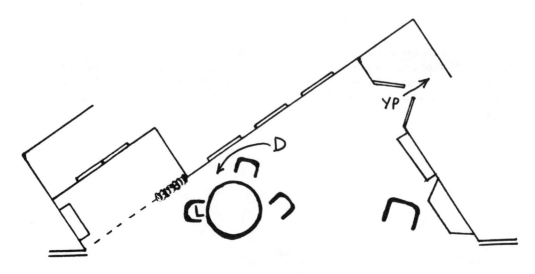

YEPIKHODOV

I'm going. (*Stumbles against a chair, which falls over.*) There! . . . pardon the expression . . . but there again . . . you see . . . bumping into another misfortune . . . it's positively remarkable . . . (YEPIKHODOV *exits.*)

DUNYASHA

You know, Yermolay Alexeyevitch, I simply must tell you, Yepikhodov has proposed to me!

LOPAKHIN

Ah.

DUNYASHA

I'm sure I don't know how . . . he's a quiet fellow, but sometimes when he begins talking, it just doesn't make sense. It's all very fine . . . makes you want to cry . . . but there's no understanding it. I kind of like him though, and he loves me madly. He's an unlucky man . . . every day something happens to him. They tease him about it . . . Twenty-Two Misfortunes, he's called.

Humor lies between the absurdity of the character and Yepikhodov's pretensions, and that he lacks the basis for these pretensions. One of the funniest experiences in the Moscow Art Theatre was the time when Nemirovitch-Danchenko stumbled off the stage. He was very distinguished, with a well-kept beard. He liked women a great deal, and he liked to be respected. But, he was short. When standing with Stanislavski to have his picture taken, he would stand on a step. Once he stumbled when walking into a room. It was so funny because he, like Yepikhodov, was pompous.

Dunyasha is embarrassed at telling Lopakhin that she likes Yepikhodov. Her talk about him comes out of Yepikhodov's exit. Dunyasha is asking Lopakhin's advice in a sense, for she likes Yepikhodov.

ЛОПАХИН

(*прислушивается*). Вот, кажется, едут . . .

ДУНЯША

Едут! Что ж это со мной . . . похолодела вся.

ЛОПАХИН

Едут, в самом деле. Пойдем встречать. Узнает ли она меня? Пять лет не видались.

ДУНЯША

(*в волнении*). Я сейчас упаду . . . Ах, упаду!

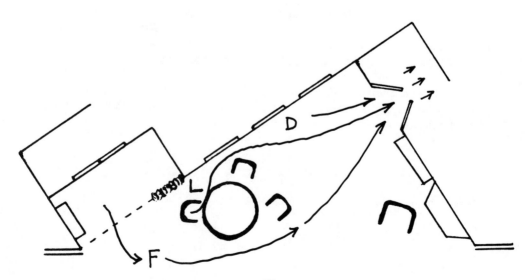

LOPAKHIN

(*Listening.*) There. I do believe they're coming.

DUNYASHA

They *are* coming! What's the matter with me . . . I'm all in a tremble!

LOPAKHIN

They really are coming. Let's go and meet them. Will she know me? It's five years since I saw her.

DUNYASHA

(*In a flutter.*) I'm going to faint . . . I know I am . . .

Actors, know what is happening in the first scene. For example, Dunyasha is trying to keep from getting even more excited. She is full of excitement about love; all sorts of men are asking her to marry them. She asks herself, 'what shall I do?'

In working with you actors, I ask you to start from yourself to create a character. It isn't just different cosmetic make-up, but a different person behind the actors' make-up and a different inner rhythm. Start from yourself and find new traits of yourself in order to create the character you play. Each role is a part of the totality, like a composition.

Слышно, как к дому подъезжают два экипажа. Лопахин и Дуняша быстро уходят. Сцена пуста. В соседних комнатах начинается шум. Через сцену, опираясь на палочку, торопливо проходит Фирс, ездивший встречать Любовь Андреевну; он в старинной ливрее и в высокой шляпе; он что-то говорит сам с собой, но нельзя разобрать ни одного слова. Шум за сценой все усиливается. Голос: " Вот пройдемте здесь . . ." Любовь Андреевна, Аня и Шарлотта Ивановна с собачкой на цепочке, одетые по-дорожному, Варя в пальто и платке, Гаев, Семеонов-Пищик, Лопахин, Дуняша с узлом и зонтиком, прислуга с вещами - все идут через комнату.

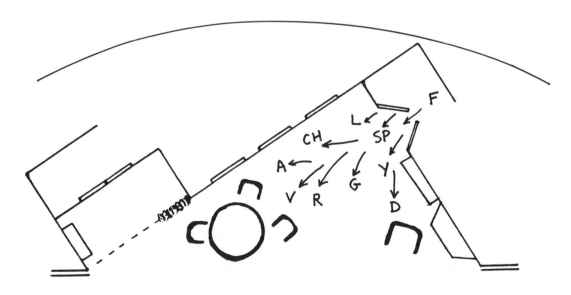

There is the sound of two carriages driving up to the house. LOPAKHIN and DUNYASHA go out quickly. The stage is left empty. A noise is heard from the adjoining rooms. FIRS, who has driven to meet LYUBOV ANDREYEVNA, crosses the stage hurriedly, leaning on a stick. He is wearing old-fashioned livery and a high hat. He says something to himself, but the words are indistinguishable. The noise behind the scene goes on increasing. A voice: "Come, let's go in here." Enter LYUBOV ANDREYEVNA, ANYA, and CHARLOTTA IVANOVNA with a pet dog on a chain; all wear traveling dresses; VARYA, in an outdoor coat with a kerchief over her head, GAYEV, SIMEONOV-PISCHIK, LOPAKHIN, DUNYASHA with bag and parasol, SERVANTS with other articles. All walk across the room.

What is Firs' inner monologue at the moment of his entrance? He thinks about the coffee; he is happy at their return. In addition, he is preoccupied with the placement of luggage, and he is displeased with the way things are done now.

Actors must be careful not to crowd the entrance. Yuri Zavadski told the cast that Stanislavski had a stage wait of a full minute before the entrance of the family. A minute seems very long to an audience; it was a daring thing to do. (Chekhov's stage directions merely state: the stage is left empty.)

Goals of the scene of arrival are reactions to the return of those returning, and reactions of those who have returned.

The arrival scene can be a problem. There must be a lot of improvisation on the arrival, just as on the second entrance of Lyubov and Gayev, but we shouldn't hear individual sentences which Chekhov has not written. The actors' ad-libbing cannot be too articulate. Each actor must find an inner motivation to be in the scene and look for the continuous uninterrupted line of action. The method is basically consecutiveness, continuity. It is important for everyone to have patience.

As characters, be aware that it's cold outside. Actors, forget yourself completely. Stanislavski called it naiveté. You must not think; a true artist will try immediately. Sitting in chairs, you should be preparing your characters. You could try it in a corner walking around. If you wish, you may have some elements of costume or props for rehearsal.

The actor may not reach the depth and power immediately, but he or she must not lose the sense of truth. Each actor is to react to each other in terms of his character, and the spontaneity of everything happening for the first time.

I would like to look only for the pantomime of the performance, the movement; to look for elements of character in movements, gestures, and in the mise-en-scène.

АНЯ

Пройдемте здесь. Ты, мама, помнишь, какая это комната?

ЛЮБОВЬ АНДРЕЕВНА

(*радостно, сквозь слезы*). Детская!

ВАРЯ

Как холодно, у меня руки закоченели. (*Любови Андреевне.*) Ваши комнаты, белая и фиолетовая, такими же и остались, мамочка.

ЛЮБОВЬ АНДРЕЕВНА

Детская, милая моя, прекрасная комната . . . Я тут спала, когда была маленькой . . . (*Плачет.*) И теперь я, как маленькая . . . (*Целует брата, Варю, потом опять брата.*) А Варя по-прежнему все такая же, на монашку похожа. И Дуняшу я узнала . . . (*целует Дуняшу.*)

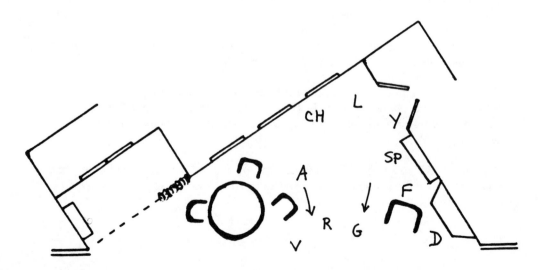

ANYA

Let's go through here. Do you remember this room, Mama?

LYUBOV

(*Joyfully, through her tears.*) The nursery!

VARYA

How cold it is! My hands are stiff! (*To* LYUBOV ANDREYEVNA.) Your rooms are just the same, Mama, the white one and the lavender.

LYUBOV

The dear old nursery! . . . Lovely room! I used to sleep here when I was a child . . . (*Cries.*) And here I am, just like a child again. (*Kisses her brother and* VARYA *and then her brother again.*) Varya's just the same as ever, like a nun. And I recognize Dunyasha. (*Kisses* DUNYASHA.)

Varya's line, 'how cold it is!', is said by her to get Mme. Ranyevsky out of the mood of crying; e.g., on 'the nursery'.

Lyubov's hands are for show, created to be kissed. Lyubov, you must be aware of your hands. I've already noticed that the American woman's gestures with her hands are somewhat energetic and masculine. Mme. Ranyevsky feels gay, but it is the gaiety of yesterday that cannot be recreated.

Varya, react to Mme. Ranyevsky's line, 'like a nun'. Your reaction is as if to say: 'you shouldn't talk about me'.

The play has to be expressed both in space and time . . . a conscious awareness combined with imagination is what I, as director, am trying to develop in you.

ГАЕВ

Поезд опоздал на два часа. Каково? Каковы порядки?

ШАРЛОТТА

(*Пищику*). Моя собака и орехи кушает.

ПИЩИК

(*удивленно*). Вы подумайте!

Уходят все, кроме Ани и Дуняши.

ДУНЯША

Заждались мы... (*Снимает с Ани пальто, шляпу.*)

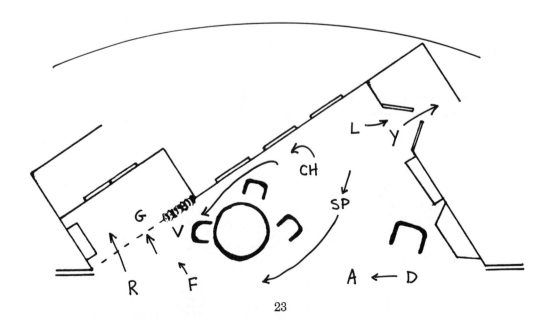

GAYEV

The train was two hours late. What do you think of that? What a way to do things!

CHARLOTTA

(*To* PISCHIK.) My dog eats nuts, too.

PISCHIK

(*Wonderingly.*) Imagine that!

They all go out, except ANYA and DUNYASHA.

DUNYASHA

We've been expecting you for hours. (*Takes* ANYA's *hat and coat.*)

Please, actors: never play just yourself. Your relationship to others is an interlocking relationship of character. A person doesn't exist by himself, but in relationship to others. This is true in life. It is only "actors" who come on stage and say, 'Here I am!'

Every word in the text helps unfold the characters. Charlotta's reference to her dog underlines her loneliness.

АНЯ

Я не спала в дороге четыре ночи . . . теперь озябла очень.

ДУНЯША

Вы уехали в великом посту, тогда был снег, был мороз, а теперь? Милая моя! (*Смеется, целует ее.*) Заждалась вас, радость моя, светик . . . Я скажу вам сейчас, одной минутки не могу утерпеть . . .

АНЯ

(*вяло*). Опять что-нибудь . . .

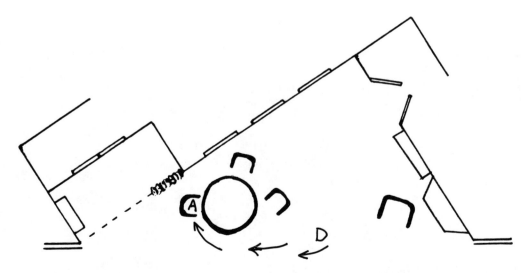

ANYA

Four whole nights I haven't slept on the train . . . and now I'm frozen . . .

DUNYASHA

It was freezing hard and snowy when you left during Lent, and now . . . my darling! (*Laughs and kisses her.*) I have missed you, my treasure, my joy! But I must tell you . . . I can't put it off another minute . ..

ANYA

(*Wearily.*) What now?

The goal of this scene is that Dunyasha wants to tell Anya, impress upon her, that Yepikhodov has proposed to her, that she's grown up now. Not too many people like Dunyasha, but Anya does.

Anya, the tiredness you have is your own tiredness. You can't play tiredness.

*I want to call the actors' attention once more to the fact that in life when you tell someone something, you have a **relationship** to what you are saying. It is the subtlety of that relationship which you have to explore: the reasons why you say it, for not a single phrase is accidental.*

ДУНЯША

Конторщик Епиходов после Святой мне предложение сделал.

АНЯ

Ты все об одном . . . (*Поправляя волосы.*) Я растеряла все шпильки . . . (*Она очень утомлена, даже пошатывается.*)

ДУНЯША

Уж не знаю, что и думать. Он меня любит, так любит!

АНЯ

(*глядит в свою дверь, нежно*). Моя комната, мои окна, как будто я не уезжала. Я дома! Завтра утром встану, побегу в сад . . . О, если бы я могла уснуть! Я не спала всю дорогу, томило меня беспокойство.

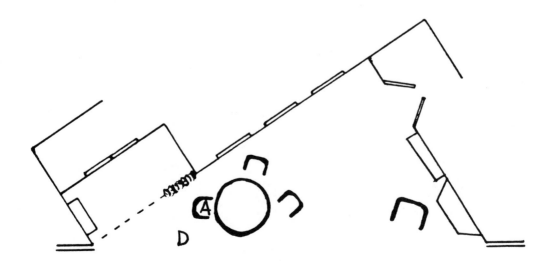

DUNYASHA

The bookkeeper, Yepikhodov, proposed to me, just after Easter.

ANYA

There you go, always the same thing. (*Straightening her hair.*) I've lost all my hairpins. (*She is staggering from exhaustion.*)

DUNYASHA

Really, I don't know what to think. He loves me . . . he does love me so!

ANYA

(*Looking toward her door, tenderly.*) My own room, my windows, just as though I'd never been away. I'm home! Tomorrow morning I shall get up and run out into the garden. Oh, if I could just get some sleep. I didn't close my eyes the whole journey . . . I was so anxious and worried.

Anya always drops her hairpins; her hair is always coming down. This is one of the keys to Anya. She is the kind of young woman who can never keep her hairpins in place.

*On Dunyasha's speech about Yepikhodov, she is asking advice of Anya: 'Should I marry him? I may hurt him. He loves me, or **does** he love me?' These are suggested subtext thoughts for Dunyasha.*

Anya, on her speech, 'my own room, my windows', is caught up in her own subjective thought, not listening to Dunyasha. Dunyasha's subtext thought to that is: 'Well, I'll ask Anya another time.'

ДУНЯША

Третьего дня Петр Сергеич приехали.

АНЯ

(*радостно*). Петя!

ДУНЯША

В бане спят, там и живут. Боюсь, говорят, стеснить. (*Взглянув на свои карманные часы.*) Надо бы их разбудить, да Варвара Михайловна не велела. Ты, говорит, его не буди.

Входит Варя, на поясе у нее вязка ключей.

ВАРЯ

Дуняша, кофе поскорей . . . Мамочка кофе просит.

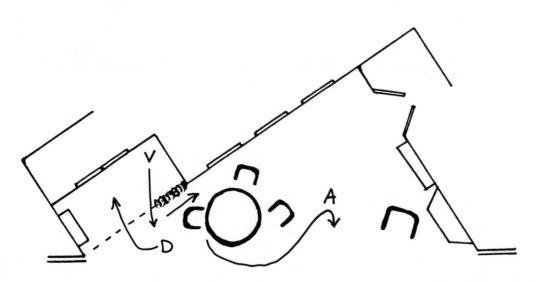

DUNYASHA

Master Trofimov came the day before yesterday.

ANYA

(*Joyfully.*) Petya!

DUNYASHA

He's sleeping in the bath house. He has settled in there. Said he was afraid of being in the way. (*Looks at her pocket watch.*) I should have waked him, but Miss Varya told me not to. "Don't you dare wake him," said she.

Enter VARYA with a bunch of keys at her waist.

VARYA

Dunyasha, coffee, quick . . . Mamotchka's asking for coffee.

As a subtext for Dunyasha when she makes reference to where Trofimov, the former tutor, is sleeping, she is thinking, 'I would have settled him to sleep in here, but Trofimov didn't want to'.

Dunyasha's telling about Trofimov's having come the day before yesterday is a secret. Dunyasha evokes her characterization from identifying with household effects.

ДУНЯША

Сию минуточку. (*Уходит.*)

ВАРЯ

Ну, слава богу, приехали. Опять ты дома. (*Ласкаясь.*) Душечка моя приехала! Красавица приехала!

АНЯ

Натерпелась я.

ВАРЯ

Воображаю!

АНЯ

Выехала я на Страстной неделе, тогда было холодно. Шарлотта всю дорогу говорит, представляет фокусы. И зачем ты навязала мне Шарлотту . . .

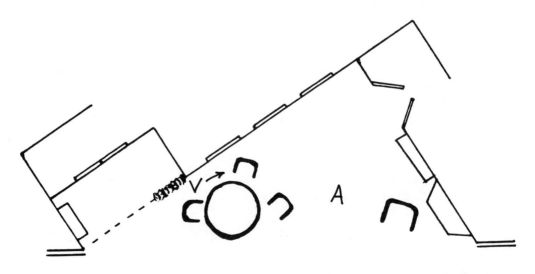

DUNYASHA

This minute. (*Exits.*)

VARYA

Well, thank God you've come.(VARYA *crosses to* ANYA.) You're home again. My pretty one's home again. (*Kissing* ANYA *on both cheeks.*)

ANYA

Oh, what I've been through!

VARYA

I can imagine.

ANYA

When we left it was Holy Week, it was cold then, and all the way Charlotta would talk and show off her tricks. What did you want to burden me with Charlotta for?

Varya's goal is to share her burden with Anya, her "child." She takes on the responsibility for the entire family. Varya is preoccupied throughout the act and busy until the scene with Gayev, when she can finally sit down and rest.

ВАРЯ

Нельзя же тебе одной ехать, душечка. В семнадцать лет!

АНЯ

Приезжаем в Париж, там холодно, снег. По-французски говорю я ужасно. Мама живет на пятом этаже, прихожу к ней, у нее какие-то французы, дамы, старый патер* с книжкой, и накурено, неуютно. Мне вдруг стало жаль мамы, так жаль, я обняла ее голову, сжала руками и не могу выпустить. Мама потом все ласкалась, плакала .

ВАРЯ

(*сквозь слезы*). Не говори, не говори . . .

* Католический священик.

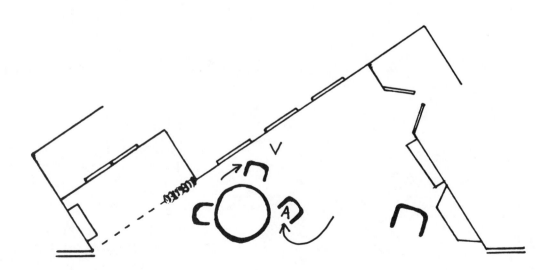

VARYA

(*Crossing to center chair above table*). You couldn't have traveled all alone, darling — at seventeen!

ANYA

We got to Paris, it was cold there, too — snowing. My French is dreadful. Mama lived on the fifth floor. She had all kinds of French people there, ladies, an old priest with a book. The place was full of smoke and so uncomfortable. Suddenly I felt so sorry for Mama — I put my arms round her and hugged her and wouldn't let her go . . . then Mama made such a fuss over me, and she kept crying . . .

VARYA

(*Through her tears.*) Don't talk about it . . . don't. . .

The goals of the scene are Varya's wish that Anya share her burden, while Anya wants to tell someone what Paris was like. Although Anya is a young lady, for Varya, Anya is a baby. When Anya is speaking about Paris: 'ladies, and a priest with a book', she should name them fast.

Anya, while talking about Paris, thinks, 'I can talk about it, but it is about my mother's life in Paris.' Varya's objective is to protect Anya from all ugliness. Varya knows life, but Anya has come into contact with life for the first time in Paris.

Anya has the best of Mme. Ranyevsky in her: her sincerity, her capacity for great happiness, and her ability to forget misfortunes. In Mme. Ranyevsky, it is light-headedness; in Anya, it is youth. Anya is actually better than Mme. Ranyevsky, quite sincere.

АНЯ

Дачу свою около Ментоны она уже продала, у нее ничего не осталось, ничего. У меня тоже не осталось ни копейки, едва доехали. И мама не понимает! Сядем на вокзале обедать, и она требует самое дорогое и на чай лакеям дает по рублю. Шарлотта тоже. Яша тоже требует себе порцию, просто ужасно. Ведь у мамы лакей Яша, мы привезли его сюда . . . .

ВАРЯ

Видела подлеца.

АНЯ

Ну что, как? Заплатили проценты?

ВАРЯ

Где там.

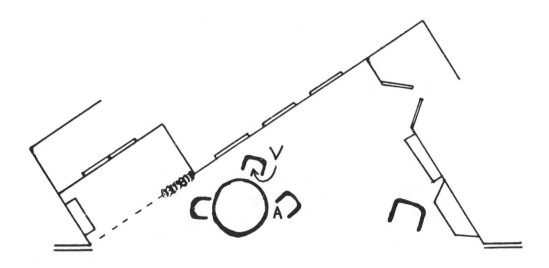

ANYA

She had sold her villa at Menton, she had nothing left, nothing. I hadn't a kopek left either, we only just had enough to get here. And Mama wouldn't understand! When we had dinner at the railway station, she always ordered the most expensive thing and gave the waiters a whole rouble. Charlotta's just the same. Yasha insisted on having everything we had — it's simply awful. You know we brought Yasha back with us, he's Mama's manservant now.

VARYA

Yes, I've seen the little wretch. (VARYA *sits.*)

ANYA

Well, tell me — have you paid the interest?

VARYA

What with?

АНЯ

Боже мой, боже мой . . .

ВАРЯ

В августе будут продавать имение . . .

АНЯ

Боже мой..

Заглядывает в дверь и мычит.

ЛОПАХИН

Ме-е-е . . . (*Уходит.*)

ВАРЯ

(*сквозь слезы*). Вот так бы и дала ему . . .
(*Грозит кулаком.*)

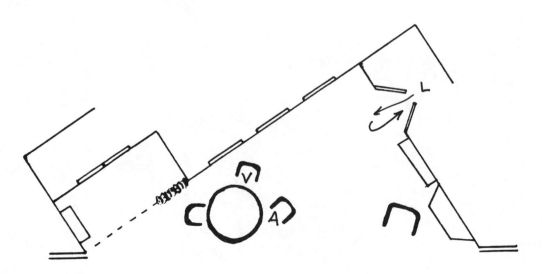

ANYA

Oh, God! Oh, God! (ANYA *sits in chair left of table.*)

VARYA

In August, they'll put the estate up for sale.

ANYA

My God!

LOPAKHIN peeps in at the door and moos like a cow.

LOPAKHIN

Moo-oo. (*Disappears.*)

VARYA

(*Weeping, shakes her fist. She rises as she weeps.*)
There — that's what I could do to him!

Lopakhin's stage business, peeping in at the door and mooing like a cow, means that Lopakhin never knows what to do.

АНЯ

(*обнимает Варю, тихо*). Варя, он сделал предложение? (*Варя отрицательно качает головой.*) Ведь он же тебя любит . . . Отчего вы не объяснитесь, чего вы ждете?

ВАРЯ

Я так думаю, ничего у нас не выйдет. У него дела много, ему не до меня . . . и внимания не обращает. Бог с ним совсем, тяжело мне его видеть . . . Все говорят о нашей свадьбе, все поздравляют, а на самом деле ничего нет, все как сон . . . (*Другим тоном.*) У тебя брошка вроде, как пчелка.

АНЯ

(*печально*). Это мама купила. (*Идет в свою комнату, говорит весело, по-детски.*) А в Париже я на воздушном шаре летала!

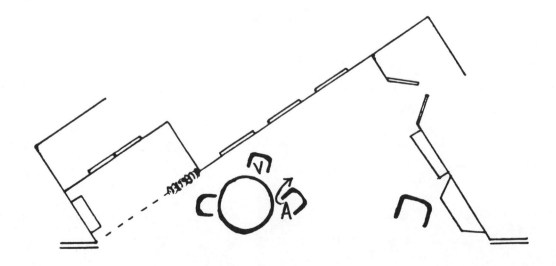

ANYA

(*Embracing* VARYA, *softly.*) Varya, has he proposed to you? (VARYA *shakes her head*) But he loves you. Why can't the two of you make up your minds? What are the two of you waiting for?

VARYA

Oh, nothing will ever come of it. He's too busy, has no time for me. . . . takes no notice of me. Somehow . . . it's hard for me to see him. They all talk about our getting married — they all congratulate me — and all the time, there's really nothing in it — it's just a dream. (*In another tone.*) You have a new brooch like a bumblebee.

ANYA

(*Mournfully.*) Mama bought it. (*She goes into her own room, and speaks gaily like a child.*) You know, in Paris I went up in a balloon.

In reference to the bumblebee brooch, the line should be done fast.

Varya, as soon as you believe you are in charge of the house, as soon as you are interested in the house (you even speak of the dust,) you, as actress, will have found one small element of Varya.

Varya is not at all a lady; she is the housekeeper.

ВАРЯ

Душечка моя приехала! Красавица приехала!

Дуняша уже вернулась с кофейником и варит кофе. Варя стоит около двери.

ВАРЯ

Хожу я, душечка, цельный день по хозяйству и все мечтаю. Выдать бы тебя за богатого человека, и я бы тогда была покойней, пошла бы себе в пустынь, потом в Киев . . . в Москву, и так бы все ходила по святым местам . . . Ходила бы и ходила. Благолепие! . . .

АНЯ

Птицы поют в саду. Который теперь час?

ВАРЯ

Должно, третий. Тебе пора спать, душечка. (*Входя в комнату к Ане.*) Благолепие!

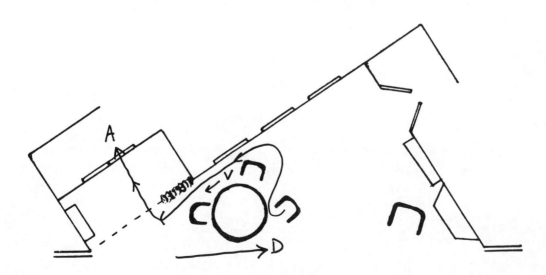

VARYA

My little one's come home, my beauty's come home again!

DUNYASHA returns with the coffee pot, and VARYA stands at the door of ANYA's room.

VARYA

All day long, darling, as I go about the house, I keep dreaming. If only we could marry you to a rich man, I should feel more at peace. Then I would go off and buy myself a pilgrimage to Kiev, to Moscow . . . I would spend my life going from one holy place to another . . . I'd go on and on . . . how blessed that would be.

ANYA

The birds are singing in the orchard. What time is it?

VARYA

It must be nearly two. Time you were asleep, darling. (VARYA *goes into* ANYA's *room.*) How blessed that would be.

I want to create the inner atmosphere, a very special atmosphere. I am plunging you into an atmosphere of half-tones. But we will succeed in getting the right atmosphere and will get valuable memories. I would like you to be permeated by this atmosphere. Chekhov is talking of the flow of human life.

There's a difference in the inner rhythm of Anya and Varya. What does Varya dream of? Going away to forget; complete renunciation of the world; to have no responsibility; just to wander around listening to church music; to leave the everyday world. Anya, however, is full of the joy of life. She has a great desire to live; she believes in life.

Входит Яша с пледом, дорожной сумочкой. Идет через сцену, деликатно.

ЯША

Тут можно пройти-с?

ДУНЯША

И не узнаешь вас, Яша. Какой вы стали за границей.

ЯША

Гм . . . А вы кто?

ДУНЯША

Когда вы уезжали отсюда, я была этакой . . . (*показывает от полу.*) Дуняша, Федора Козоедова дочь. Вы не помните!

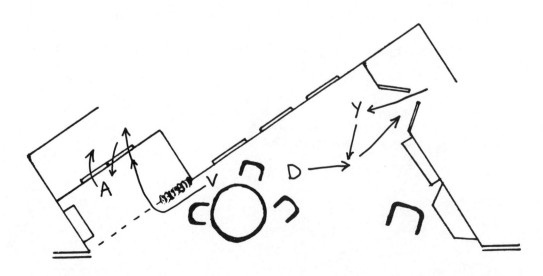

YASHA enters with a rug and a traveling bag. He crosses the stage delicately.

YASHA

May one come in here, pray?

DUNYASHA

Yasha! I didn't know you! How you've changed abroad.

YASHA

Hm-m . . . and who are you?

DUNYASHA

When you went away, I was that high. (*Indicates distance from floor.*) Dunyasha — Fyodor's daughter . . . Don't you remember?

On Yasha's entrance, Dunyasha thinks of him as an extraordinary person. Perhaps he is the man? On her speech, 'Fyodor's daughter,' Dunyasha is thinking, 'Yasha's a higher being. He's extraordinary!' Dunyasha compares Yasha to Yepikhodov, finding Yepikhodov uncouth.

Dunyasha's skirt should be short, but a little longer than Anya's. Throughout Act One, Dunyasha is wondering how to arrange her life.

Yepikhodov is heard singing offstage. Dunyasha's reaction to hearing it should be a big reaction.

ЯША

Гм.. Огурчик! (*Оглядывается и обнимает ее: она вскрикивает и роняет блюдечко. Яша быстро уходит.*)

ВАРЯ

(*в дверях, недовольным голосом*). Что еще тут?

ДУНЯША

(*сквозь слезы*). Блюдечко разбила . . .

ВАРЯ

Это к добру.

АНЯ

(*выйдя из своей комнаты*). Надо бы маму предупредить: Петя здесь . . .

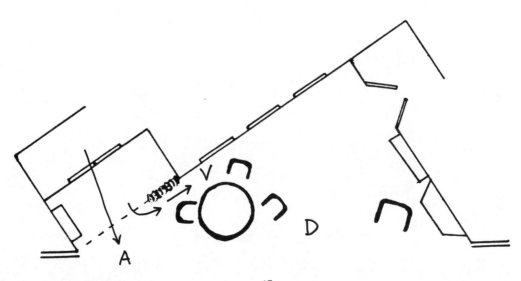

YASHA

H'm! What a peach! (*He looks round and then embraces her. She shrieks and drops a saucer.* YASHA *goes out quickly.*)

VARYA

(*In the doorway, in a tone of vexation.*) What's going on here?

DUNYASHA

(*Through tears.*) I've broken a saucer.

VARYA

(VARYA *crosses upstage center.*) Oh, well, that's good luck.

ANYA

(*Coming out of her room.*) We should warn Mama Petya's here.

Dunyasha takes the candle off with her when she has broken the saucer.

When we're onstage as actors unfortunately, we know all the words. We must be able not so much to play the text as to react to it. One should play not parts, but the interrelationship between people. I want to produce in you the desire to talk to each other. One reacts immediately to simple things, such as, 'do you want tea?' But in more complex circumstances, it takes a moment to understand, to comprehend, as when a person has died. We are trying to reach for different characters.

ВАРЯ

Я приказала его не будить.

АНЯ

(*задумчиво*). Шесть лет тому назад умер отец, через месяц утонул в реке брат Гриша, хорошенький семилетний мальчик. Мама не перенесла, ушла, ушла без оглядки . . . (*Вздрагивает.*) Как я ее понимаю если бы она знала! (*Пауза.*) А Петя Трофимов был учителем Гриши, он может напомнить . . .

Входит Фирс: он в пиджаке и белом жилете.

ФИРС

(*идет к кофейнику, озабоченно*). Барыня здесь будут кушать . . . (*Надевает белые перчатки.*) Готов кофий? (*Строго Дуняше.*) Ты! А сливки?

ДУНЯША

Ах, боже мой . . . (*Быстро уходит.*)

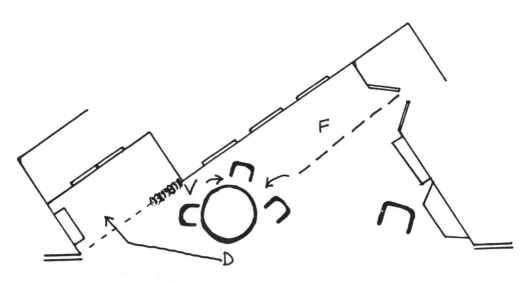

VARYA

I left orders not to wake him.

ANYA

(*Pensively.*) Six years ago father died. A month later, brother Grisha drowned in the river. A cute seven-year-old boy. Mama didn't get over it. She went away and never looked back. (*Trembling.*) I understand her so well, if only she knew! (*Pause.*) And Petya Trofimov was Grisha's tutor. He might remind her.

Enter FIRS wearing a tie, a frock coat, with white gloves and a white waistcoat.

FIRS

(*Goes up to the coffee pot anxiously.*) The mistress will be served here. (*Puts on white gloves.*) Is the coffee ready? (*Sternly to* DUNYASHA.) Ech, you! Where's the cream?

DUNYASHA

Oh, my God! (DUNYASHA *follows* FIRS *upstage of the table and goes out quickly.*)

Anya, some things are important in passing. Don't look at Varya in, 'I understand mama so well.' That refers to Grisha.

Between Mme. Ranyevsky and Firs there is an inner relationship. Firs' goal is that nothing changes; he wants to please the mistress to prove his worth. Firs' major job is to see to the other rooms. Stanislavski used to call these the mechanical elements.

Firs has two costumes; one is the livery of a footman, the other is for the home, a black coat with a vest and white gloves.

ФИРС

(*хлопочет около кофейника.*) Эх, ты, недотепа . . . (*бормочет про себя.*) Приехали из Парижа . . . И барин когда-то ездил в Париж . . . на лошадях . . . (*Смеется.*)

ВАРЯ

Фирс, ты о чем?

ФИРС

Чего изволите? (*Радостно.*) Барыня моя приехала! Дождался! теперь хоть и помереть . . . (*Плачет от радости.*)

Входят Любовь Андреевна, Гаев и Симеонов - Пищик; Симеонов - Пищик в поддевке из тонкого сукна и шароварах. Гаев, входя, руками и туловищем делает движения, как будто играет на бильярде.

ЛЮБОВЬ АНДРЕЕВНА

Как это? Дай-ка вспомнить . . . Желтого в угол! Дуплет в середину!

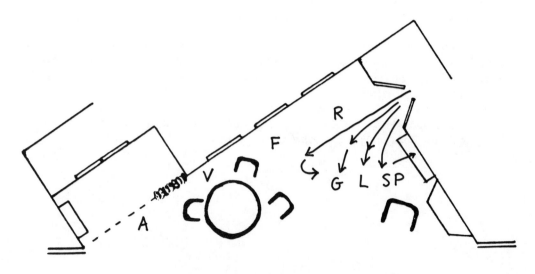

FIRS

(*Fusses around the coffee-pot, muttering to himself.*)
Ech, you good-for-nothing! Home from Paris. And the
old master used to go to Paris too . . . horses all the
way. (*He laughs.*)

VARYA

Firs, what are you muttering about?

FIRS

What is your wish? (*Joyfully.*) My mistress has come
home, and I have lived to see it! Now I can die. (*Weeps
with joy.*)

Enter LYUBOV ANDREYEVNA, GAYEV, and SIMEONOV-PISHCHIK. The latter is
in a short-waisted, full coat of fine cloth, and full trousers. GAYEV, as he
comes in makes a gesture with his arms and body, as though he were playing
billiards.

LYUBOV

Let's see, how does it go? Carom off the red!

*Simeonov-Pishchik had been at the train with the others awaiting for the
arrival of Mme. Ranyevsky. He is very much the peasant, but he's very
prosperous. Although as a man, Pishchik's interest is in the soil in his way
of thinking and feeling, he is not the subhuman stereotype of a peasant. He
may dress richly, but it is in a 'kulak' or rich peasant style.*

*Firs, be specific. It is in the shoulders where Firs has the rheumatism.
Stanislavski called these elements the mechanical part of the work, but they
should become habitual for you. You should not **play** the feelings. If you start
right, these feelings will come to you. If you start showing your feelings right
away, you will kill them. Work on action and business. They are more closely
related.*

Firs knows he is in his last days. He is dying soon.

ГАЕВ

Режу в угол! Когда-то мы с тобой, сестра, спали вот в этой самой комнате, а теперь мне уже пятьдесят один год, как это ни странно . . .

ЛОПАХИН

Да, время идет.

ГАЕВ

Кого!

ЛОПАХИН

Время, говорю, идет.

ГАЕВ

А здесь пачулями *пахнет.

* Небольшое ост-индокитайское растение из семейства губоцветных.

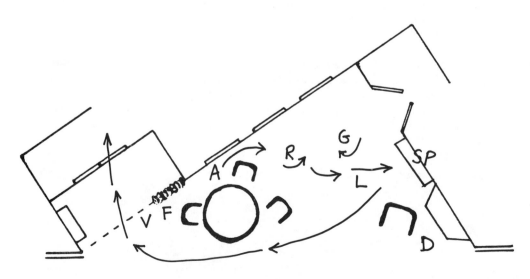

GAYEV

That's it — in off the white! Once upon a time, sister, you and I used to sleep in this very room, and now I'm fifty-one, strange as it may seem.

LOPAKHIN[*]

Yes, time flies.

GAYEV

Who?

LOPAKHIN

Time, I say, flies.

GAYEV

Posh! What a smell of patchouli!

[*] — There is no stage direction from Chekhov indicating Lopakhin's return. It is assumed that he enters with Lyubov Andreyvna, Gayev and Simeonov-Pishchik.

Gayev has moments when he is serious and comprehending. He is not a fool, but he plays the fool, almost a clown. On Gayev's 'who?', please, all actors listen to everyone. One talks, and others listen. You all hear everything, and all react. Only then will you have the whole.

АНЯ

Я спать пойду. Спокойной ночи, мама. (*Целует мать.*)

ЛЮБОВЬ АНДРЕЕВНА

Ненаглядная дитюся моя. (*Целует ей руки.*) Ты рада, что ты дома? Я никак в себя не приду.

АНЯ

Прощай, дядя.

ГАЕВ

(*целует ей лицо, руки*). Господь с тобой. Как ты похожа на свою мать! (*Сестре.*) Ты, Люба, в ее годы была точно такая.

Аня подает руку Лопахину и Пищику, уходит и затворяет за собой дверь.

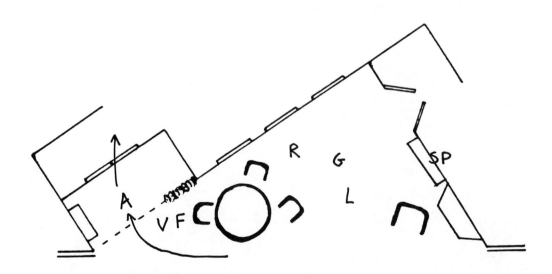

ANYA

I'm going to bed. Good night, Mama. (*Kisses her mother.*)

LYUBOV

My precious child! (*Kisses her hands.*) Are you happy to be home? I can't believe it's true.

ANYA

Good night, uncle.

GAYEV

(*Kissing her face and hands.*) God bless you, how like your mother you are! (*To his sister.*) At her age, Lyuba, you looked just like her.

ANYA shakes hands with LOPAKHIN and PISHCHIK then goes out, shutting the door after her.

Feelings will come as a result of the whole work. Search for a deeper motivation of all your actions. Search as much as you can for the reasons for transitions. Make them your own. That is the work of yourselves.

Anya, not too big a smile on, 'good night, mama.'

ЛЮБОВЬ АНДРЕЕВНА

Она утомилась очень.

ПИЩИК

Дорога, небось, длинная.

ВАРЯ

(*Лопахину и Пищику*). Что ж, господа? Третий час, пора и честь знать.

ЛЮБОВЬ АНДРЕЕВНА

(*смеется*). Ты все такая же, Варя, (*Привлекает ее к себе и целует.*) Вот выпью кофе, тогда все уйдем. (*Фирс кладет ей под ноги подушечку.*) Спасибо, родной. Я привыкла к кофе. Пью его и днем и ночью. Спасибо, мой старичок. (*Целует Фирса.*)

ВАРЯ

Поглядеть, все ли вещи привезли . . . (*Уходит.*)

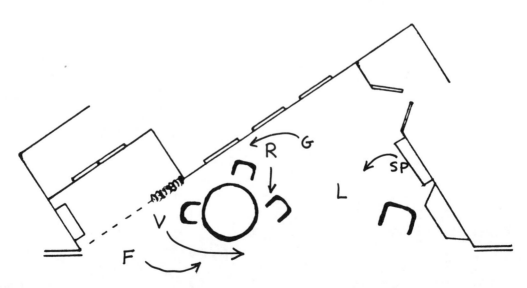

LYUBOV

She's very tired.

PISHCHIK

Well, it's a long journey. (*Rises.*)

VARYA

(*Crossing down left. To* LOPAKHIN *and* PISCHIK.) How about it gentlemen? It's past two o'clock — time you were going.

LYUBOV

(*Laughs.*) You're just the same as ever, Varya. (*Draws her to him and kisses her.*) I'll drink my coffee and then we'll all say goodnight. (FIRS *puts a cushion under her feet.*) Thank you my friend . . . thanks. I can't live without coffee. I drink it day and night. (*Kisses* FIRS.) You sweet little old man.

VARYA

I'd better see if all of the things have been brought in. (*She goes out.*)

Pishchik start to rise as Varya says, 'how about it, gentlemen.' Mme. Ranyevsky stops him.

As you understand and believe in the circumstances, your image is developed into something you can believe. Each day it must be clearer and closer to you.

ЛЮБОВЬ АНДРЕЕВНА

Неужели это я сижу? (*Смеется.*) Мне хочется прыгать, размахивать руками. (*Закрывает лицо руками.*) А вдруг я сплю! Видит бог, я люблю родину, люблю нежно, я не могла смотреть из вагона, все плакала. (*Сквозь слезы.*) Однакоже, надо пить кофе. Спасибо тебе, Фирс, спасибо, мой старичок. Я так рада, что ты еще жив.

ФИРС

Позавчера.

ГАЕВ

Он плохо слышит.

ЛОПАХИН

Мне сейчас, в пятом часу утра, в Харьков ехать. Такая досада! Хотелось поглядеть на вас, поговорить... Вы все такая же великолепная.

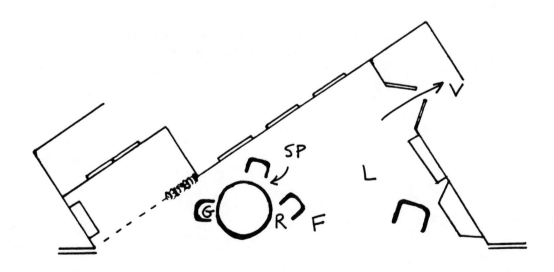

LYUBOV

Can it really be me sitting here? (*She laughs.*) I feel like dancing and clapping my hands. And yet in a second, I could be fast asleep. God knows I love my country, I love it tenderly; I couldn't look out of the window in the train, I kept crying so. However, I must drink my coffee. Thank you, Firs, thank you dear old man. I'm so happy that you're still alive.

FIRS

Day before yesterday.

GAYEV

He's grown very deaf.

LOPAKHIN

I must go in a minute. I'm leaving for Kharkov at five o'clock. So tiresome. I'd like to go on looking at you; I'd like to go on talking . . . you're just as magnificent as ever.

*Mme. Ranyevsky's speech at the top of this page provides atmosphere. It may be old, but remember to listen, remember, to affect the others is the **only** reason for talking. If only actors would remember that!*

In the course of the role, the actor should change both his inner and outer image. If the actor starts to play the outer image too early, the actor will leave the inner core untouched. Actually, things on the stage are never real. But now, believe this: 'this is your desk, your table,' etc. Translate the rehearsal into truth.

ПИЩИК

(*тяжело дышит*). Даже похорошела . . . Одета по-парижскому . . . пропадай моя телега, все четыре колеса . . .

ЛОПАХИН

Ваш брат, вот Леонид Андреич, говорит про меня, что я хам, я кулак, но это мне решительно все равно. Пускай говорит. Хотелось бы только, чтобы вы мне верили по-прежнему, чтобы ваши удивительные, трогательные глаза глядели на меня, как прежде. Боже милосердный! Мой отец был крепостным у вашего деда и отца, но вы, собственно вы, сделали для меня когда-то так много, что я забыл все и люблю вас, как родную . . . больше чем родную.

ЛЮБОВЬ АНДРЕЕВНА

Я не могу усидеть, не в состоянии . . . (*Вскакивает и ходит в сильном волнении.*) Я не переживу этой радости . . . Смейтесь надо мной, я глупая . . . Шкафчик мой родной . . . (*Целует шкаф.*) Столик мой . . .

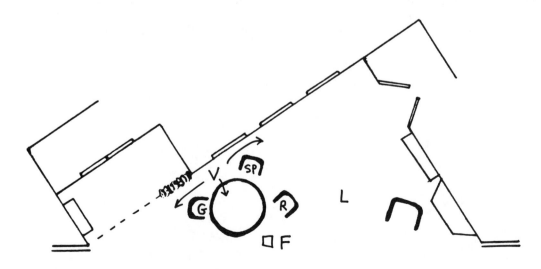

PISHCHIK

(*Breathing heavily.*) She's grown even better-looking
... dressed in the Paris fashion ... (*Hums.*) "I'd sell
my wagon and all for wheels ... "

YASHA is standing upstage; VARYA moves about serving coffee.

LOPAKHIN

Your brother here (*Gesturing to himself.*) calls me a
vulgar kulak. But what do I care ... let him talk. As
long as you believe in me as you used to ... as long
as you look at me with those gentle beautiful eyes of
yours, as you used to in the old days. Merciful God!
To think my father was a serf ... your grandfather's
and your father's serf ... but you ... you were so good
to me, you did so much for me once — so much —
you've made me forget all that ... I love you so deeply
... I feel so bound to you ... as a brother might ...
no, even more than that.

LYUBOV

I can't sit still, I simply can't ... (*Jumps up and walks
about in violent agitation.*) I'm much too happy ...!
Laugh at me, I know I'm silly! My own little cupboard! My little table!

An actor must know how to talk and also how to listen. Time is a key to
the play.

ГАЕВ

А без тебя здесь няня умерла.

ЛЮБОВЬ АНДРЕЕВНА

(*садится и пьет кофе*). Да, царство небесное. Мне писали.

ГАЕВ

И Анастасий умер. Петрушка Косой от меня ушел и теперь в городе у пристава живет. (*Вынимает из кармана коробку с леденцами, сосет.*)

ПИЩИК

Дочка моя, Дашенька . . . вам кланяется . . .

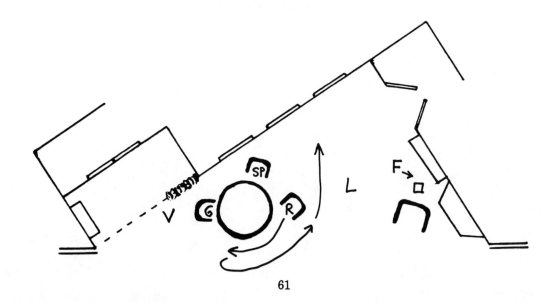

GAYEV

Nurse died while you were away.

LYUBOV

(*Sits down and drinks her coffee.*) Yes, God rest her soul. They wrote me about it.

GAYEV

And Anastasy is dead. And then Petrushka Kosdy left me, and is now in town working for the police. (*Takes a box of sweets out of his pocket and sucks one.*)

PISHCHIK

My little daughter Dashenka sends her regards to you.

ЛОПАХИН

Мне хочется сказать вам что-нибудь очень приятное, веселое. (*Взглянув на часы.*) Сейчас уеду, некогда разговаривать . . . ну, да я в двух-трех словах. Вам уже известно, вишневый сад ваш продается за долги, на двадцать второе августа назначены торги, но вы не беспокойтесь, моя дорогая, спите себе спокойно, выход есть . . . Вот мой проект. Прошу внимания! Ваше имение находится только в двадцати верстах от города, возле прошла железная дорога, и если вишневый сад и землю по реке разбить на дачные участки и отдавать потом в аренду под дачи, то вы будете иметь самое малое двадцать пять тысяч в год дохода.

ГАЕВ

Извините, какая чепуха!

ЛЮБОВЬ АНДРЕЕВНА

Я вас не совсем понимаю, Ермолай Алексеич.

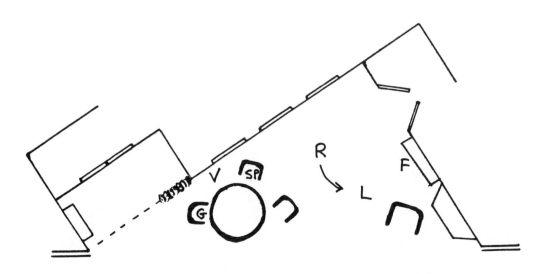

LOPAKHIN

I have something to tell you, some really good news. (*He looks at his watch*.) There's not much time to talk . . . Well, I can tell you in a couple of words. As you already know, your cherry orchard is to be sold to pay your debts. The sale is to be on the twenty-second of August; but don't you worry, my dear lady, you may sleep in peace; there is a way out. This is my plan: I beg your attention! Your estate is only twenty miles from the town; the railway runs close by it; and if the cherry orchard and the land along the river bank were cut up into building lots and then let on lease for summer dachas, you would make an income of at least 25,000 roubles a year out of it.

GAYEV

Forgive me . . . that's just nonsense.

LYUBOV

I don't quite understand you, Yermolay Alexeyevitch.

Lopakhin is thinking: 'I must tell them, how bad things are . . . it's difficult . . . how happy I am to see them . . . how proud I am of my success . . . will they notice . . .'

In my Director's Studio, we often do this exercise: 'what did you do today and why?' Sometimes, between the sentences we speak aloud, the thoughts which are usually unexpressed, showing the continuous uninterrupted flow of life, come out while you are telling me something and I am giving you an answer.

ЛОПАХИН

Вы будете брать с дачников самое малое по двадцать пять рублей в год за десятину, и если теперь же объявите, то я ручаюсь чем угодно, у вас до осени не останется ни одного свободного клочка, все разберут. Одним словом, поздравляю, вы спасены. Местоположение чудесное, река глубокая. Только, конечно, нужно поубрать, почистить . . . например, скажем, снести все старые постройки, вот этот дом, который уже никуда не годится, вырубить старый вишневый сад . . .

ЛЮБОВЬ АНДРЕЕВНА

Вырубить? Милый мой, простите, вы ничего не понимаете. Если во всей губернии есть что-нибудь интересное, даже замечательное, так это только наш вишневый сад.

ЛОПАХИН

Замечательного в этом саду только то, что он очень большой. Вишня родится раз в два года, да и ту девать некуда, никто не покупает.

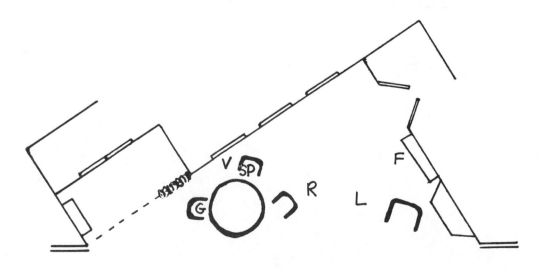

LOPAKHIN

You'll get a rent of at least twenty-five roubles a year
for each lot. They'll all be taken. In a word, I congratulate you. You are saved. And I'll bet you what
you like there won't be one vacant lot left by autumn.
Congratulations! You see — you're saved! It's a perfect site by that deep river . . . only of course it must
be cleared . . . all of the old buildings must be torn
down . . . this old house too, which is really worthless
. . . you'll have to cut down the old cherry orchard.

LYUBOV

Cut down! My dear fellow, forgive me, but you don't
know what you're talking about. If there's only one
thing in the whole province that's interesting at all,
even wonderful, then it's our cherry orchard.

LOPAKHIN

The only remarkable thing about this orchard is that
it's a very large one. There's a crop of cherries every
two years, but nothing's ever done with them; no one
buys them.

*"There were wonderful sessions of improvisation under Zavadski. They
differed from improvisation in rehearsal or workshops in theatre here.
Zavadski had us individually pick out spots all around the seating area of
the theatre. He'd say, 'now, lie down, and then wake up as you woke up as
your character in* **Cherry Orchard**, *the morning of the first act of the play.
Each did it. Individually. The improvisation was for us actors. We were not
doing it for a teacher, a director; nobody was particularly watching us
improvise."* [Robert Stattel's interview from **Actors Talk: About Styles of
Acting**.]

ГАЕВ

И в "Энциклопедическом Словаре" упоминается про этот сад.

ЛОПАХИН

(*взглянув на часы*). Если ничего не придумаем и ни к чему не придем, то двадцать второго августа и вишневый сад и все имение будут продавать с аукциона. Решайтесь же! Другого выхода нет, клянусь вам. Нет и нет.

ФИРС

В прежнее время, лет сорок-пятьдесят назад, вишню сушили, мочили, мариновали, варенье варили и, бывало . . .

ГАЕВ

Помолчи, Фирс.

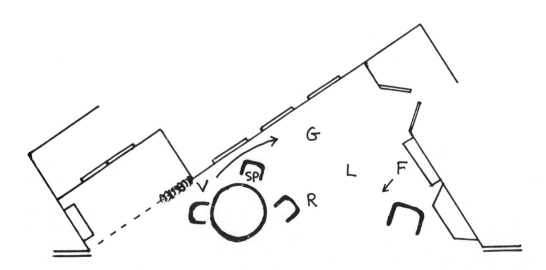

GAYEV

This orchard is mentioned in the Encyclopedia[*].

LOPAKHIN

(*Glancing at his watch.*) If we can't think of a solution, if we don't decide on something on the twenty-second of August, the cherry orchard and your entire estate will be sold at auction. Make up your minds — it's the only way out — I swear it!

FIRS

In the old days, forty or fifty years ago, the cherries would be dried, soaked, pickled, and made into jam, too, and frequently . . .

GAYEV

Be quiet, Firs.

[*] - Most likely the *Brockhaus and Efron Encyclopedia*, an 86-volume set issued between 1890-1907.

Firs' goal: 'listen, these were the good old days. Bring them back.' Firs hears only what they say about the cherry orchard.

"Mr. Zavadski worked so that each line had not only its own meaning, but its meaning **under** *the meaning. It was layer upon layer upon layer of meaning and fullness and depth, until in the end the actors were the characters they were playing." [From the actress Elena Karam playing Charlotta.]*

ФИРС

И бывало, сушеную вишню возами отправляли в Москву и в Харьков. Денег было! И сушеная вишня тогда была мягкая, сочная, сладкая, душистая . . . Способ тогда знали . . .

ЛЮБОВЬ АНДРЕЕВНА

А где же теперь этот способ?

ФИРС

Забыли. Никто не помнит.

ПИЩИК

(*Любови Андреевне*). Что в Париже? Как? Ели лягушек?

ЛЮБОВЬ АНДРЕЕВНА

Крокодилов ела.

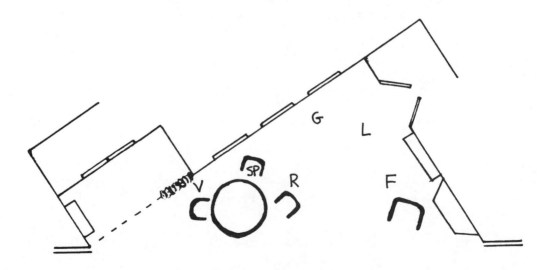

FIRS

And frequently, the preserve cherries would be sent in cartloads to Moscow and to Kharkov; they made money out of them. They made money then! And the preserve cherries in those days were soft and juicy, sweet and fragrant . . . they knew the recipe then .. .

LYUBOV

And where is the recipe now?

FIRS

Forgotten. Nobody remembers it.

PISHCHIK

(*To* LYUBOV.) What about Paris. Did you eat frogs there?

LYUBOV

I ate crocodiles.

Lyubov embraces Firs first after his line, 'where's the recipe now?'

*To summarize our work a little: what have I been working on? In the past, I have been acquainting you with a method of work, essentially preparing you, the actors, for the work ahead. I've been preparing **myself** by getting acquainted with you, the actors.*

ПИЩИК

Вы подумайте . . .

ЛОПАХИН

До сих пор в деревне были только господа да мужики, а теперь появились еще дачники. Все города, даже самые небольшие, окружены теперь дачами. И можно сказать, дачник лет через двадцать размножится до необычайности. Теперь он только чай пьет на балконе, но ведь может случиться, что на своей одной десятине он займется хозяйством, и тогда ваш вишневый сад станет счастливым, богатым, роскошным..

ГАЕВ

(*возмущаясь*). Какая чепуха!

Входят Варя и Яша.

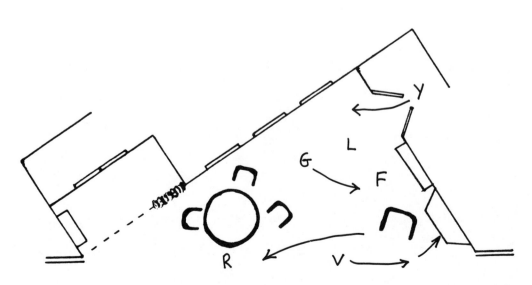

PISHCHIK

Just imagine!

LOPAKHIN

In the old days, there were only land owners and peasants in the country, but lately, these summer visitors have appeared on the scene. All the towns, even the small ones, are surrounded by their dachas, and there's no doubt that in another twenty years, they'll be everywhere. Right now, these visitors do nothing but sit on their porches drinking tea, but, who knows, maybe they'll start cultivating their bit of land too, and then your cherry orchard will become happy, rich, and prosperous.

GAYEV

(*Annoyed.*) What nonsense!

Enter VARYA and YASHA. VARYA crosses up left to the old-fashioned bookcase, takes out her keys and opens the bookcase with a loud crack; she takes a telegram and gives it to MME. RANYEVSKY.

"There was an aspect of the rehearsals which was hard to define. The atmosphere of all the rehearsals was, as it were, highly charged. The actor's entire being had become highly sensitive, quick to respond to emotions required by the scene, and the characters' subtext as used in each scene." [Comment of an actor of the cast of **Cherry Orchard**.]

ВАРЯ

Тут, мамочка, вам две телеграммы. (*Выбирает ключ и со звоном отпирает старинный шкаф.*) Вот они.

ЛЮБОВЬ АНДРЕЕВНА

Это из Парижа. (*Рвет телеграммы не прочитав.*) С Парижем кончено . . .

ГАЕВ

А ты знаешь, Люба, сколько этому шкафу лет? Неделю назад я выдвинул нижний ящик, гляжу, а там выжжены цифры. Шкаф сделан ровно сто лет тому назад. Каково? А? Можно было бы юбилей отпраздновать. Предмет неодушевленный, а все-таки, как-никак, книжный шкаф.

ПИЩИК

(*удивленно*). Сто лет . . . Вы подумайте!

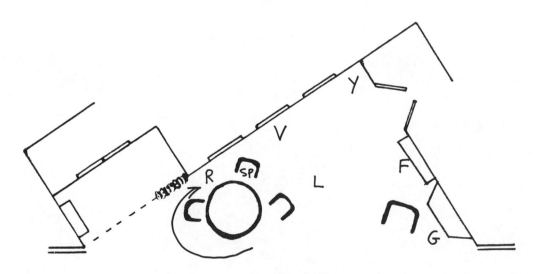

VARYA

There are two telegrams for you, Mamotchka. Here they are.

VARYA is up right of MME. RANYEVSKY.

LYUBOV

From Paris. (*Tears up the telegrams without reading them.*) I'm through with Paris.

GAYEV

Do you know, Lyuba, how old this bookcase is? Last week I pulled out the drawer and I found the date branded on it. The bookcase was made exactly a hundred years ago. Think of that! We might have celebrated its jubilee. True, it's an inanimate object, but nevertheless, a bookcase.

PISHCHIK

(*Amazed.*) A hundred years! Just imagine!

Gayev's goal is 'I can't tell Lyubov how things are, although her conduct in Paris was shameful. How am I to keep from talking about that?' Lyubov's goal is 'I don't want to think about Paris; I want to live again as if I'd never met that man. I'm now home — again.'

Gayev must not give a lecture with this speech. If he thinks out loud, we get the full concept of this world of the play. Stanislavski used to say, "You're not speaking of this thing." The actor onstage must always play from desires, wishes, motivations.

ГАЕВ

Да . . . Это вещь . . . (*Ощупав шкаф*). Дорогой, многоуважаемый шкаф! Приветствую твое существование, которое вот уже больше ста лет было направлено к светлым идеалам добра и справедливости. Твой молчаливый призыв к плодотворной работе не ослабевал в течении ста лет, поддерживая (*сквозь слезы*) в поколениях нашего рода бодрость, веру в лучшее будущее и воспитывая в нас идеалы добра и общественного самосознания. (*Пауза.*)

ЛОПАХИН

Да· . . .

ЛЮБОВЬ АНДРЕЕВНА

Ты все такой же, Леня.

ГАЕВ

(*немного сконфуженный*). От шара направо в угол! Режу в среднюю!

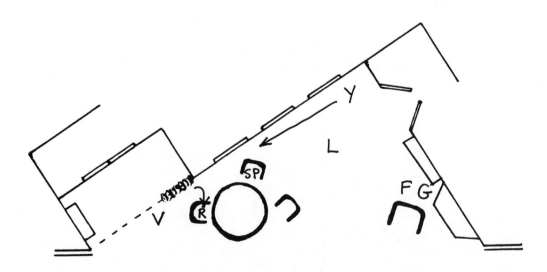

GAYEV

Yes, (*Tapping it.*) It's a venerable thing! . . . dear, honored bookcase, hail to thee, though, for more than a hundred years, it has served the pure ideals of Truth and Justice! Thy silent call to fruitful labor has never weakened in all those hundred years, maintaining (*Fighting tears.*) through succeeding generations of mankind, courage and faith in a better future and fostering in us ideals of social consciousness . . . (*Pause.*)

LOPAKHIN

Yes . . .

LYUBOV

You're just the same as ever, Leonid.

GAYEV

(*A little embarrassed.*) Carom off the right, into the pocket.

VARYA crosses left of LYUBOV.

There are people who love to philosophize, to make beautiful speeches. Gayev is sure he is saying very wise things in his speech to the bookcase. Some of these traits of his are repeated in a distorted fashion in the scene between Yepikhodov and Pishchik.

ЛОПАХИН

(*поглядев на часы*). Ну, мне пора.

ЯША

(*подает Любови Андреевне лекарства*). Может, примете сейчас пилюли . . .

ПИЩИК

Не надо принимать медикаменты, милейшая . . . от них ни вреда, ни пользы . . . Дайте-ка сюда . . . многоуважаемая. (*Берет пилюли, высыпает их себе на ладонь, дует на них, кладет в рот и запивает квасом.*) Вот!

ЛЮБОВЬ АНДРЕЕВНА

(*испуганно*). Да вы с ума сошли!

ПИЛЬЩИК

Все пилюли принял.

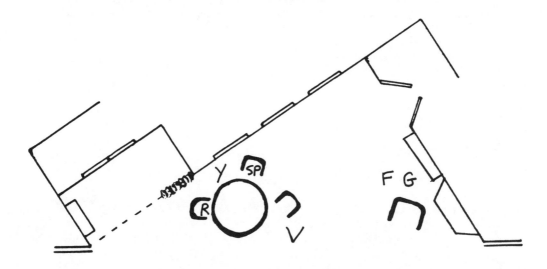

ACT ONE

LOPAKHIN

(*Looks at his watch.*) Well, it's time I was off . . .

YASHA

(*Handing* LYUBOV ANDREYEVNA *some medicine.*)
Maybe you'll take your pills now.

PISHCHIK

One shouldn't take medicines, my dearest lady, they
do neither harm nor good . . . give them here, honored
lady . . . (*He rises, takes the pillbox, pours the pills
into his hand, blows on them, puts them into his
mouth, and drinks off some kvass.*) There!

LYUBOV

(*In alarm.*) You must be out of your mind!

PISHCHIK

I've taken all the pills.

On Pishchik's line, 'one shouldn't take medicines,' Pishchik does this
ridiculous thing to cover his embarrassment somewhat. This is a scene full
of surprise for the characters — and, we hope, for the audience. The scene is
a challenge, as well, to the actor playing Pishchik.

If I propose something to an actor, don't try to put it into practice
immediately. The actor won't be able to achieve it at once. Do it tomorrow. I
may even have to show you something. As a rule, disciples of Stanislavski
don't show actors what to do; we don't want the actor to ape us; rather we
want to open the actor up. I have to find the character in each of you as an
individual interpreter. I don't have an abstract image of each character and
thus mold you into it. My task is to change you.

ЛОПАХИН

Экая прорва. (*Все смеются.*)

ФИРС

Они были у нас на Святой, полведра огурцов скушали . . . (*Бормочет.*)

ЛЮБОВЬ АНДРЕЕВНА

О чем это он?

ВАРЯ

Уж три года так бормочет. Мы привыкли.

ЯША

Преклонный возраст.

Шарлотта Ивановна в белом платье, очень худая, стянутая, с лорнеткой на поясе, проходит через сцену.

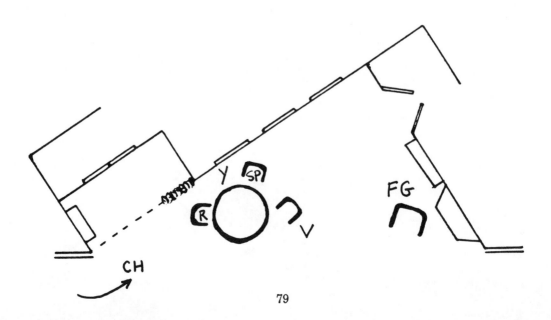

LOPAKHIN

The old glutton! (*They all laugh.*)

FIRS

Stayed with us in Easter week . . . ate half a pail of cucumbers . . . (*Mutters.*)

LYUBOV

What's he talking about?

VARYA

He's taken to muttering like that for the last three years — we're used to it.

YASHA

His declining years!

CHARLOTTA IVANOVNA, in a white dress, very thin and slender, with a lorgnette at her waist, crosses the stage.

ЛОПАХИН

Простите, Шарлотта Ивановна, я не успел еще поздороваться с вами. (*Хочет поцеловать у нее руку.*)

ШАРЛОТТА

(*отнимая руку*). Если позволить вам поцеловать руку, то вы потом пожелаете в локоть, потом в плечо . . .

ЛОПАХИН

Не везет мне сегодня. (*Все смеются.*) Шарлотта Ивановна, покажите фокус!

ЛЮБОВЬ АНДРЕЕВНА

Шарлотта, покажите фокус!

ШАРЛОТТА

Не надо. Я спать желаю. (*Уходит.*)

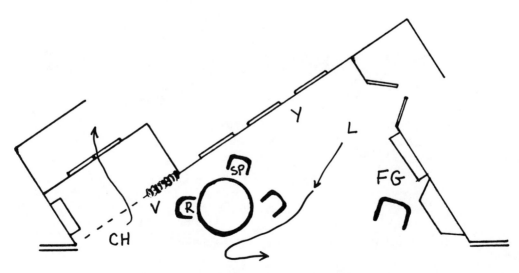

LOPAKHIN

Forgive me, Charlotta Ivanovna, I've not had time to greet you. (*Tries to kiss her hand.*)

CHARLOTTA

(*Pulling away her hand.*) If I let you kiss my hand, you'll be wanting to kiss my elbow and then my shoulder.

LOPAKHIN

I've no luck today. (*They all laugh.*) Charlotta Ivanovna, show us a trick.

LYUBOV

Charlotta, do show us a trick.

CHARLOTTA

Quite unnecessary. I wish to sleep. (*She goes out.*)

Sometimes, the actors listen badly; they don't listen to each other. In order to get to the core of the play, the atmosphere we discussed at the beginning, we have to realize there's a lot of concentrated work needed.

ЛОПАХИН

Через три недели увидимся. (*Целует Любови Андреевне руку.*) Пока прощайте. Пора. (*Гаеву.*) До свидания. (*Целуется с Пильщиком.*) До свидания. (*Подает руку Варе, потом Фирсу и Яше.*) Не хочется уезжать. (*Любови Андреевне.*) Ежели надумаете насчет дач и решите, тогда дайте знать, я взаймы тысяч пятьдесят достану. Серьезно подумайте.

ВАРЯ

(*сердито*). Да уходите же наконец!

ЛОПАХИН

Ухожу, ухожу...(*Уходит.*)

ГАЕВ

Хам. Впрочем, пардон . . . Варя выходит за него замуж, это Варин женишок.

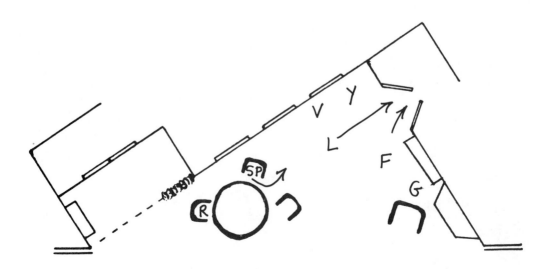

LOPAKHIN

In three weeks, we'll meet again. (*Kisses* LYUBOV ANDREYEVNA's *hand.*) Good-bye till then. I must go. (*To* GAYEV.) Good-bye. (*He kisses* PISHCHIK.) Good-bye. (*Gives his hand to* VARYA, *then to* FIRS *and* YASHA.) I don't want to go. (*To* LYUBOV.) If you think over my plan for the dachas and make up your mind, let me know; I'll get you a loan of fifty thousand roubles. Think it over seriously.

VARYA

(*Angrily.*) Well, do go for goodness' sake.

LOPAKHIN

I'm going, I'm going. (*He goes out.*)

GAYEV

Lout! I beg pardon though ... Varya is going to marry him, he is Varya's young man.

For a new stage of our work, remember the suggestions as to movement which are still tentative. We will have to do it in a most precise and subtle way, but we will create precision of movement as a result of improvisation. I will have to present each of you with a series of problems, quite difficult to solve. Therefore, I ask patience with the fact that I am much sterner. Not that I like discipline, but in a sense, under certain circumstances, only then are things possible. (One aspect of the Stanislavski system actually is contradictory to a casual attitude towards the work!)

Consider the difference between the way you yourself get up in the morning, and the way the character you are playing gets up. Also the character's attitude to food and to nature ... this will be an inner exercise ... I will watch what you set in motion inside, which part of the core of you really participates in this work. I'm listening to you not only with my ear.

ВАРЯ

Не говорите, дядечка, лишнего.

ЛЮБОВЬ АНДРЕЕВНА

Что ж, Варя, я буду очень рада. Он хороший человек.

ПИЩИК

Человек, надо правду говорить . . . достойнейший . . . И моя Дашенька . . . тоже говорит, что . . . разные слова говорит. (*Храпит, но тотчас же просыпается.*) А все-таки, многоуважаемая, одолжите мне . . . взаймы двести сорок рублей . . . завтра по закладной *проценты платить . . .

ВАРЯ

(*испуганно*). Нету, нету!

* Официальный письменный акт о заложенном имуществе, преимущественно недвижимом, обеспечивающий права кредитора, то есть лица или учреждения, дающего что-либо в долг.

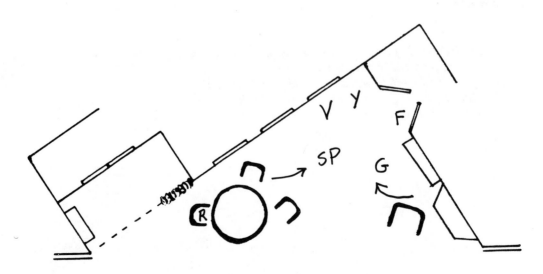

VARYA

Don't talk nonsense, Uncle.

LYUBOV

Well, Varya, I shall be delighted. He's a good man.

PISHCHIK

Yes, one must admit he's a most worthy man. And my Dashenka . . . also says that . . . she says various things. (*Snores, but at once wakes up.*) But never mind that. Honored lady, could you oblige me . . . with a loan of 240 rubles . . . to pay the interest on my mortgage tomorrow . . .

VARYA

(*Dismayed.*) No, no!

In the first act, the basic goal for Pishchik is, 'how can I approach the question of borrowing money?' A second goal is his reacting to all those who have stayed, and to make company with all those who have returned from Paris. Pishchik has been sitting on the porcelain stove. When Pishchik snores and wakes up at once it's due to the fact that he almost falls off the porcelain stove. Pishchik, you are always sort of hot, sweaty. With your money you sweat not only because it is hot but because of your money.

Do not judge the character. I demand now from you sincerity, all sincerity. That is Chekhov's wisdom, that he looks at the world, understands all, and he is good to man. He has compassion.

ЛЮБОВЬ АНДРЕЕВНА

У меня в самом деле нет ничего.

ПИЩИК

Найдутся. (*Смеется.*) Не теряю никогда надежды. Вот, думаю, уж все пропало, погиб, ан глядь, - железная дорога по моей земле прошла, и . . . мне заплатили. А там, гляди, еще что-нибудь случится не сегодня - завтра . . . Двести тысяч выиграет Дашенька... у нее билет есть.

ЛЮБОВЬ АНДРЕЕВНА

Кофе выпит, можно на покой.

ФИРС

(*чистит щеткой Гаева, наставительно*). Опять не те брючки надели. И что мне с вами делать!

ВАРЯ

(*тихо*). Аня спит (*тихо отворяет окно.*) Уже взошло солнце, не холодно. Взгляните, мамочка, какие чудесные деревья! Боже мой, воздух! Скворцы поют!

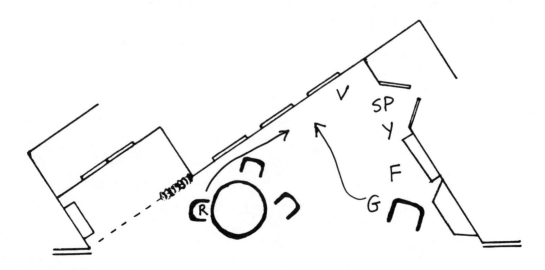

LYUBOV

I really haven't any money.

PISHCHIK

It'll turn up. (*Laughs.*) I never lose hope. I thought everything was over, I was a ruined man, when, lo and behold! The railway passed through my land . . . and I was paid for it . . . and something else will turn up again, if not today, then tomorrow . . . Dashenka will win 200,000 . . . she's got a lottery ticket. (*He goes to sleep.*)

LYUBOV

We've finished our coffee, now let's go to bed. (*She rises from her chair.* VARYA *crosses to* ANYA's *room.*)

FIRS

(*Brushes* GAYEV *reprovingly.*) You've got the wrong trousers on again. What am I to do with you?

VARYA

(*She is left of the windows. Softly.*) Anya's asleep. (*Gently opens a window.*) Now that the sun's coming up it's not a bit cold. Look, Mamotchka, how beautiful the trees are! And the air is so fresh! The starlings are singing!

ГАЕВ

(*отворяет другое окно.*) Сад весь белый. Ты не забыла, Люба? Вот эта длинная аллея идет прямо-прямо, точно протянутый ремень, она блестит в лунные ночи. Ты помнишь? Не забыла?

ЛЮБОВЬ АНДРЕЕВНА

(*глядит в окно на сад*). О, мое детство, чистота моя! В этой детской я спала, глядела отсюда в сад, счастье просыпалось вместе со мною каждое утро, и тогда он был точно таким, ничто не изменилось. (*Смеется от радости.*) Весь, весь белый! О, сад мой! После темной ненастной осени и холодной зимы опять ты молод, полон счастья, ангелы небесные не покинули тебя . . . Если бы снять с груди и плеч моих тяжелый камень, если бы я могла забыть мое прошлое!

ГАЕВ

Да, и сад продадут за долги, как это ни странно . . .

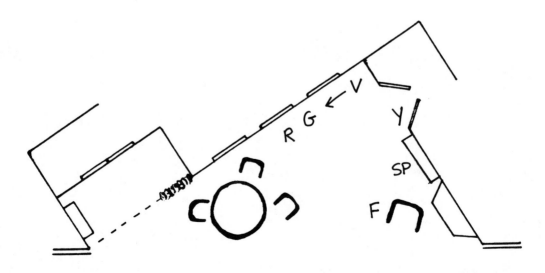

GAYEV

(*Opens the other window.*) The orchard is all white. You've not forgotten, Lyuba? That's the long avenue that runs straight, straight as an arrow, do you remember how it shines on a moonlit night? Do you remember? You've not forgotten?

LYUBOV

(*Looking out of the window into the garden.*) Oh, my childhood, my innocence! I used to sleep in this nursery — look out into the orchard, happiness waked with me every morning, the orchard was just the same then . . . nothing has changed. (*She laughs with happiness.*) All, all white! Oh, my orchard! After the dark, stormy autumn and the cold winter, you are young again, and full of happiness, the heavenly angels have never left you . . . if I could only escape from this burden that weighs on my heart, if I could forget my past!

GAYEV

Yes, and the orchard will be sold to pay our debts, strange as it may seem . . .

Gayev's and Lyubov's goals are 'if only we were children again without a care.'

Stanislavski would say, 'One has to play from within not **to** within.' He would sometimes drive an actor into a panic: 'All right, your legs are all right; what about your hands? What about your breathing? Now your legs have gone wrong again. Now you're not functioning again. You forgot your characterization!' At the end the actor wouldn't understand a thing. Stanislavski always experimented!

ЛЮБОВЬ АНДРЕЕВНА

Посмотрите, покойная мама идет по саду . . . в белом платье! (*Смеется от радости.*) то она.

ГАЕВ

Где?

ВАРЯ

Господь с вами, мамочка.

ЛЮБОВЬ АНДРЕЕВНА

Никого нет, мне показалось. Направо, на повороте к беседке, белое деревцо склонилось, похоже на женщину . . .

Входит Трофимов в поношенном студенческом мундире, в очках.

ЛЮБОВЬ АНДРЕЕВНА

Какой изумительный сад! Белые массы цветов, голубое небо . . .

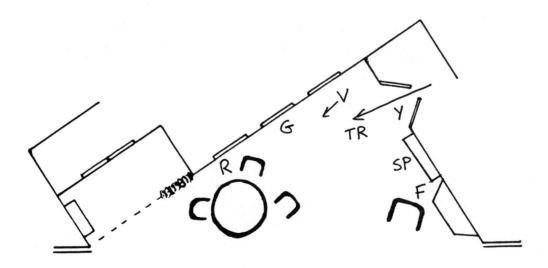

LYUBOV

Look! There is our deceased mother walking in the orchard . . . all in white . . . (*She laughs with delight.*) It is she!

GAYEV

Where?

VARYA

Oh, please! The Lord be with you, Mamotchka!

LYUBOV

There isn't anyone, I just imagined it. To the right, by the path to the arbor, there's a little white tree, bending like a woman . . .

Enter TROFIMOV, wearing a shabby student's uniform and spectacles. Some straw on him.

LYUBOV

What an amazing orchard! White masses of blossom, a blue sky . . .

When Lyubov Andreyevna speaks of her countryside, Pishchik and Gayev should have big reactions. I will reveal a small secret. I never come with a ready-made plan. I have put on quite a number of plays, and I believe it is very important to create the production jointly with the actors. The interrelation between you, the actors, and me as director is very important. I don't want you to look upon me as a teacher; I am not a headmaster.

ТРОФИМОВ

Любовь Андреевна! (*Она оглянулась на него.*) Я только поклонюсь вам и тотчас же уйду. (*Горячо целует руку.*) Мне приказано было ждать до утра, но у меня не хватило терпения . . .

ВАРЯ

(*сквозь слезы*). Это Петя Трофимов . . .

ТРОФИМОВ

Петя Трофимов, бывший учитель вашего Гриши . . . Неужели я так изменился?

Любовь Андреевна обнимает его и тихо плачет.

ГАЕВ

(*смущенно*). Полно, полно, Люба.

ВАРЯ

(*плачет*). Говорила ведь, Петя, чтобы погодили до завтра.

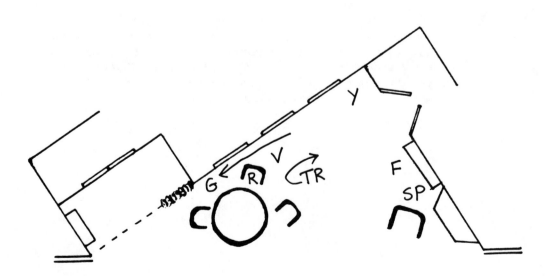

TROFIMOV

Lyubov Andreyevna! (*She looks round at him.*) I just want to pay my respects to you, then leave you at once. (*Kisses her hand warmly.*) I was told to wait until later in the morning, but I hadn't the patience . . . (LYUBOV ANDREYEVNA *looks at him in perplexity.*)

VARYA

(*Through tears.*) It's Petya Trofimov, Mamotchka . . ..

TROFIMOV

Petya Trofimov, who was your Grisha's tutor . . . can I have changed so much?

LYUBOV embraces him and weeps quietly.

GAYEV

There, there, Lyuba.

VARYA

(*Hitting* PETYA *and crying.*) I told you, Petya, to wait until tomorrow.

At the meeting between Lyubov and Trofimov, they weep. But, it is very important to understand this: you play it so as to produce tears in the audience each time; aim for the audience's reaction to the whole rather than to Lyubov's tears. It is important to reach what Stanislavski referred to as 'a feeling of true measure'.

This scene is wonderful; a harmony of comedy and tragedy combined in Chekhov. Lyubov remembers Grisha, her little son who drowned. There has always been a tacit understanding that Grisha should not be mentioned in her presence.

ЛЮБОВЬ АНДРЕЕВНА

Гриша мой . . . мой мальчик . . . Гриша . . . сын...

ВАРЯ

Что же делать, мамочка. Воля божья.

ТРОФИМОВ

(*мягко, сквозь слезы*). Будет, будет . . .

ЛЮБОВЬ АНДРЕЕВНА

(*тихо плачет*). Мальчик погиб, утонул . . . Для чего? Для чего, мой друг? (*Тише.*) Там Аня спит, а я громко говорю . . . поднимаю шум . . . Что же, Петя? Отчего вы так подурнели? Отчего постарели?

ТРОФИМОВ

Меня в вагоне одна баба назвала так : облезлый барин.

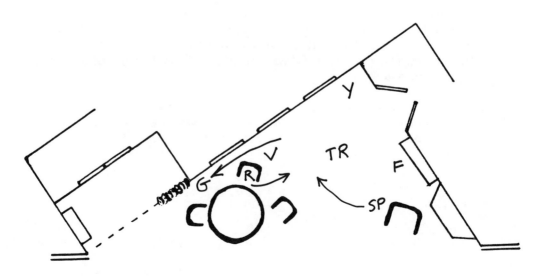

LYUBOV

My Grisha . . . my little boy . . . Grisha — my son!

VARYA

What can one do, Mamotchka, it's God's will.

TROFIMOV

(*Softly, through his tears.*) There . . . .there.

LYUBOV

(*Weeping quietly.*) My little boy was lost . . . drowned
What for? What for, my friend? (*More quietly.*) Anya's
asleep in there and here I am talking so loud making
all this noise . . . but, Petya? Why have you grown so
ugly? Why have you grown so old?

TROFIMOV

In the train, a peasant woman called me a moth-
eaten gentleman.

Trofimov's goal is, "I want to be near Anya. Maybe they'll let me take the place of Grisha?" He thinks, "Anya is more wonderful — and more necessary to me — than I had anticipated." Chekhov said to his wife, who created the role of Mme. Ranyevesky in Cherry Orchard, 'Don't cry. When people have a really deep sorrow, they don't cry. They pause to think.' So Mme. Ranyevesky, don't cry.

Varya, your "it's God's will" comes from your soul; they're not just words, they're soul. When we are reading, always try to understand the sense, the image, and always for what are we talking. Lyubov, why do you pronounce these words? What for? "Why" may be quite near. It may happen immediately. Sometimes it has its grounds in the past.

ЛЮБОВЬ АНДРЕЕВНА

Вы были тогда совсем мальчиком, милым студентиком, а теперь волосы негустые, очки, Неужели вы все еще студент? (*Идет к двери.*)

ТРОФИМОВ

Должно быть, я буду вечным студентом.

ЛЮБОВЬ АНДРЕЕВНА

(*целует брата, потом Варю*). Ну, идите спать . . . Постарел и ты, Леонид.

ПИЩИК

(*идет за ней*). Значит, теперь спать . . . Ох, подагра моя. Я у вас останусь . . . Мне бы, Любовь Андреевна, душа моя, завтра утречком . . . двести сорок рублей . . .

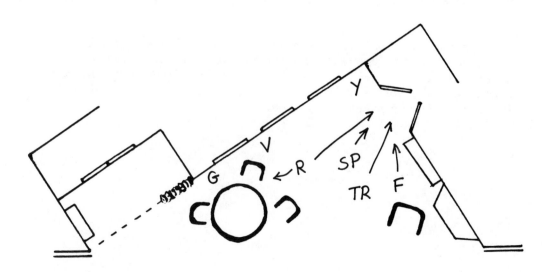

LYUBOV

You were quite a boy then, just a young student, and now your hair's thin — and you've got on glasses! Is it possible you're still a student? (*She goes towards the door.*)

TROFIMOV

I'll most likely be an eternal student.

LYUBOV

(*Kisses her brother, then* VARYA.) Now, go to bed . . . you look older too, Leonid.

PISHCHIK

(*Goes to her.*) Yes, it's time we were asleep. Ouch, my gout! (*To* VARYA.) I'm staying the night. Lyubov Andreyevna, my dear soul, if you could . . . tomorrow morning . . . two hundred and forty roubles.

Trofimov's characterization must be made whole. My task is to change you into the character. I compare growth within an actor to the growth within a flower. In life you start with a seed — an inside world. To help create this inner world is my first task.

It is my feeling that art is a great force, capable of bringing people closer together. The artist who thinks himself unique and self-sufficient is not worth much. Stanislavski also felt that art is the means of communication between people.

ГАЕВ

А этот все свое.

ПИЩИК

Двести сорок рублей . . . проценты по закладной платить.

ЛЮБОВЬ АНДРЕЕВНА

Нет у меня денег, голубчик.

ПИЩИК

Отдам, милая . . . Сумма пустяшная . . .

ЛЮБОВЬ АНДРЕЕВНА

Ну, хорошо, Леонид даст . . . Ты дай, Леонид.

ГАЕВ

Дам я ему, держи карман.

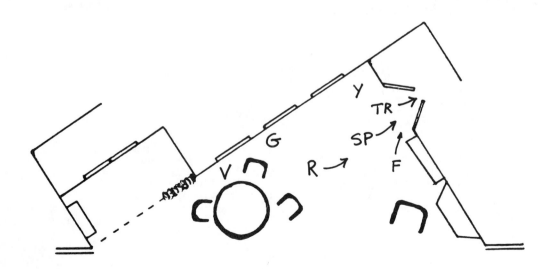

GAYEV

There he goes again . . . the same old story.

PISHCHIK

Two hundred and forty roubles . . . to pay the interest on my mortgage.

LYUBOV

My darling man, I have no money.

PISHCHIK

I'll give it back, my dear . . . it's a trifling sum.

LYUBOV

All right, Leonid will give it to you. Go on, you give it to him Leonid.

GAYEV

I'll give it to him. Hah! Don't hold your breath!

ЛЮБОВЬ АНДРЕЕВНА

Что же делать, дай . . . Ему нужно . . . Он отдаст.

Любовь Андреевна, Трофимов, Пищик и Фирс уходят. Остаются Гаев, Варя и Яша.

ГАЕВ

Сестра не отвыкла еще сорить деньгами. (*Яше*). Отойди, любезный, от тебя курицей пахнет.

ЯША

(*с усмешкой*). А вы, Леонид Андреевич, все такой же, как были.

ГАЕВ

Кого? (*Варе.*) Что он сказал?

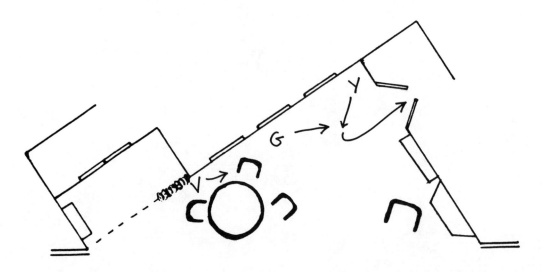

LYUBOV

It can't be helped. Give it to him! He needs it. He'll
pay it back.

LYUBOV, TROFIMOV, PISHCHIK and FIRS go out. GAYEV, VARYA and YASHA
remain.

GAYEV

Sister hasn't got out of the habit of flinging away her
money. (*To* YASHA.) Get away, my good fellow, you
smell of the barnyard

YASHA

(*With a grin.*) And you, Leonid Andreyevitch, are just
the same as ever.

GAYEV

Who? (*To* VARYA.) What did he say?

*Gayev's goal is "now I can speak my mind about my sister." Varya is the
family confidante.*

*I focus on the actor's instrument through improvisation and rehearsal.
The development of the actor's art comes from the development of a scene.
The elements of the craft are what we are most interested in, and will try to
solve something new each time. There are no recipes in art.*

ВАРЯ

(*Яше*). Твоя мать пришла из деревни, со вчерашнего дня сидит в людской, хочет повидаться . . .

ЯША

Бог с ней совсем!

ВАРЯ

Ах, бесстыдник!

ЯША

Очень нужно. Могла бы и завтра прийти. (*Уходит.*)

ВАРЯ

Мамочка такая же, как была, нисколько не изменилась. Если бы ей волю, она бы все раздала.

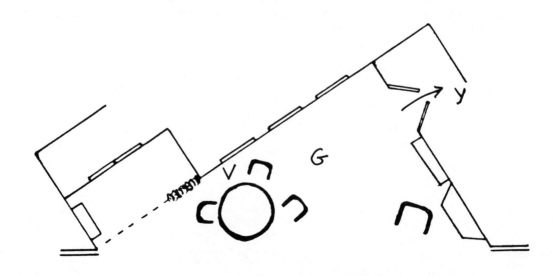

VARYA

(*To* YASHA.) Your mother's come from the village; she's been sitting in the servant's room since yesterday, waiting to see you.

YASHA

Ach! That old nuisance!

VARYA

For shame!

YASHA

As if I needed her! She could have come tomorrow. (*Goes out.*)

VARYA

Mamotchka's just the same as ever; she hasn't changed a bit. If she had her own way she'd give away everything.

Yasha, return the cup to the table before going off to see your mother.

Sometimes actors get very used to each other, and this adds a touch of the commonplace to the work, an air of indifference, of taking the work for granted. Only the best and most splendid actors retain their self-dicipline and continue to work for themselves. I like to repeat the thought that I can help you learn things for yourself, but I can't teach you.

ГАЕВ

Да . . . (*Пауза.*) Если против какой-нибудь болезни предлагается очень много средств, это значит, что болезнь неизлечима. Я думаю, напрягаю мозги, у меня много средств, очень много и, значит, в сущности, ни одного. Хорошо бы получить от кого-нибудь наследство, хорошо бы выдать нашу Аню за очень богатого человека, хорошо бы поехать в Ярославль и попытать счастья у тетушки-графини. Тетка ведь очень, очень богата.

ВАРЯ

(*плачет*). Если бы бог помог.

ГАЕВ

Не реви. Тетка очень богата, но нас она не любит. Сестра, во-первых, вышла замуж за присяжного поверенного*, не дворянина . . .

Аня показывается в дверях.

* Адвоката

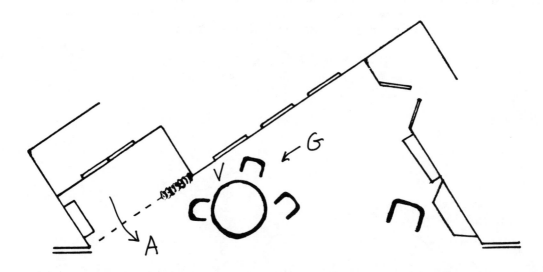

GAYEV

Yes. (*Pause.*) If a great many remedies are suggested for some disease, it means that the disease is incurable; I keep thinking and racking my brains; I have thought of many remedies, a great many, and that really amounts to none. We might come in for a legacy from somebody; we might marry Anya to a very rich man; or we might go to Yaroslavl and try our luck with our aunt, the countess. Auntie's very, very rich, you know . . .

VARYA

(*Weeping.*) If only God would help us!

GAYEV

Stop bawling. Aunt's very rich, but she doesn't like us. In the first place, sister married a lawyer instead of a nobleman . . .

ANYA appears in the doorway, she is wearing a dark shawl.

ГАЕВ

Вышла за не дворянина и вела себя, нельзя сказать, чтобы очень добродетельно. Она хорошая, добрая, славная, я ее очень люблю, но, как там ни придумывай смягчающие обстоятельства, все же, надо сознаться, она порочна. Это чувствуется в ее малейшем движении.

ВАРЯ

(*шепотом*). Аня стоит в дверях.

ГАЕВ

Кого? (*Пауза.*) Удивительно, мне что-то в правый глаз попало . . . плохо стал видеть. И в четверг, когда я был в окружном суде..

Входит Аня.

ВАРЯ

Что же ты не спишь, Аня?

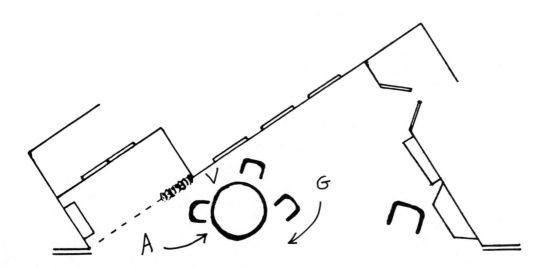

GAYEV

Married a man who was beneath her . . . and her behavior has been anything but virtuous. She's good, kind, sweet, and I love her, but however one allows for extenuating circumstances, there's no denying she's an immoral woman. One feels it in her slightest gesture.

VARYA

(*In a whisper.*) Anya's in the doorway.

GAYEV

Who? (*Pause.*) Most extraordinary, I seem to have something in my right eye . . . I can't see out of it . . . and on Thursday, when I was in the district court . . .

Enter ANYA. VARYA crosses to left of GAYEV.

VARYA

Why aren't you asleep, Anya?

I add layer upon layer to the inside of the character, to the actor's imagination, to his awareness of the life of the play, the times, the rhythm, in short, the spirit of the character. Sometimes for the actor, it's so cumulative as to become almost unbearable: the inner life of the character, and the meaning of the play and the characters' effect upon one another.

АНЯ

Не спится. Не могу.

ГАЕВ

Крошка моя. (*Целует Ане лицо, руки.*) Дитя мое . . . (*Сквозь слезы.*) Ты не племянница, ты мой ангел, ты для меня все. Верь мне, верь . . .

АНЯ

Я верю тебе, дядя. Тебя все любят, уважают... но, милый дядя, тебе надо молчать, только молчать. Что ты говорил только что про мою маму, про свою сестру? Для чего ты это говорил?

ГАЕВ

Да, да . . . (*Ее рукой закрывает себе лицо.*) В самом деле, это ужасно! Боже мой! Боже, спаси меня! И сегодня я речь говорил перед шкафом . . . так глупо! И только когда кончил, понял, что глупо.

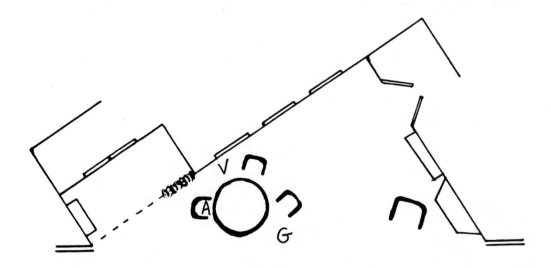

ANYA

I can't get to sleep, I can't.

VARYA crosses down left.

GAYEV

My little pet! (*He kisses* ANYA's *face and hands.*) My child! (*Weeps.*) You are not my niece, you're my angel! You're everything to me. Believe me, believe . . .

ANYA

I believe you, Uncle. Everyone loves you and respects you . . . but, dear Uncle, you should be silent . . . . simply be silent. What were you saying just now about my mother. Your own sister? What made you say that?

GAYEV

Yes, yes . . . (*Puts his hand over his face.*) Really, that was awful! God help me! And just now I made a speech to the bookcase . . . so stupid! It wasn't until I finished I realized how stupid it was.

VARYA crossing to left of GAYEV.

Anya's goal is 'I must defend my mother' and Gayev's goal is 'oh, dear, I'll solve everything . . . Chekhov takes the extraordinary moments of life. To understand these moments the actor has to be both an artist and a great person, to understand, to feel and to love the extraordinary moment; not with the mind, but with the whole body, the whole self. The actor is to dig, to find a frame of reference to the Chekhovian character that is a special understanding of life.

ВАРЯ

Правда, дядечка, вам надо бы молчать. Молчите себе и все.

АНЯ

Если будешь молчать, то тебе же самому будет покойнее.

ГАЕВ

Молчу. (*Целует Ане и Варе руки.*) Молчу. Только вот о деле. В четверг я был в окружном суде, ну, сошлась компания, начался разговор о том, о сем, пятое-десятое, и, кажется, вот можно будет устроить заем под векселя, чтобы заплатить проценты в банк.

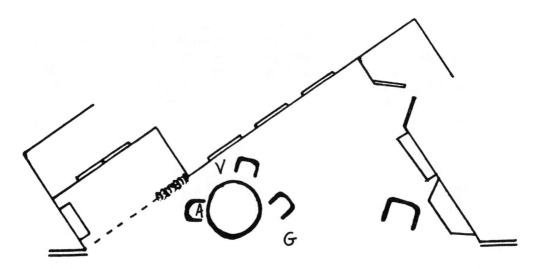

VARYA

It's true, Uncle. You ought to keep quiet. Just don't talk, that's all.

ANYA

If you could only keep silent, it would make things easier for you too . . .

GAYEV

I'll be silent. (*Kisses* ANYA *and* VARYA*'s hands.*) Quite silent. Only this is about business. On Thursday I was in the district court; well, there was a large party of us there, and we began talking of one thing and another, and this and that, and do you know, I believe it will be possible to raise a loan with what they call a promissory note to pay off the interest to the bank.

I have tried this approach where I look only for the movement, only the pantomime of the performance and elements of characterization in the mise-en-scène.

People think the Method is a set of rules. It is only a key to the understanding. It is quite possible for actors who have never heard of a word to be using it. Or vice versa: they may think they know the Method, but that is why, when the Method is badly understood, it becomes its opposite. It creates a self-confident, know-it-all attitude when you really know nothing.

ВАРЯ

Если бы господь помог!

ГАЕВ

Во вторник поеду, еще раз поговорю. (*Варе.*) Не реви. (*Ане.*) Твоя мама поговорит с Лопахиным, он, конечно, ей не откажет . . . А ты, как отдохнешь, поедешь в Ярославль к графине, твоей бабушке. Вот так и будем действовать с трех концов - и дело наше в шляпе. Проценты мы заплатим, я убежден . . . (*Кладет в рот леденец.*) Честью моей, чем хочешь клянусь! Вот тебе моя рука, назови меня тогда дрянным, бесчестным человеком, если я допущу до аукциона! Всем существом моим клянусь!

АНЯ

(*спокойное настроение вернулось к ней, она счастлива*). Какой ты хороший, дядя, какой умный! (*Обнимает дядю.*) Я теперь покойна! Я покойна! Я счастлива!

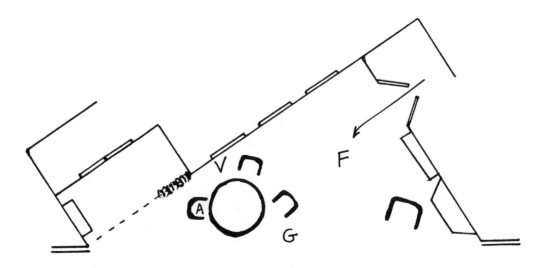

VARYA

(*Crossing to left of* ANYA.) If only the Lord would help us!

GAYEV

On Tuesday I'll go and talk of it again. (*To* VARYA.) Do stop bawling. (*To* ANYA.) Your mama will get Lopakhin to help, of course he won't refuse her . . . and as soon as you're rested, you'll go to Yaroslavl to the Countess, your great-aunt. So we'll all set to work in three directions at once, and the business is as good as settled. We shall pay off the interest . . . I'm convinced of it. (*Puts a sweet in his mouth.*) I swear by my honor, I swear by anything you like, the estate shan't be sold. (*Excitedly.*) By my own happiness, I swear it! Here's my hand on it, you can call me a cheat and a scoundrel if I let it come to an auction! With all my soul I swear!

ANYA

(*Quite happy again.*) How good you are, Uncle, and how clever! (*She embraces her uncle.*) Now I'm at peace, quite at peace, I'm happy.

Stanislavski had a great philosophical idea of practical value: There is no today, there is no tomorrow — only a movement from yesterday to tomorrow. From the point of view of the actors, yesterday is what you left behind you in the country; tomorrow, what you have to go see. Be specific, actors. Bring your past biography and what you want to accomplish in life to the character you are playing. This is the understanding of the artist when he has a very big yesterday: culture, history, and a great feeling for tomorrow.

Chekhov was permeated with the Russian culture and he was pushing Russia into the future.

Входит Фирс.

ФИРС

(*укоризненно*). Леонид Андреич, бога вы не боитесь! Когда же спать?

ГАЕВ

Сейчас, сейчас. Ты уходи, Фирс. Я уж, так и быть, сам разденусь. Ну, детки, бай-бай... Подробности завтра, а теперь идите спать. (*Целует Аню и Варю.*) Я человек восьмидесятых годов . . . Не хвалят это время, но все же, могу сказать, за убеждения мне доставалось немало в жизни. Недаром меня мужик любит. Мужика надо знать! Надо знать, с какой..

АНЯ

Опять ты, дядя!

ВАРЯ

Вы, дядечка, молчите.

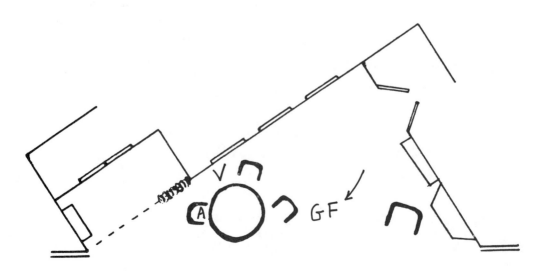

Enter FIRS.

FIRS

(*Reproachfully.*) Leonid Andreyevitch, have you no fear of God? When are you going to bed?

GAYEV

Directly, directly. Go away, Firs, I'll . . . yes, I will undress myself. Now, children, bye-bye. We'll go into details tomorrow, but now go to sleep. (*Kisses* ANYA *and* VARYA.) I am a man of the 'eighties'; nowadays they don't appreciate that . . . . Nevertheless, in the course of my life I have suffered not a little for my convictions. It's not for nothing that the peasants love me; one should know the peasants; one should know from which . . . .

ANYA

There you go again, Uncle.

VARYA

Uncle dear, be quiet.

Varya's thoughts throughout her scenes are: "The things you hear about me aren't true. I'd make a good wife for Lopakhin." Varya rationalizes these as sub-text thoughts.

We should play Chekhov so that even the audience should see anew with clear eyes. We play not only within our own souls, but also in the souls of our audience. So, the audience goes through what our own souls are going through onstage. It is the power of Stanislavski's art. You, the actors, create a unity of actor and audience.

ФИРС

(*сердито*). Леонид Андреич!

ГАЕВ

Иду, иду... Ложитесь. От двух бортов в середину! Кладу чистого ... (*Уходит, за ним семенит Фирс.*)

АНЯ

Я теперь покойна. В Ярославль ехать не хочется, я не люблю бабушку, но все же я покойна. Спасибо дяде. (*Садится.*)

ВАРЯ

Надо спать. Пойду. А тут без тебя было неудовольствие. В старой людской, как тебе известно, живут одни старые слуги: Ефимьюшка, Поля, Евстигней, ну и Карп. Стали они пускать к себе ночевать каких-то проходимцев - я промолчала. Только вот, слышу, распустили слух, будто я велела кормить их одним только горохом. От скупости, видишь ли ... И это все Евстигней ... Хорошо, думаю. Коли так, думаю, то погоди же. Зову я Евстигнея ... (*Зевает.*) Приходит ... Как же ты, говорю, Евстигней ... дурак ты этакой ...

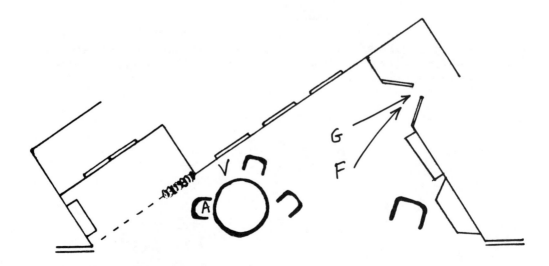

FIRS

(*Angrily.*) Leonid Andreyevitch!

GAYEV

I'm coming, I'm coming! Go to bed! Potted the shot —
clean as a whistle — a beaut! (*He goes out,* FIRS
hobbling after him.)

ANYA

I feel easier now. I don't want to go to Yaroslavl — I
don't like my great-aunt, but still, I feel easier,
thanks to Uncle.

She sits down. VARYA is behind ANYA's chair.

VARYA

I must get some sleep. I'm going now. While you were
away, something unpleasant happened. In the old
servants' quarters there are only the old servants as
you know: Yefimyushka, Palyla, Yevstignei, Karp.
They began letting in all sorts of tramps to spend the
night . . . I didn't say anything. Then I heard they'd
been spreading a report that I gave them nothing but
dried peas to eat — out of stinginess, you know . . .
and it was all Yefstignei's doing . . . all right, I
thought, if that's how it is, I thought, wait a bit. I sent
for Yefstignei . . . (*Yawns.*) He comes . . . . "How's this,"
I said, "you could be such a fool as to . . . "

*On the last exit, Firs mumbles more as he walks out with Gayev. We've
talked about everything. Soon I think it will be easier for you to play when
you know where you are, when you are sure of the lines. This, actors, is not
the last word or the final form.*

ВАРЯ

(*Поглядев на Аню.*) Аничка!.. (*Пауза.*) Заснула..
. (*Берет Аню под руку.*) Пойдем в постельку . .
. Пойдем!.. (*Ведет ее.*) Душечка моя уснула!
Пойдем.. (*Идут.*)

Далеко за садом пастух играет на свирели.* Трофимов идет через сцену и, увидев Варю и Аню, останавливается.

ВАРЯ

Тсс . . . Она спит . . . спит . . . Пойдем, родная.

АНЯ

(*тихо, в полусне*). Я так устала . . . все колокольчики . . . Дядя . . . милый, и мама и дядя . . .

ВАРЯ

Пойдем, родная, пойдем . . . (*Уходит в комнату Ани.*)

ТРОФИМОВ

(*в умилении*). Солнышко мое! Весна моя!

* Народный музыкальный инструмент в виде дудки из дерева или тростника.

ЗАНАВЕС

(VARYA)

(*Looking at* ANYA.) Anitchka! (*Pause.*)She's asleep.
(*Puts her arm around* ANYA.) Come to your little bed
.... come ... (*Leads her.*) My darling has fallen asleep
... come along!

They go. Far away beyond the orchard a shepherd plays on a pipe. TROFIMOV
crosses the stage, and seeing VARYA and ANYA, stands still.

VARYA

Sh! She's asleep ... asleep ... come, my own.

ANYA

(*Softly, half asleep.*) I'm so tired. All those bells ...
uncle ... dear ... mama and uncle ...

VARYA

Come, my own, come along. (*They go into* ANYA's
room.)

TROFIMOV

(*Tenderly, with emotion.*) My sunshine, my spring!

CURTAIN

" . . . The bookkeeper, Yepikhodov, proposed to me just after Easter . . ." **Dunyasha**, at left, (Annette Hunt) confides in **Anya** (Patricia Peardon.)

From l. to r.: **Lyubov** *(Margaret Draper),* **Pischik** *(Graham Jarvis),* **Yasha** *(Stephen Daley),* **Firs** *(Eugene Wood), and* **Gayev** *(Frederick Rolf) in Act One of* **Cherry Orchard***.*

Yepikhodov, *at left, (Niels Miller) and* ***Lopakhin*** *(Bill Berger) discuss the cherry orchard while* ***Gayev****(Frederick Rolf) looks on.*

*Trofimov (Roger Newman) speaks with **Lyubov Andreyevna** (Muriel Higgins.)*

*L. to r.: **Pischik**, on stove, (Stephen Daley), **Yasha** (Eric Tavares), **Firs** (William Whedbee), **Varya** (Miriam Mitchell), **Gayev** (Jack Eddleman), **Lopakhin** (MIchael Durrell) and **Lyubov**, seated, (Muriel Higgins) in IASTA's Denver Festival production of **Cherry Orchard**.*

ACT TWO

Although Yuri Zavadski made the decision within the time limit of his work with the American professional actors at IASTA to stage only Act One and Act Four, he did read through the whole of **Cherry Orchard** with the cast. He made significant comments from time to time on the characterization and things relative to **Cherry Orchard** for Act Two and for Act Three. These are the things which he said to start off Act Two.

There are several ways of approaching rehearsal for Acts One and Two. For Chekhov's **Cherry Orchard** *we have to get into the full text of the play, but please, while reading through Act Two and Act Three do so without any acting. Slowly pass over each word so you understand what the word means.*

One has to know how to read the play. This is not a radio show where you read aloud for expression. Stanislavski used to say of such readings: 'You are not playing, you are reading with gestures. Above all, you should not try to read the way you think you will say the lines in the end in performance.'

Every word has a different meaning for each of us. For example the word "book" for one person means one thing, for another something quite different.

On facing pages: Moscow Arts Theatre production of **Cherry Orchard***, Act Two.*

125

We are surrounded by an external world full of people, things, phenomena. Each person takes from the world what interests him and creates his own relationship to the world around him. This attempt to find a relationship to Chekhov's words will be our first step to the part. What does this word mean for each of you as the character? All this unfolds gradually within the text of the play.

On Tuesday, March 31st, 1959, I attended my first rehearsal at the Moscow Art Theatre in Moscow. This, and the succeeding rehearsals touched me deeply. There was an added excitement observing rehearsal at this legendary Moscow theatre.

The rehearsal I observed was under the direction of Victor Stanitsyn, a people's artist of the USSR. He was a distinguished actor of the Moscow Art Theatre. He told me that he was also the actor to have first played the role of the brother, Andra, in Chekhov's **Three Sisters.**

Stanitsyn later came with the Moscow Art Theatre to New York and performed **Cherry Orchard** in repertory at the New York City Center. It was the Moscow Art Theatre's *mise-en-scène* used for Act Two and Act Three for the revival of **Cherry Orchard** in the International Theatre Festival in Denver. Stanitsyn, of course, was the director for **Cherry Orchard**.

ДЕЙСТВИЕ ВТОРОЕ

Поле. Старая, покривившаяся, давно заброшенная часовенка, возле нее колодец, большие камни, когда-то бывшие, по-видимому, могильными плитами, и старая скамья. Видна дорога в усадьбу Гаева. В стороне, возвышаясь, темнеют тополи: Там начинается вишневый сад. Вдали ряд телеграфных столбов, и далеко-далеко на горизонте неясно обозначается большой город, который бывает виден только в очень хорошую, ясную погоду.

Скоро сядет солнце. Шарлотта, Яша и Дуняша сидят на скамье; Епиходов стоит возле и играет на гитаре (что-то грустное)*, все сидят задумавшись. Шарлотта в старой фуражке; она сняла с плеч ружье и поправляет пряжку на ремне.

* Слова, заключенные в скобки, взяты из текста первого прижизненного издания пьесы Сб. "Знание" 1904, 2.

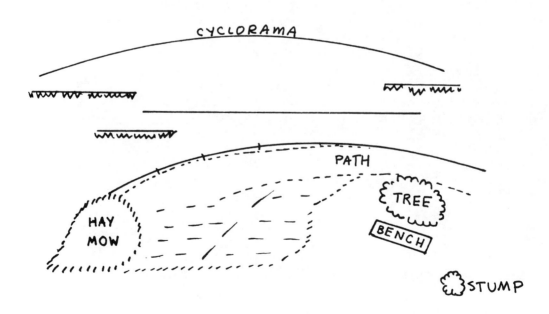

ACT TWO

In open country stands an old wayside shrine; it leans slightly to one side and has evidently been abandoned. Beside it there are a well, an old seat and a number of large stones which apparently have served as gravestones in the past. A road leads to GAYEV's estate. On one side and some distance away is a row of dark poplars, and it is there that the cherry orchard begins. Farther away is seen a line of telegraph poles and beyond them, on the horizon, the vague outlines of a large town, visible only in very good, clear weather.

The sun is about to set. CHARLOTTA, YASHA and DUNYASHA are sitting on the bench. YEPIKHODOV is standing near playing a guitar. They all sit, lost in thought. CHARLOTTA wears an old forage cap. She has taken a gun from her shoulder and is tightening the buckle on the strap.

[Yuri Zavadski added, away in the distance one can see the spires of churches of the town.]

At the Moscow Art Theatre for Act Two, sheepskins had been dyed green and thus were used effectively to suggest grassy hillocks in the park of the estate. We noted, when it was been pointed out to us, that wicker baskets covered with a blanket of hay became realistic haycocks. The setting, at close range backstage, was tastefully and imaginatively realistic. On a batten above our heads, lighting units were mounted backstage for projecting clouds onto the painted backdrop.

ШАРЛОТТА

(*в раздумье*). У меня нет настоящего паспорта, я не знаю, сколько мне лет, и мне все кажется, что я молоденькая. Когда я была маленькой девочкой, то мой отец и мамаша ездили по ярмаркам и давали представления, очень хорошие. А я прыгала сальто-мортале* и разные штучки. И когда папаша и мамаша умерли, меня взяла к себе одна немецкая госпожа и стала меня учить. Хорошо. Я выросла, потом пошла в гувернантки**. А откуда я и кто я, - не знаю . . . Кто мои родители, может, они не венчались . . . не знаю. (*Достает из кармана огурец и ест.*) Ничего не знаю. (*Пауза.*) Так хочется поговорить, а не с кем . . . Никого у меня нет.

ЕПИХОДОВ

(*играет на гитаре и поет*). "Что мне до шумного света, что мне друзья и враги . . ." Как приятно играть на мандолине!

* Сальто-мортале (итальянск.) буквально - смертельный прыжок. Акробатический прыжок с перевертыванием тела в воздухе.

** Воспитательница детей в дворянских и буржуазных семьях.

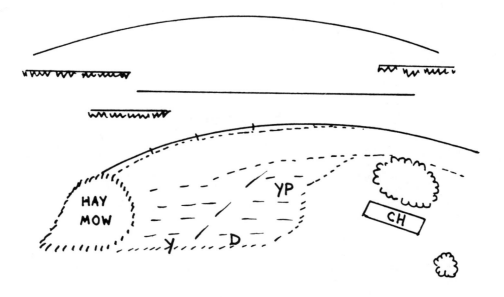

CHARLOTTA

(*Pensively*.) I haven't a real passport, and I've no idea
how old I am. But I always feel I must be young. When
I was a little girl, my father and mother used to travel
about to fairs and give performances — very good
ones. And I used to jump the *Salto Mortale** and all
sorts of other things. And when Papa and Mama died,
a German lady adopted me and had me educated. So
far so good. Then I grew up and became a governess.
But where I came from and who I am, I don't know .
. . who my parents were — perhaps they weren't even
married . . . I don't know. (*Takes a cucumber out of
her pocket and eats it.*) I don't know anything.
(*Pause.*) One wants so much to talk and there isn't
anyone to talk to . . . I haven't anybody.

YEPIKHODOV plays on the guitar and sings.

YEPIKHODOV

"What do I care for the noisy world, What do I care
for friends or foes" . . . How pleasant it is to play the
mandolin.

* *Salto Mortale* means, literally in Italian, a mortal leap, a daring circus
act.

*The scheme of time passing goes through the play. The desire to hold onto
time — to stop it — is the inner rhythm of the play. Sometimes it comes out
sharply, sometimes it almost disappears. In life we forget [that time has
passed,] then we meet somebody [who we haven't seen in years.]*

*What is time? That's what the play is about. It is less understandable for
young people.*

ДУНЯША

Это гитара, а не мандолина. (*Глядится в зеркальце и пудрится.*)

ЕПИХОДОВ

Для безумца, который влюблен, это мандолина ... (*Напевает.*) "Было бы сердце согрето жаром взаимной любви ..." (*Яша подпевает.*)

ШАРЛОТТА

Ужасно поют эти люди ... фуй! Как шакалы.

ДУНЯША

(*Яше*). Все-таки какое счастье побывать за границей.

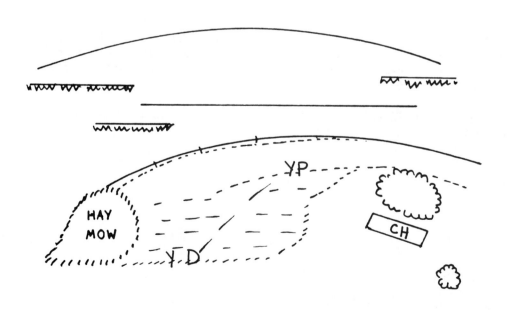

DUNYASHA

That's a guitar, not a mandolin. (*Looks in a hand mirror and powders herself.*)

YEPIKHODOV

To a man mad with love it's a mandolin. (*Sings.*) "Were her heart but aglow with love's mutual flame . . ." (YASHA *joins in.*)

CHARLOTTA

How horribly these people sing. Phoo! Like jackals!

DUNYASHA

(*To* YASHA.) How wonderful, though, to visit foreign lands.

YZ: Dunyasha listens to Yepikhodov's serenade and enjoys it.

Remember, a simple scene can be very complex.

It is a custom at the Moscow Art Theatre for an accurate cueing to the lines of dialogue as written; either a director, or other actors, or the prompter keeps the actors to the exact words and phrases of the script.

VS: Today we are to spend an hour, most likely, on just three pages of script. There will be frequent interruptions by myself as director.

ЯША

Да, конечно. Не могу с вами не согласиться. (*Зевает, потом закуривает сигару.*)

ЕПИХОДОВ

Понятное дело. За границей все давно уже в полной комплекции.

ЯША

Само собой.

ЕПИХОДОВ

Я развитой человек, читаю разные замечательные книги, но никак не могу понять направления, чего мне собственно хочется, жить мне или застрелиться, собственно говоря, но тем не менее, я всегда ношу при себе револьвер. Вот он . . . (*Показывает револьвер.*)

ШАРЛОТТА

Кончила. Теперь пойду. (*Надевает ружье.*)

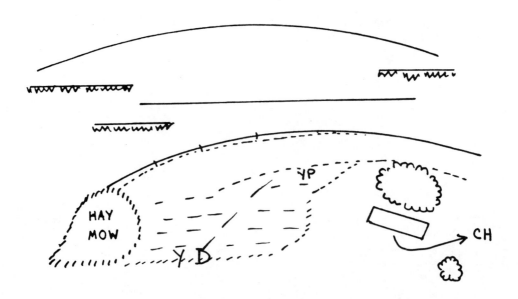

YASHA

Ah yes, I cannot but agree with you there. (*He yawns and lights a cigar.*)

YEPIKHODOV

That's understandable. In foreign lands, everything has long since reached its peak.

YASHA

Of course, that's obvious.

YEPIKHODOV

I'm a cultivated man, I read all kinds of remarkable books. I can never decide which path of life I'm impelled to follow — should I live, or should I shoot myself, strictly speaking. Nevertheless, I always carry a revolver . . . here it is . . . (*Shows revolver.*)

CHARLOTTA

I've had enough, I'm going. (*Puts gun over her shoulder.*)

ШАРЛОТТА

Ты, Епиходов, очень умный человек и очень страшный; тебя должны безумно любить женщины. Бррр!. (*Идет.*) Эти умники все такие глупые, не с кем мне поговорить . . . Все одна, одна, никого у меня нет и . . . кто я, зачем я, неизвестно . . . (*Уходит неспеша.*)

ЕПИХОДОВ

Собственно говоря, не касаясь других предметов, я должен выразиться о себе, между прочим, что судьба относится ко мне без сожаления, как буря к небольшому кораблю. Если, допустим, я ошибаюсь, тогда зачем же сегодня утром я просыпаюсь, к примеру сказать, гляжу, а у меня на груди страшной величины паук . . . Вот такой. (*Показывает обеими руками.*) И тоже квасу возьмешь, чтобы напиться, а там глядишь, что-нибудь в высшей степени неприличное вроде таракана. (*Пауза.*) Вы читали Бокля?* (*Пауза.*) Я желаю побеспокоить вас, Авдотья Федоровна, на пару слов.

* Английский либерально - буржуазный историк и социолог.

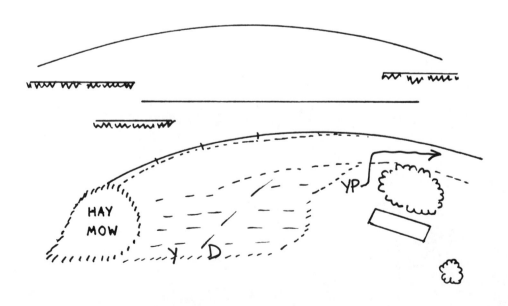

135

(CHARLOTTA)

You, Yepikhodov, are very clever, and very terrifying; all the women must be wild about you. Br-r-r! (*Starts to go.*) These clever men are all so stupid; there's no one for me to talk to . . . always alone, alone, I haven't anybody . . . and who I am, and why I am, nobody knows. (CHARLOTTA *goes out slowly*.)

YEPIKHODOV

Speaking personally, not touching upon other subjects, I am forced to the conclusion that fate behaves mercilessly to me, as a storm to a little boat. If I'm incorrect in this supposition, then why, for example, did I wake up this morning, and find here on my chest, a spider of fearful magnitude . . . like this . . . Again, I take up a jug of kvass to quench my thirst and in it there is something highly indecent in the nature of a cockroach. (*Pause.*) Have you read Buckle?* (*Pause.*) I am desirous of troubling you, Dunyasha, with a couple of words.

*Buckle, Henry Thomas (1821-1862) English historian, author of **History of Civilization in England.** Buckle believed that, "the progress of every people is regulated by principles . . . as certain of those that govern the physical world." [**Encyclopedia Britannica**, Volume 4, 1962 Edition, p.321.]

"But youthful curiosity also led him [Chekhov] into tackling the tougher intellectual matter of Buckle, Schopenhauer, and Humboldt." [Ernest J. Simmons, **Chekhov: A Biography.** Boston: Little, Brown & Company, 1962, p.26.]

YZ: *Yepikhodov thinks he is smart, only he has bad luck. Yepikhodov is like the character in Gogol's* **Dead Souls** *who read books without understanding a word.*

ДУНЯША

Говорите.

ЕПИХОДОВ

Мне бы желательно с вами наедине . . . (*Вздыхает.*)

ДУНЯША

(*смущенно*). Хорошо . . . только сначала принесите мне мою тальмочку* . . . Она около шкафа . . . тут немножко сыро . . .

ЕПИХОДОВ

Хорошо-с . . . принесу-с . . . Теперь я знаю, что мне делать с моим револьвером . . . (*Берет гитару и уходит наигрывая.*)

ЯША

Двадцать два несчастья! Глупый человек, между нами говоря. (*Зевает.*)

* Женская длинная накидка без рукавов.

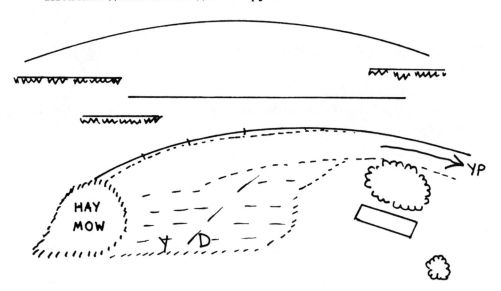

137

DUNYASHA

Well, speak.

YEPIKHODOV

I should be desirous to speak with you alone. (*Sighs.*)

DUNYASHA

(*Embarrassed.*) Very well — only first bring me my little cape. You'll find it by the cupboard. It's rather damp here.

YEPIKHODOV

Certainly, madame; I will fetch it, madame. Now I know what I must do with my revolver. (*Takes guitar and goes off playing it.*)

YASHA

Twenty-Two Misfortunes! Between ourselves, he's a fool. (*He yawns.*)

YZ: *Yepikhodov could be a Charlie Chaplin character. On Yepikhodov's speech, 'I should be desirous to speak with you alone', Dunyasha remembers his proposal. She must see the humor of the situation the three of them are in.*

During this exchange between Dunyasha and Yasha, Yepikhodov makes no impression on Dunyasha, despite his playing of the guitar for her benefit.

On Dunyasha's embarrassed speech, 'very well — only first . . .,' Dunyasha feels very delicate.

ДУНЯША

Не дай бог застрелится. (*Пауза.*) Я стала тревожная, все беспокоюсь. Меня еще девочкой взяли к господам, я теперь отвыкла от простой жизни, и вот руки белые, белые, как у барышни. Нежная стала, такая деликатная, благородная, всего боюсь . . . Страшно так. И если вы, Яша, обманете меня, то я не знаю, что будет с моими нервами.

ЯША

(*целует ее*). Огурчик! Конечно, каждая девушка должна себя помнить, и я больше всего не люблю, ежели девушка дурного поведения.

ДУНЯША

Я страстно полюбила вас, вы образованный, можете обо всем рассуждать. (*Пауза.*)

ЯША

(*зевает*). Да-с . . . По-моему, так : ежели девушка кого любит, то она, значит, безнравственная. (*Пауза.*)

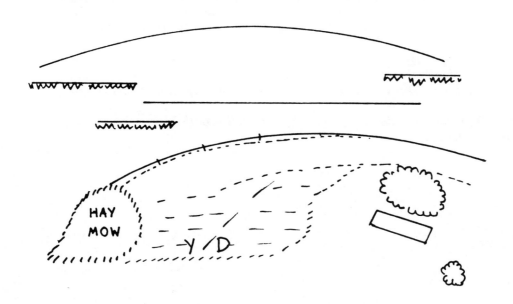

DUNYASHA

Pray God he doesn't shoot himself! (*Pause.*) I've become so nervous, I'm always in a flutter. I was quite a little girl when I was taken into the master's house. I've grown quite unused to simple ways, and my hands are white — as white as a lady's. I've become so refined. I'm such a delicate, sensitive creature, I'm afraid of everything. I'm so frightened; and if you deceive me, Yasha, I don't know what will happen to my nerves.

YASHA

(YASHA *kisses her.*) You're a peach! Of course, a nice girl should never forget herself; what I dislike more than anything is a girl who is flighty in her behavior.

DUNYASHA

I'm passionately in love with you, Yasha; you're a man of culture — you can discuss anything.

YASHA

(*Yawns.*) Yes, my girl, that's so. Now in my opinion, it's like this: if a girl loves anyone, it means she has no morals. (*Pause.*)

YZ: *On Dunyasha's speech, 'I've become so nervous . . . ,' Dunyasha wants to appear very fragile. She is thinking, 'Yasha, love me. I am no different from your French girls. A better girl you won't find. My soul is delicate. I have nerves. Not everyone does.'*

On Dunyasha's speech, 'I'm passionately in love . . ,' Dunyasha is striving to convince Yasha that he should love her.

On Yasha's line, 'You're a peach', Dunyasha thinks, 'Yasha is so sensitive and clever, he is as strong as a cucumber!'

ЯША

Приятно выкурить сигару на чистом воздухе . . . (*Прислушивается.*) Сюда идут . . . Это господа. (*Дуняша порывисто обнимает его*). Идите домой, будто ходили на реку купаться, идите этой дорожкой, а то встретятся и подумают про меня, будто я с вами на свидании. Терпеть этого не могу.

ДУНЯША

(*тихо кашляет*). У меня от сигары голова разболелась . . . (*Уходит.*)

Яша остается, сидит возле часовни. Входит Любовь Андреевна, Гаев и Лопахин.

ЛОПАХИН

Надо окончательно решить, - время не ждет. Вопрос ведь совсем пустой. Согласны вы отдать землю под дачи или нет? Ответьте одно слово : да или нет? Только одно слово!

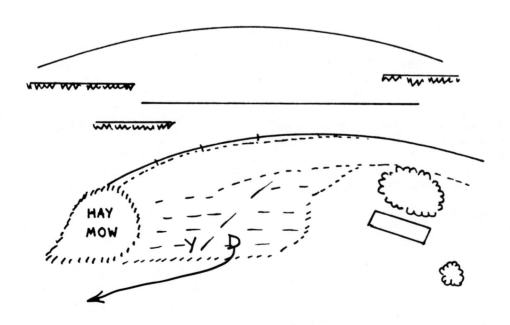

(YASHA)

It's pleasant smoking a cigar in the open air. (*Listens*.) Someone's coming this way . . . it's them! (DUNYASHA *embraces him impulsively*.) You go home, as though you'd been to the river to bathe, go by the little path, or else they'll meet you and suspect me of having made an appointment with you here. That I can't endure.

DUNYASHA

(*Coughing softly*.) The cigar's made my head ache.

DUNYASHA goes off. Enter LYUBOV ANDREYEVNA, GAYEV and LOPAKHIN.

LOPAKHIN

You must make up your mind once and for all — there's no time to lose. It's quite a simple question, you know. Will you lease your land for building purposes or not? Answer one word, yes or no; only one word!

YZ: *On Dunyasha's speech, 'the cigar's made my head ache,' Yasha's talk has been disturbing to Dunyasha, for she is naïve. Dunyasha wants to marry Yasha.*

VS: *Concentrate on the part, strive for relaxation, and, of course, constant interreacting.*

ЛЮБОВЬ АНДРЕЕВНА

Кто это здесь курит отвратительные сигары . . . (*Садится.*)

ГАЕВ

Вот железную дорогу построили, и стало удобно. (*Садится.*) Съездили в город и позавтракали . . . желтого в середину! Мне бы сначала пойти в дом, сыграть одну партию . . .

ЛЮБОВЬ АНДРЕЕВНА

Успеешь.

ЛОПАХИН

Только одно слово! (*Умоляюще.*) Дайте же мне ответ!

ГАЕВ

(*зевая*). Кого?

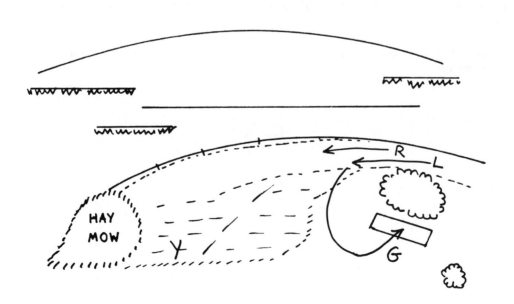

LYUBOV

Who's smoking such abominable cigars here? (*Sits down.*)

GAYEV

Now that the railway line has been brought near it's made things very convenient. (*Sits.*) We went over and lunched in town, and we are home again already. Carom off the white . . . I feel like going and playing just one game.

LYUBOV

You have plenty of time.

LOPAKHIN

Only one word! (*Imploringly.*) Do give me an answer!

GAYEV

(*Yawning.*) Who?

YZ: *I'm only proposing this to you to get it bit by bit. And then it will all fuse together: a new transmutation of the quantity to quality. The most difficult thing to do is to search — to know yourself, your character, before you come to rehearsal.*

Contrast the domestic Gayev and the philosopher Gayev. The possibility of marrying Anya to a rich man is just his imagination.

ЛЮБОВЬ АНДРЕЕВНА

(*глядит в свое портмоне*). Вчера было много денег, а сегодня совсем мало. Бедная моя Варя из экономии кормит всех молочным супом, на кухне старикам дают один горох, а я трачу как-то бессмысленно . . . (*Уронила портмоне, рассыпала золотые.*) Ну, посыпались . . . (*Ей досадно.*)

ЯША

Позвольте, я сейчас подберу. (*Собирает монеты.*)

ЛЮБОВЬ АНДРЕЕВНА

Будьте добры. Яша. И зачем я поехала завтракать . . . Дрянной ваш ресторан с музыкой, скатерти пахнут мылом . . . Зачем так много пить, Леня? Зачем так много есть? Зачем так много говорить? Сегодня в ресторане ты говорил опять много и все некстати. О семидесятых годах, о декадентах. И кому? Половым говорить о декадентах!

ЛОПАХИН

Да.

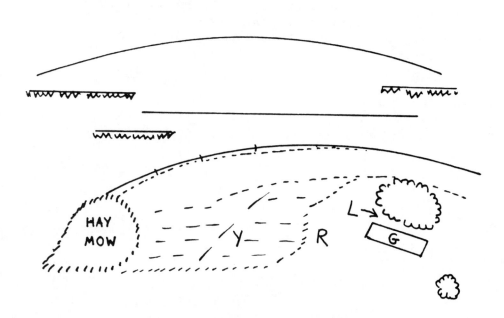

LYUBOV

(*Looks in her purse.*) Yesterday this was nearly full, and now it's almost empty. My poor Varya tries to economize; she feeds us all on milk soup! In the kitchen the old people get nothing but dried peas to eat, and yet I squander my money like a fool — (*She drops the purse, scattering gold pieces.*) There . . . you see . . . (*She is annoyed.*)

YASHA

Allow me — I'll pick them up at once. (*He picks up the money.*)

LYUBOV

There's a good boy, Yasha. And why did I go to lunch in town? Your nasty little restaurant, with its music and the tablecloths smelling of soap . . . why drink so much Leonid? Why eat so much? Why talk so much? Today you talked a great deal again, and all so pointlessly — about the 'seventies', about the 'Decadence!' And to whom? To the waiters! Talking to waiters about decadence.

LOPAKHIN

Yes.

YZ: *In our understanding, a play is created through the creation of each part; as each character unfolds, the play unfolds. It is very important that each individual role be only a part of the whole we are trying to create. Each person will have a different concept of the character. We don't even know ourselves, however.*

ГАЕВ

(*машет рукой*). Я неисправим, это очевидно. (*Раздраженно Яше.*) Что такое, постоянно вертишься перед глазами . . .

ЯША

(*смеется*). Я не могу без смеха вашего голоса слышать.

ГАЕВ

(*сестре*). Или я, или он . . .

ЛЮБОВЬ АНДРЕЕВНА

Уходите, Яша, ступайте . . .

ЯША

(*отдает Любови Андреевне кошелек*). Сейчас уйду. (*Едва удерживается от смеха.*) Сию минуту . . . (*Уходит.*)

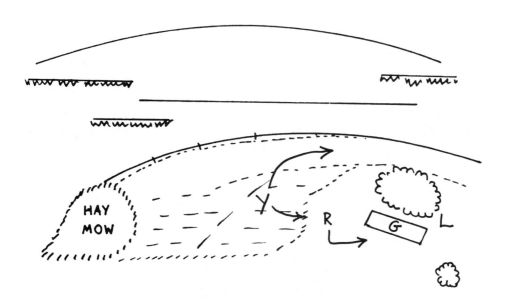

GAYEV

(*Waving his hand*.) I'm incorrigible; that's evident. (*Irritably to* YASHA.) Will you stop fidgeting about in front of us?

YASHA

(*Laughs*.) I can't hear your voice without laughing.

GAYEV

(*To* LYUBOV.) Either he or I . . .

LYUBOV

Get along — go away, Yasha.

YASHA

(*Giving* LYUBOV *her purse*.) I'm going this minute — this minute . . . (*Hardly able to suppress his laughter, he goes*.)

ЛОПАХИН

Ваше имение собирается купить богач Дериганов.
На торги, говорят, приедет сам лично.

ЛЮБОВЬ АНДРЕЕВНА

А вы откуда слышали?

ЛОПАХИН

В городе говорят.

ГАЕВ

Ярославская тетушка обещала прислать, а когда
и сколько пришлет, неизвестно . . .

ЛОПАХИН

Сколько она пришлет? Тысяч сто? Двести?

ЛЮБОВЬ АНДРЕЕВНА

Ну . . . Тысяч десять - пятнадцать, и на том
спасибо.

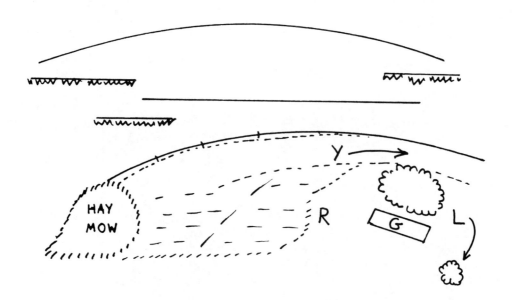

LOPAKHIN

That rich man, Deriganov, means to buy your estate.
They say he's coming to the sale himself.

LYUBOV

Where did you hear that?

LOPAKHIN

That's what they say in town.

GAYEV

Our aunt from Yaroslavl has promised to send help;
but when and how much she will send, no one knows.

LOPAKHIN

How much *will* she send? A hundred thousand? Two
hundred?

LYUBOV

Oh well . . . ten or fifteen thousand; and we must be
thankful to get that.

As played by the Moscow Art Theatre Company, the character Lopakhin in Cherry Orchard is sensitive but tempestuous. He was Mikhail Zimin. In Moscow, he had played the taciturn and ineffectual brother, André, in **Three Sisters**. *In Gorky's* **The Lower Depths**, *(more accurately translated as* **On The Bottom**,*) the actor plays the heavy, glowering locksmith. It was interesting to see the shading and variety this actor brings to contrasting characters.*

ЛОПАХИН

Простите, таких легкомысленных людей, как вы, господа, таких неделовых, странных, я еще не встречал. Вам говорят русским языком, имение ваше продается, а вы точно не понимаете.

ЛЮБОВЬ АНДРЕЕВНА

Что же нам делать? Научите, что?

ЛОПАХИН

Я вас каждый день учу. Каждый день я говорю одно и тоже. И вишневый сад, и землю необходимо отдать в аренду под дачи, сделать это теперь же, поскорее, - аукцион на носу! Поймите! Раз окончательно решите, чтоб были дачи, так денег вам дадут сколько угодно, и вы тогда спасены.

ЛЮБОВЬ АНДРЕЕВНА

Дачи и дачники - это так пошло, простите.

ГАЕВ

Совершенно с тобой согласен.

ЛОПАХИН

Я или зарыдаю, или закричу, или в обморок упаду. Не могу! Вы меня замучили! (*Гаеву.*) Баба вы!

LOPAKHIN

Forgive me, but I've never in my life known such frivolous people as you are — so strange and un-businesslike! You're told in plain language your estate is going to be sold and you behave as if you didn't grasp it.

LYUBOV

What are we to do? Tell us what to do.

LOPAKHIN

(*Crosses down to stage left of bench.*) I do tell you, every day; every day I say the same thing; the cherry orchard and land must be leased to build dachas, and as soon as possible — immediately. The auction's right on top of us. Please understand! Decide once and for all to let there be dachas, then you could raise as much money as you like and you are saved.

LYUBOV

Dachas — summer visitors — forgive me, but it's all so cheap and vulgar. (*Crosses to grassy mound; sits.*)

GAYEV

I absolutely agree with you.

LOPAKHIN

(*Turning away from them.*) I shall either sob or scream or have a fit! I can't stand it! You're driving me mad! (*Sits on stump. To* GAYEV.) You're an old woman!

YZ: Lopakhin can't understand why they won't listen to his plan. The whole play shows lack of communication between people.

VS: Show a transition from rage to quietness.

ГАЕВ

Кого?

ЛОПАХИН

Баба! (*Хочет уйти.*)

ЛЮБОВЬ АНДРЕЕВНА

(*испуганно*). Нет, не уходите, останьтесь, голубчик. Прошу вас. Может быть, надумаем что-нибудь!

ЛОПАХИН

О чем тут думать!

ЛЮБОВЬ АНДРЕЕВНП

Не уходите, прошу вас. С вами все-таки веселее ... (*Пауза.*) Я все жду чего-то, как-будто над нами должен обвалиться дом.

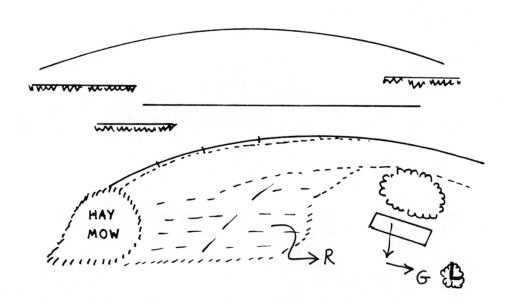

GAYEV

Who?

LOPAKHIN

An old woman! (*Gets up to go.*)

LYUBOV

(*Alarmed. Rises.*) No, don't go! Please stay. I beg you. Perhaps we shall think of something.

LOPAKHIN

What is there to think of?

LYUBOV

(*Taking a step towards him.*) Don't go, I entreat you, somehow it's more cheerful with you here. (*Pause.*) (*Returns and sits.*) I keep expecting something, as if the house were going to fall about our ears.

ГАЕВ

(*в глубоком раздумье*). Дуплет в угол . . . Краузе в середину . . .

ЛЮБОВЬ АНДРЕЕВНА

Уж очень много мы грешили . . .

ЛОПАХИН

Какие у вас грехи . . .

ГАЕВ

(*кладет в рот леденец*). Говорят, что я все свое состояние проел на леденцах . . . (*Смеется.*)

ЛЮБОВЬ АНДРЕЕВНА

О, мои грехи . . . Я всегда сорила деньгами без удержу, как сумасшедшая, и вышла замуж за человека, который делал одни только долги. Мой муж умер от шампанского, - он страшно пил, - и на несчастье я полюбила другого, сошлась, и как раз в это время, - это было первое наказание, удар прямо в голову, - вот тут на реке . . . утонул мой мальчик, и я уехала за границу, совсем уехала, чтобы никогда не возвращаться, не видеть этой реки . . .

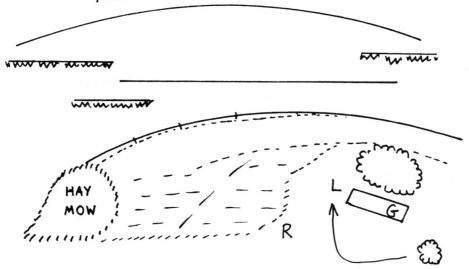

GAYEV

(*Crossing a step downstage. In profound dejection.*)
Potted the white — it fails — a kiss . . .

LYUBOV

We have been great sinners . . .

LOPAKHIN

What sins have you to repent?

GAYEV

(*Turning to* LOPAKHIN. *Puts a sweet in his mouth.*)
They say I've eaten up my property in sweets!
(*Laughs.*)

LYUBOV

Oh my sins, my sins! I've always frittered my money
away recklessly, like a lunatic. I married a man who
did nothing but get into debt. He died of champagne,
drank horribly. To my shame, I fell in love with
another man, and I lived with him. Then immediately, that was my first punishment — inexorably —
the blow fell: here in the river, my little boy was
drowned . . . And I went abroad, went away forever
. . . never to come back, never to see this river
again . . .

YZ: *Gayev is an idealist, but a parasite.*

ЛЮБОВЬ АНДРЕЕВНА

Я закрыла глаза, бежала, себя не помня, а он за мной . . . безжалостно, грубо. Купила я дачу возле Ментоны, так как он заболел там, и три года я не знала отдыха ни днем ни ночью; больной измучил меня, душа моя высохла. А в прошлом году, когда дачу продали за долги, я уехала в Париж, и там он обобрал меня, бросил, сошелся с другой, я пробовала отравиться . . . Так глупо, так стыдно . . . И потянуло вдруг в Россию, на родину, к девочке моей . . . (*Утирает слезы.*) Господи, господи, будь милостив, прости мне грехи мои! Не наказывай меня больше! (*Достает из кармана телеграмму.*) Получила сегодня из Парижа . . . Просит прощения, умоляет вернуться . . . (*Рвет телеграмму.*) Словно где-то музыка. (*Прислушивается.*)

ГАЕВ

Это наш знаменитый еврейский оркестр. Помнишь, четыре скрипки, флейта и контрабас.

ЛЮБОВЬ АНДРЕЕВНА

Он еще существует? Его бы к нам зазвать как-нибудь, устроить вечерок.

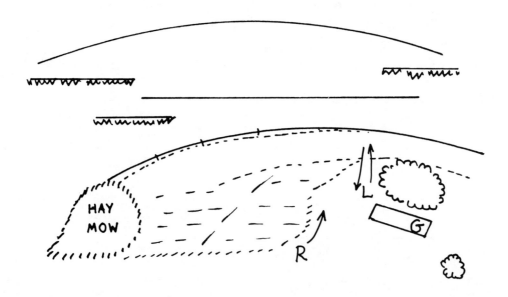

(LYUBOV)

. . . I closed my eyes and fled, distracted . . . but he followed me — pitiless, brutal. I bought a villa near Menton, because he fell ill there; and for three years, day and night I knew neither peace nor rest. Ill as he was, he tormented me — my soul grew parched and withered. Then last year, when the villa was sold to pay the debts — I went to Paris, and there he robbed me, abandoned me and went to live with another woman. I tried to poison myself — so stupid, so shameful — and then suddenly I felt irresistibly drawn back to Russia — back to my own country — to my little girl. (*Wiping away tears.*) Lord, Oh Lord! Be merciful, forgive me my sins — don't punish me anymore! (*Takes a telegram out of her purse.*) This came today from Paris — he begs me to forgive him, implores me to come back.(*She tears up the telegram.*) Don't I hear music somewhere? (*Listens.*)

GAYEV

That's our famous Jewish orchestra, you remember? Four violins, a flute and a double bass.

VARYA and CHARLOTTA cross from upstage left to upstage right.

LYUBOV

Does that still exist? We ought to send for them some evening and give a dance.

YZ: *Lyubov, each role is not a straight line, but a line with ups and downs, with contradictions. Yet it has a development of its own. These contradictions within a role are very interesting to develop . . . You can do everything pale, not fully expressed, wilted, if you don't find all the riches of the part. Chekhov gives you much to work with, both for your fortissimo and for your piano.*

You will see each rehearsal as not just a repetition. It is new and then, once again, new. Every phrase is something. The whole has to permeate you.

ЛОПАХИН

(*прислушивается*). Не слыхать . . . (*Тихо напевает.*) "И за деньги русака немцы офрацузят". (*Смеется.*) Какую я вчера пьесу смотрел в театре, очень смешно.

ЛЮБОВЬ АНДРЕЕВНА

И, наверное, ничего нет смешного. Вам не пьесы смотреть, а смотреть бы чаще на самих себя. Как вы все серо живете, как много говорите ненужного.

ЛОПАХИН

то правда. Надо прямо говорить, жизнь у нас дурацкая . . . (*Пауза.*) Мой папаша был мужик, идиот, ничего не понимал, меня не учил, а только бил спьяна, и все палкой. В сущности, и я такой же болван и идиот. Ничему не обучался, почерк у меня скверный, пишу я так, что от людей совестно, как свинья.

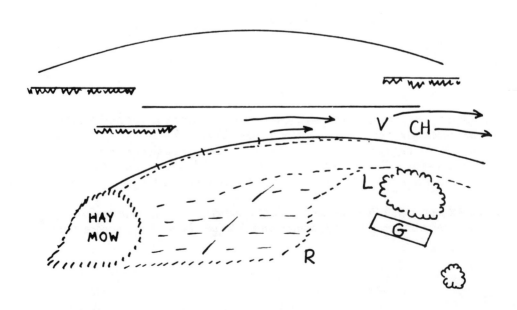

LOPAKHIN

(*Listens.*) I don't hear anything. And for money, the Germans will turn Russians into Frenchman . . . (*Hums softly.*) I saw a wonderful play at the theatre yesterday — very funny.

LYUBOV

There was probably nothing funny about it. You shouldn't look at plays, you should look at yourselves, more often. How drab your lives are — how full of unnecessary talk.

LOPAKHIN

That's true; come to think of it we do live like fools. (*Pause.*) My father was a peasant, almost an idiot; he understood nothing, never taught me anything; all he did was beat me when he was drunk, and always with a stick. And when you come down to it, I'm just the same; a dumb idiot. I never learned anything — my writing is so bad I feel ashamed before people, like a pig.*

* Anton Chekhov wrote of his earliest memories, "my father began my education or, to put it more simply, began to beat me, before I reached the age of five . . . every morning as I awoke, my first thought was: will I be beaten today?" [Henri Troyat, **Chekhov**.]

"The peasant proverb: Beat your wife as you beat your old sheepskin coat . . . Chekhov wrote his brother Alexander years later, how their father's despotism and lies ruined their mother's youth and spoiled their own childhood." [Ernest J. Simmons, **Chekhov: A Biography**.]

ЛЮБОВЬ АНДРЕЕВНА

Жениться вам нужно, мой друг.

ЛОПАХИН

Да . . . Это правда.

ЛЮБОВЬ АНДРЕЕВНА

На нашей бы Варе. Она хорошая девушка.

ЛОПАХИН

Да.

ЛЮБОВЬ АНДРЕЕВНА

Она у меня из простых, работает целый день, а главное вас любит. Да и вам-то давно нравится.

ЛОПАХИН

Что же? Я непрочь . . . Она хорошая девушка. (*Пауза.*)

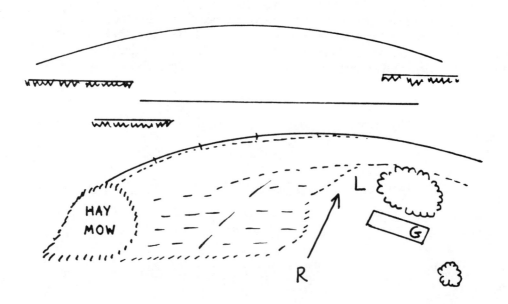

LYUBOV

(*Crossing up to* LOPAKHIN.) You should get married, my friend.

LOPAKHIN

Yes . . . that's true.

LYUBOV

To our Varya, she's a good girl.

LOPAKHIN

Yes.

LYUBOV

She's a nice, simple girl, she's busy all day long; but the main thing is, she loves you. Besides, you've liked her for a long time now.

LOPAKHIN

Well, why not? She's a good girl. (*Pause.*)

VS: *Strive for a stream of conscious thought appropriate to the character both in the immediate scene and in the total context of the play. Fight clichés and line readings, in gestures, in movements.*

ГАЕВ

Мне предлагают место в банке. Шесть тысяч в год
. . . Слыхала?

ЛЮБОВЬ АНДРЕЕВНА

Где тебе! Сиди уж . . .

Фирс входит, он принес пальто.

ФИРС

(*Гаеву*). Извольте, сударь, надеть, а то сыро.

ГАЕВ

(*надевает пальто*). Надоел ты, брат.

ФИРС

Нечего там . . . Утром уехали не сказавшись.
(*Оглядывает его.*)

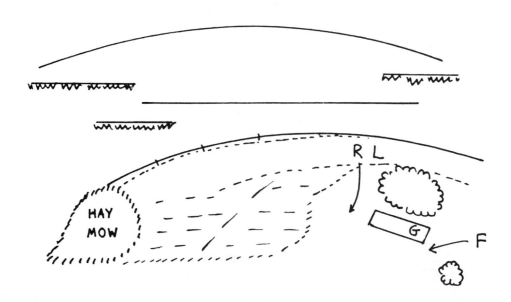

GAYEV

I've been offered a place in the bank — 6,000 roubles
a year — have you heard?

LYUBOV

That would never do for you. You'd better stay here.

Enter FIRS with overcoat.

FIRS

Allow me to put this on, sir, it's damp.

GAYEV

(*Putting it on.*) You bother me, old fellow.

FIRS

Never mind about that. This morning you went out
without leaving word. (*Looks him over.*)

VS: *Chekhov's* **Three Sisters** *had been directed originally as a painful, anguished dream not to be realized. In the later day, shifting of emphasis of the play,* **Three Sisters** *became not a play of frustration but a vision of the future and of young people striving for it. I say that the character Vershinin of* **Three Sisters** *has also been played in Russia as a man of the future, but I think that this has not been correct. Vershinin, in my view, is still locked in the past. It's only the young characters of* **Three Sisters** *— as in Cherry Orchard — who are positive and have a solid vision.*

ЛЮБОВЬ АНДРЕЕВНА

Как ты постарел, Фирс!

ФИРС

Чего изволите?

ЛОПАХИН

Говорят, ты постарел очень!

ФИРС

Живу давно. Меня женить собрались, а вашего папаши еще на свете не было . . . (*Смеется.*) А воля вышла, я уже старшим камердинером был. Тогда я не согласился на волю, остался при господах . . . (*Пауза.*) И помню, все рады, а чему рады, и сами не знают.

ЛОПАХИН

Прежде очень хорошо было. По крайней мере, драли.

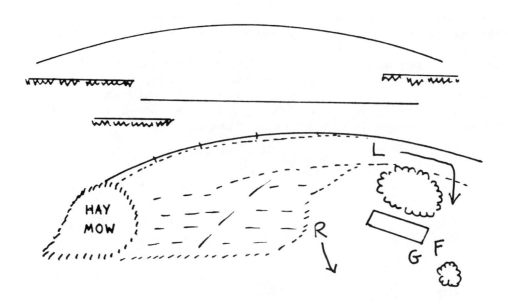

LYUBOV

How old you look, Firs!

FIRS

What is your wish?

LOPAKHIN

She said, how old you look.

FIRS

I've had a long life; they were arranging my wedding before your papa was born. (*Laughs*.) I was already head footman when the Emancipation* came. I wouldn't consent to be set free then; I stayed on with the old master . . . (*Pause*.) I remember they were all very happy, but why they were happy they didn't know themselves.

LOPAKHIN

The good old days! There was flogging, anyway!

---

* The Emancipation refers to the Tzar's freeing of the serfs in the 19th Century.

Echoes of Chekhov's peasant background: 'A grandfather Yegor Mikhailovich Chekhov, coming from a long line of serfs . . . began this process of self-emancipation. Shrewd, driving, and thrifty, he was transferred from work in the fields to his master's sugar beet factory, where he soon became foreman . . . In 1841, at the age of 42, . . . he realized the dream of his life — he bought his freedom and that of his wife and sons for thirty-five hundred roubles . . . The sum was not large enough to include his only daughter in the deal. However, his owner, Count A. D. Chertkov [!] . . "generously" threw in the girl . . . Once free, grandfather Chekhov lost no time in thrusting his sons out in the world to make good the liberty he had bought for them . . . [Ernest J. Simmons, *Chekhov: A Biography*.]

ФИРС

(*не расслышав*). А еще бы. Мужики при господах, господа при мужиках, а теперь все враздробь, не поймешь ничего.

ГАЕВ

Помолчи, Фирс. Завтро мне нужно в город. Обещали познакомить с одним генералом, который может дать под вексель.

ЛОПАХИН

Ничего у вас не выйдет. И не заплатите вы процентов, будьте покойны.

ЛЮБОВЬ АНДРЕЕВНА

Это он бредит. Никаких генералов нет.

Входят Трофимов, Аня и Варя.

ГАЕВ

А вот и наши идут.

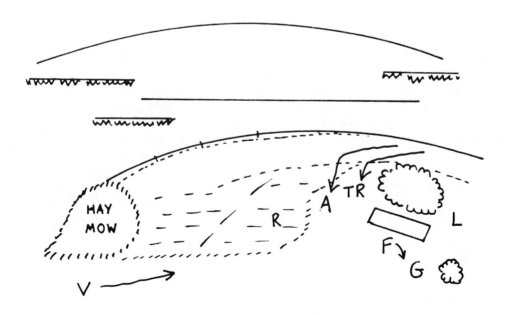

FIRS

(*Not hearing.*) To be sure. The peasants knew their masters, the masters knew their peasants; but now everything's all broken up, there's no making it out.

GAYEV

Be quiet, Firs. I must go to town tomorrow. They've promised to introduce me to a general who might let us have a loan.

LOPAKHIN

Nothing will come of that. You won't even be able to pay the interest, make no mistake about that.

LYUBOV

(*Sits right, on mound.*) He's raving, there is no such general.

Enter TROFIMOV, ANYA and VARYA. ANYA enters from stage right and goes up, and then, down right of haycock.

GAYEV

Here come the girls.

АНЯ

Мама сидит.

ЛЮБОВЬ АНДРЕЕВНА

(*нежно*). Иди, иди . . . Родные мои . . . (*Обнимая Аню и Варю.*) Если бы вы обе знали, как я вас люблю. Садитесь рядом, вот так. (*Все усаживаются.*)

ЛОПАХИН

Наш вечный студент все с барышнями ходит.

ТРОФИМОВ

Не ваше дело.

ЛОПАХИН

Ему пятьдесят лет скоро, а он все еще студент.

ТРОФИМОВ

Оставьте ваши дурацкие шутки.

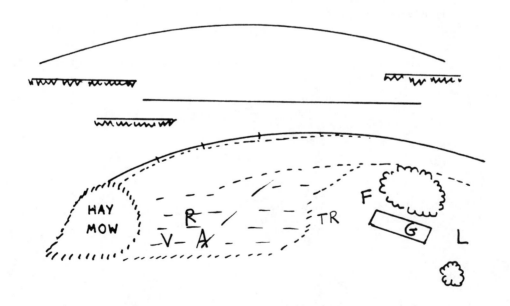

ANYA

There's Mama . . .

LYUBOV

(*Tenderly*.) Come here, come along, my darlings. (VARYA *crosses to* MME. RANYEVSKY, *below haycock. Embraces* ANYA *and* VARYA. VARYA *sits*.) If you only knew how I love you both! Sit beside me — there, like that.

LOPAKHIN

Our eternal student is always with the young ladies.

TROFIMOV

That's not your business.

LOPAKHIN

He'll soon be fifty, and he's still a student!

TROFIMOV

Stop your silly jokes.

We have letters of Chekhov in which he guides us [about Trofimov's character.] In one of Chekhov's letters, he stressed that the young student, Trofimov of **Cherry Orchard**, *was a man who had been in and out of jail in the revolutionary period; Chekhov in the same letter wrote that he did not know how to put that background information on Trofimov into the context of the play.*

ЛОПАХИН

Что же ты, чудак, сердишься?

ТРОФИМОВ

А ты не приставай.

ЛОПАХИН

(*смеется*). Позвольте вас спросить, как вы обо мне понимаете?

ТРОФИМОВ

Я, Ермолай Алексеич, так понимаю - вы богатый человек, будете скоро миллионером. Вот так в смысле обмена веществ нужен хищный зверь, который съедает все, что попадается ему на пути, так и ты нужен. (*Все смеются.*)

ВАРЯ

Вы, Петя, расскажите лучше о планетах.

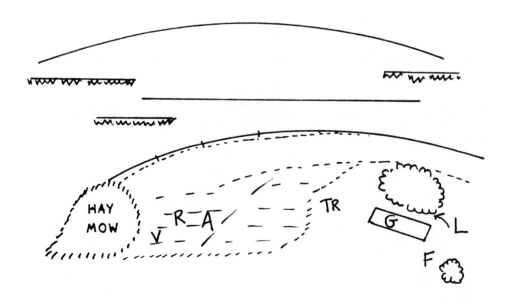

LOPAKHIN

What are you so cross about, you funny fellow?

TROFIMOV

Oh, leave me alone . . .

LOPAKHIN

(*Laughs*.) Allow me to ask you, what's your real opinion of me?

TROFIMOV

My real opinion of you, Yermolay Alexeyevitch, is that you are a rich man who will soon be a millionaire. Well, just as in the economy of nature a wild beast is necessary, who devours everything that comes in his way, so you, too, have your uses. (*They all laugh*.)

VARYA

Better tell us something about the planets, Petya.

ЛЮБОВЬ АНДРЕЕВНА

Нет, давайте продолжим вчерашний разговор.

ТРОФИМОВ

О чем это?

ГАЕВ

О гордом человеке.

ТРОФИМОВ

Мы вчера говорили долго, но ни к чему не пришли. В гордом человеке, в вашем смысле, есть что-то мистическое. Быть может, вы и правы по-своему, но если рассуждать попросту, без затей, то какая там гордость, есть ли в ней смысл, если человек физиологически устроен неважно, если в своем громадном большинстве он груб, неумен, глубоко несчастлив. Надо перестать восхищаться собой. Надо бы только работать.

ГАЕВ

Все равно умрешь.

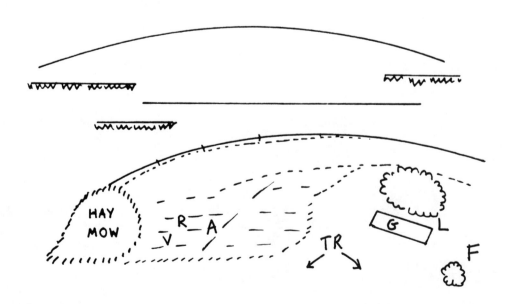

LYUBOV

No, let's get on with yesterday's conversation.

TROFIMOV

What was it about? (*Sits center stage on grass.*)

GAYEV

About the pride of man.

TROFIMOV

Yes, we talked a long time, but we came to no conclusion. In pride, as you understand it, there is something mystical. Perhaps you're right, from your personal point of view. But if one discusses it in the abstract, simply and without prejudice, then what kind of pride can there be, since man is physiologically so imperfect, since, in the great majority of cases, he is coarse, unintelligent and profoundly unhappy? We should stop admiring ourselves — we should work, and nothing else.

GAYEV

We must die in any case.

ТРОФИМОВ

Кто знает? И что значит - умрешь? Быть может, у человека сто чувств, и со смертью погибает только пять, известных нам, а остальные девяносто пять остаются живы.

ЛЮБОВЬ АНДРЕЕВНА

Какой вы умный, Петя!

ЛОПАХИН

(*иронически*). Страсть!

ТРОФИМОВ

Человечество идет вперед, совершенствуя свои силы. Все, что недосягаемо для него теперь, когда-нибудь станет близким, понятным, только вот надо работать, помогать всеми силами тем, кто ищет истину. У нас, в России, работают пока очень немногие. Громадное большинство той интеллигенции, какую я знаю, ничего не ищет, ничего не делает и к труду пока не способно.

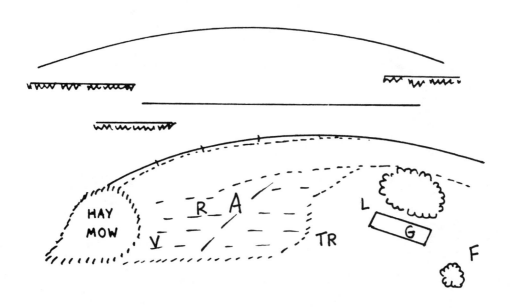

TROFIMOV

Who knows? And what does it mean — to die? Perhaps man has a hundred senses, and at his death only the five we know will perish, while the other ninety-five remain alive.

LYUBOV

How clever you are, Petya.

LOPAKHIN

(*Sarcastically.*) Fearfully clever!

TROFIMOV

Humanity progresses, perfecting its powers. Everything that seems unattainable now, will one day become familiar and comprehensible; only we must work — helping with all our strength those who seek the truth. Among us, here in Russia, such workers are few as yet. Most of the "intelligentsia," as they like to call themselves, do nothing — are totally unfit for work of any kind. They are patronizing to their servants, treat the peasants like animals, they never study or read anything serious — they do absolutely nothing at all!

YZ: *The theme of Chekhov is work, work, work. Do remember always what I told you, we have not only today, we have the movement from yesterday to tomorrow. You must know, as artists, what will be the future of the character you are playing.*

The Moscow Arts Theatre uses primary sources as a basis for creating optimism in **Cherry Orchard,** *and for pointing up Trofimov as a man with a future.*

ТРОФИМОВ

Называют себя интеллигенцией, а прислуге говорят "ты", с мужиками обращаются, как с животными, учатся плохо, серьезно ничего не читают, ровно ничего не делают, о науках только говорят, в искусстве понимают мало. Все серьезны, у всех строгие лица, все говорят только о важном, философствуют, а между тем (у всех на глазах рабочие едят отвратительно, спят без подушек, по тридцати, по сорока в одной комнате), везде клопы, смрад, сырость, нравственная нечистота . . . И, очевидно, все хорошие разговоры у нас для того только, чтобы отвести глаза себе и другим. Укажите мне, где у нас ясли, о которых говорят так много и часто, где читальни? О них только в романах пишут, на деле же их нет совсем. Есть только грязь, пошлость, азиатчина . . . Я боюсь и не люблю очень серьезных физиономий, боюсь серьезных разговоров. Лучше помолчим!

ЛОПАХИН

Знаете, я встаю в пятом часу утра, работаю с утра до вечера, ну, у меня постоянно деньги свои и чужие, и я вижу, какие кругом люди. Надо только начать делать что-нибудь, чтобы понять, как мало честных, порядочных людей. Иной раз, когда не спится, я думаю - "Господи, ты дал нам громадные леса, необъятные поля, глубочайшие горизонты, и, живя тут, мы сами должны бы по-настоящему быть великанами . . ."

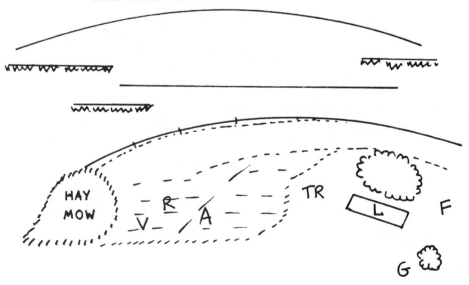

(TROFIMOV)

They only talk about Science and have very little understanding of the Arts. They are all very solemn, they put on severe faces, they philosophize and talk of weighty matters, yet all the time anyone can see that our peasants are abominably fed and have to sleep without proper beds, thirty or forty to a room, with bed bugs, bad smells, dampness, and immorality everywhere. It's obvious; the only purpose of our fine talk is to divert our attention from the realities. What about these day nurseries, these free libraries we hear so much about?* We read about them in novels — in reality they don't exist. There's nothing but dirt, vulgarity, Asiatic fatalism. I hate serious faces — I'm afraid of them — I'm afraid of serious conversations. We'd far better be silent! (*He sits.*)

LOPAKHIN

You know, I get up at five o'clock, I work from morning to night; and I've money, my own and other people's, always passing through my hands; I see what humanity is really like. You've only to start doing things to see how few honest, decent people there are. Sometimes lying awake at night, I think, "Oh, Lord, thou has given us immense forests, boundless plains, the widest horizons; living in such surroundings we ourselves ought to be giants."

* Upon the liberation of the serfs, the government had promised, for the freed serfs, schools, libraries, hospitals, etc. At the time of Chekhov, they were gravely lacking in these things that had been promised.

Trofimov understands it is pointless to live only for one's self, that every human being is part of a larger process and should make his own contribution to life. He is the eternal student, but if he is only an intellect, that is not Trofimov. Trofimov, when he speaks, speaks not only for himself, but also for the people he shares his castle with; the whole movement.

ЛЮБОВЬ АНДРЕЕВНА

Вам понадобились великаны . . . Они только в сказках хороши, а так они пугают.

В глубине сцены проходит Епиходов и (*тихо, грустно*) играет на гитаре.

ЛЮБОВЬ АНДРЕЕВНА

(*задумчиво*). Епиходов идет . . .

АНЯ

(*задумчиво*). Епиходов идет.

ГАЕВ

Солнце село, господа.

ТРОФИМОВ

Да.

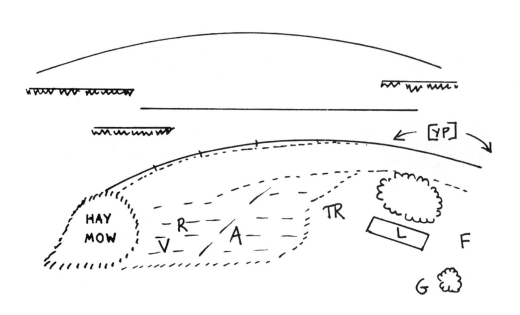

LYUBOV

You ask for giants! They're only good in fairy tales;
in real life they're frightening.

YEPIKHODOV crosses in the background playing on the guitar.

LYUBOV

There goes Yepikhodov.

ANYA

(*Dreamily*.) There goes Yepikhodov.

GAYEV

(*Rising; looking offstage left*.) Gentlemen, ladies, the
sun has set.

TROFIMOV

Yes.

VS: *Lyubov, suffer inside — think — then say the lines simply. Think the
line before saying the line. Lopakhin, do not use long phrases. The character
should utilize short phrases to indicate his inner struggle.*

YZ: *I see you are trying to give performances in your early readings of the
text of the play. If you are so talented, there's nothing for me to do.*

*I compare growth within an actor with the growth of a flower. In an
artificial flower you prepare the petals and glue them together before it is
dead. In an organic flower you start with a seed which doesn't look at all like
the flower that is to come out of it. For a long time nothing, then a bud, a
leaf, and finally the flower. And here I have to create a whole bouquet of
flowers!*

*How little time we have: to grow, to flower together, for me to take you by
the hand around this stage.*

ГАЕВ

(*негромко, как бы декламируя*). О, природа, дивная, ты блещешь вечным сиянием, прекрасная и равнодушная, ты, которую мы называем матерью, сочетаешь в себе бытие и смерть, ты живешь и разрушаешь . . .

ВАРЯ

(*умоляюще*). Дядечка!

АНЯ

Дядя, ты опять!

ТРОФИМОВ

Вы лучше желтого в середину дуплетом.

ГАЕВ

Я молчу, молчу.

Все сидят, задумались. Тишина. Слышно только, как тихо бормочет Фирс. Вдруг раздается отдаленный звук, точно с неба, звук лопнувшей струны, замирающий, печальный.

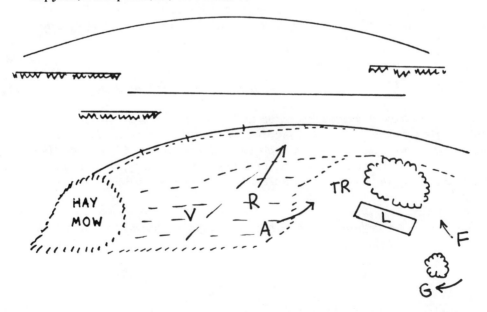

GAYEV

(*Not loud, but declaiming.*) Oh nature, divine nature, thou shinest with eternal radiance, beautiful and indifferent! Thou, whom we call our mother, thou dost unite within thee life and death! Thou givest life, and dost destroy.

VARYA

(*Pleadingly.*) Uncle!

ANYA

Uncle, you're at it again!

TROFIMOV

You'd be better off 'carom-ing off the doublet.'

GAYEV

I'm silent . . . I'm silent.

They all sit plunged in thought. Perfect stillness. The only thing audible is the muttering of FIRS. Suddenly there is a sound in the distance — as if it were from the sky — the sound of a breaking harp-string, mournfully dying away.

YZ: *A great deal is revealed in Chekhov through the characters' attitude toward nature. It is important to convey the feeling of life in Act II, where you feel the cherry orchard is onstage, so to speak. The environment is important. Please, I want the cherry orchard, nature, to be in the play as well as people.*

Each person reacts differently to the sound of the harp string.

ЛЮБОВЬ АНДРЕЕВНА

Это что?

ЛОПАХИН

Не знаю. Где-нибудь далеко в шахтах сорвалась бадья. Но где-нибудь очень далеко.

ГАЕВ

А может быть птица какая-нибудь ... вроде цапли.

ТРОФИМОВ

Или филин.

ЛЮБОВЬ АНДРЕЕВНА

(*вздрагивает*). Неприятно почему-то. (*Пауза.*)

ФИРС

Перед несчастьем тоже было: и сова кричала, и самовар гудел бесперечь.

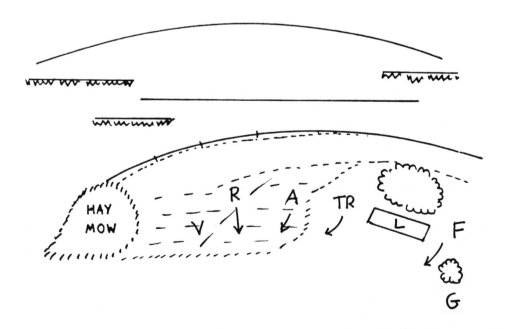

LYUBOV

What is that?

LOPAKHIN

I don't know. Somewhere in the pits a bucket's broken loose and fallen in the quarry; but somewhere very far away.

GAYEV

Or it might be some sort of bird, perhaps a heron.

TROFIMOV

Or an owl.

LYUBOV

(*Shudders.*) It's unsettling somehow. (*Pause.*)

FIRS

Before the misfortune, the same thing happened — the owl screeched, and the samovar hissed all the time.

*YZ: The play is really about the flow of time; about how people change, how youth passes. Start to add to the inner world of your characters so you can think about it outside the hours of rehearsal. The theme of **Cherry Orchard** is "time cannot stop". The inner life of the character can be better played if you know as much as possible of the complete reality in which it happened.*

ГАЕВ

Перед каким несчастьем?

ФИРС

Перед волей.

ЛЮБОВЬ АНДРЕЕВНА

Знаете, друзья, пойдемте, уже вечереет. (*Ане.*) У тебя на глазах слезы . . . Что ты, девочка? (*Обнимает ее.*)

АНЯ

Это так, мама. Ничего.

ТРОФИМОВ

Кто-то идет.

Показывается прохожий в белой потасканной фуражке, в пальто, он слегка пьян.

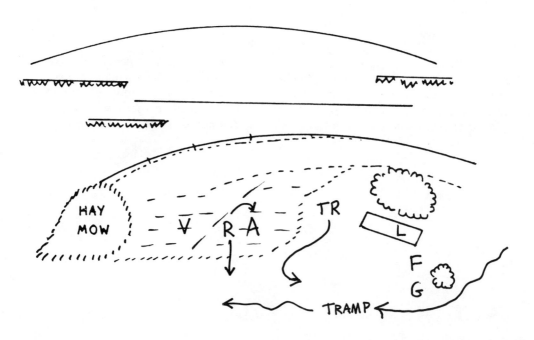

GAYEV

Before what misfortune?

FIRS

Before the Emancipation. (*Pause.*)

LYUBOV

Come, my friends, let's be going. It's getting dark. (*To* ANYA.) You have tears in your eyes. What is it, my little one? (*Embraces her.*)

ANYA

I don't know, Mama; it's nothing.

TROFIMOV

Somebody is coming.

A TRAMP appears in a shabby white forage cap and an overcoat. He is slightly drunk.

VS: *Don't play the end before it comes. The sense of art does not lie in empty self-expression; unreceived, complacent art is dead art. Art is the straightest path to mutual understanding.*

Repertory theatre can give actors an opportunity to open up their talents. Under these conditions, we can have a blossoming out of poetry in the theatre; it shimmers through the productions.

ПРОХОЖИЙ

Позвольте вас спросить, могу ли я пройти здесь прямо на стацию.

ГАЕВ

Можете. Идите по этой дороге.

ПРОХОЖИЙ

Чувствительно вам благодарен. (*Кашлянув.*) Погода превосходная . . .(*Декламирует.*) Брат мой, страдающий брат* . . .Выдь на Волгу, чей стон . . . (*Варе.*) Мадемуазель, позвольте голодному россиянину копеек тридцать . . .

Варя испугалась, вскрикивает.

ЛОПАХИН

(*сердито.*) Всякому безобразию есть свое приличие.

* Слова из стихотворения С,Я, Надсона " Друг мой, брат мой, усталый, страдающий брат".

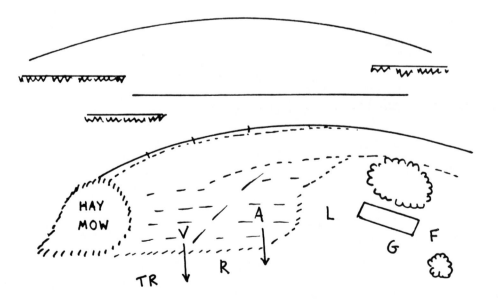

TRAMP

Allow me to inquire, may I take this short cut to the station?

GAYEV

You may. Just follow that road.

TRAMP

My heartfelt thanks. (*He coughs.*) The weather is beautiful. (*He declaims.*) 'My brother, my suffering brother . . . go to the Volga! Whose groans do you hear?' (*To* VARYA.) Mademoiselle, be so kind: a hungry Russian, thirty kopeks . . .

VARYA, rising with ANYA, utters a shriek of alarm. VARYA crosses.

LOPAKHIN

(*Angrily.*) If you must behave outrageously, at least . . .

VS: *On the tramp's lines, each character reacts differently. The sound and the tramp have both been symbols of fate.*

To the actor playing the tramp, I don't understand your attitude; you did not show me that you were for the first time among these people.

ЛЮБОВЬ АНДРЕЕВНА

(*оторопев*). Возьмите . . . вот вам . . . (*Ищет в портмоне.*) Серебра нет . . . Все равно, вот вам золотой . . .

ПРОХОЖИЙ

Чувствительно вам благодарен! (*Уходит.*)

Смех.

ВАРЯ

(*испуганная*). Я уйду . . . я уйду . . . Ах, мамочка, дома людям есть нечего, а вы ему отдали золотой.

ЛЮБОВЬ АНДРЕЕВНА

Что ж со мной, глупой, делать! Я тебе дома отдам все, что у меня есть. Ермолай Алексеич, дайте мне еще взаймы!..

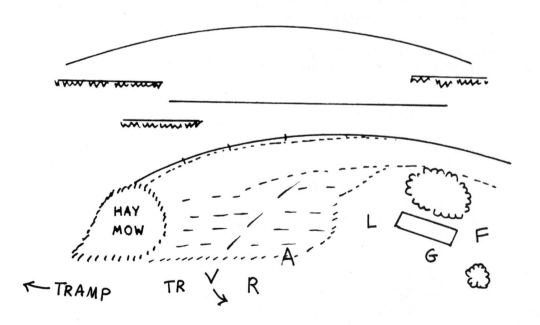

LYUBOV

(*Rising, as* TROFIMOV *comes to her.*) (*Hurriedly.*) Here, take this. (*Looks in her purse.*) There isn't any silver . . . never mind, here's gold.

TRAMP

My heartfelt thanks. (*He goes off. Laughter.*)

VARYA

(*Frightened.*) I'm going home — I'm going . . . Oh, Mamotchka, at home the servants have nothing to eat, and you gave him gold!

LYUBOV

What is to be done with such a fool like me? When we get home, I'll give you everything I have. Yermolay Alexeyevitch, you'll lend me some more, won't you? . . .

ЛОПАХИН

Слушаю.

ЛЮБОВЬ АНДРЕЕВНА

Пойдемте, господа, пора. А тут, Варя, мы тебя совсем просватали, поздравляю.

ВАРЯ

(*сквозь слезы*). Этим, мама, шутить нельзя.

ЛОПАХИН

Охмелия, иди в монастырь..*

ГАЕВ

А у меня   дрожат руки: давно не играл на бильярде.

* Искаженные слова Гамлета из одноименной трагедии Шекспира.

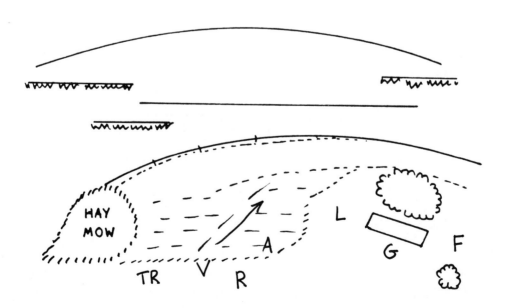

LOPAKHIN

Of course.

LYUBOV

Come gentlemen, ladies, it's time to be going. Oh! Varya, we've arranged a marriage for you. Congratulations!

VARYA

(*Through tears.*) Really, Mama, that's not a joking matter.

VARYA crosses down stage center; she looks stage right.

LOPAKHIN

'Ophelia, get thee to a nunnery . . .'

GAYEV

And do you know, my hands are trembling; it's because I haven't played billiards for so long.

The theatre can try very bold experiments; it can even work on a play which will never be produced. This is very important and, in the light of the Moscow Art Theatre, there were several occasions at rehearsals that this happened: a production would be brought almost to the end of rehearsals, and Stanislavski would not show it. But the work on these productions enriched the whole future of the theatre.

ЛОПАХИН

Охмелия, о, нимфа, помяни меня в твоих молитвах!*

ЛЮБОВЬ АНДРЕЕВНА

Идемте, господа. Скоро ужинать.

ВАРЯ

Напугал он меня. Сердце так и стучит.

ЛОПАХИН

Напоминаю вам, господа: двадцать второго августа будет продаваться вишневый сад. Думайте об этом! . . . Думайте! . . .

Уходят все, кроме Трофимова и Ани.

* Искаженные слова Гамлета.

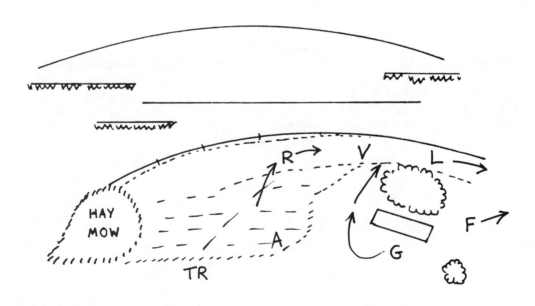

LOPAKHIN

'Ophelia, oh nymph, in your prayers, remember me!'

LYUBOV

Let's go, it's almost suppertime.

VARYA

He frightened me! My heart's pounding.

VARYA exits stage left without looking at LOPAKHIN.

LOPAKHIN

Let me remind you, ladies and gentlemen, on the twenty-second of August, the cherry orchard will be put up for sale. Think about that! Think about it!

They all go off except TROFIMOV and ANYA.

VS: *There was too much conscious styling.*

АНЯ

(*смеясь*). Спасибо прохожему, напугал Варю, теперь мы одни.

ТРОФИМОВ

Варя боится, а вдруг мы полюбим друг друга, и целые дни не отходит от нас. Она своей узкой головой не может понять, что мы выше любви. Обойти то мелкое и призрачное, что мешает быть свободным и счастливым, вот цель и смысл нашей жизни. Вперед! Мы идем неудержимо к яркой звезде, которая горит там вдали! Вперед! Не отставай, друзья!

АНЯ

(*всплескивая руками*). Как хорошо вы говорите! (*Пауза.*) Сегодня здесь дивно!

ТРОФИМОВ

Да, погода удивительная.

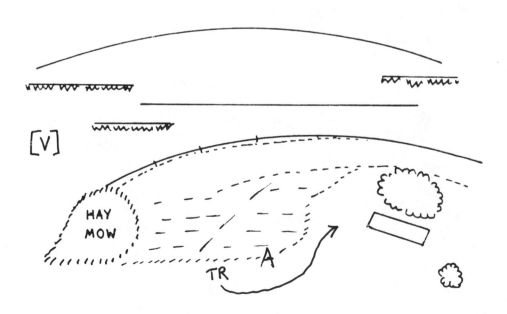

ANYA

(*Laughs.*) I'm grateful to that awful man . . . he frightened Varya and so we're alone.

TROFIMOV

Varya's afraid we shall fall in love with each other. She hasn't left us alone for days. She's so narrow-minded, she can't grasp that we're above love. To eliminate the petty and transitory, which prevents us from being free and happy — that is the end and meaning of our life. Forward! We go forward irresistibly, towards the bright star that shines in the distance. Forward! Do not fall behind, friends!

ANYA

(*Claps her hands.*) How well you speak! (*Pause.*) It's divine here today.

TROFIMOV

Yes, the weather's wonderful.

VS: *The actress must communicate to the audience the awakening of the character, her relationship with Trofimov.*

АНЯ

Что вы со мной сделали, Петя, отчего я уже не люблю вишневого сада, как прежде. Я любила его так нежно, мне казалось, на земле нет лучше места, как наш сад.

ТРОФИМОВ

Вся Россия наш сад. Земля велика и прекрасна, есть на ней много чудесных мест. (*Пауза.*) Подумайте, Аня: ваш дед, прадед и все ваши предки были крепостники, владевшие живыми душами, и неужели с каждой вишни в саду, с каждого листка, с каждого ствола не глядят на вас человеческие существа, неужели вы не слышите голосов . . . (Владеть живыми душами - ведь это переродило всех вас, живших раньше и теперь живущих, так, что ваша мать, вы, дядя уже не замечаете, что вы живете в долг, на чужой счет, на счет тех людей, которых вы не пускаете дальше передней . . .)* Мы отстали, по крайней мере, лет на двести, у нас нет еще ровно ничего, нет определенного отношения к прошлому, мы только философствуем, жалуемся на тоску или пьем водку. Ведь так ясно, чтобы начать жить в настоящем, надо сначала искупить наше прошлое, покончить с ним, а искупить его можно только страданием, только необычайным, непрерывным трудом. Поймите это, Аня.

* Слова в скобках из издательства 1903 года.

ANYA

What have you done to me, Petya? Why do I not love the cherry orchard as I used to? I loved it so tenderly. It seemed to me there was no spot on earth lovelier than our orchard.

TROFIMOV

All Russia is our orchard. Our land is vast and beautiful — there are many beautiful places in it. (*Pause.*) Think of it Anya, your grandfather, your great-grandfather and all your ancestors were owners of serfs — the owners of living souls. And from every cherry in the orchard, from every leaf, from every trunk there are human creatures looking at you. Don't you hear their voices? [To own live souls — that has changed all of you, both living before and living now so that your mother, you, your uncle already don't notice that you live on credit at somebody else's expense, at the expense of those people whom you don't let pass beyond your entrance hall.] *It's terrifying! Your orchard is a fearful thing, and when in the evening or at night one passes through the orchard, the old cherry trees gleam faintly through the dusk; they seem to be dreaming of centuries gone by, and haunted by ghastly visions. What can one say? We're at least two hundred years behind, we've really gained nothing yet — we have no definite relation to the past, we only philosophize, complain of our nostalgia, or drink vodka. It's all so clear — in order to live in the present, we should first expiate our past, finish with it — and we can expiate it only through suffering, only through extraordinary, unceasing laboring. Remember that, Anya.

*These lines were brought by Yuri Zavadski and added to the text. He said that they were among papers left by Chekhov for **Cherry Orchard**.

АНЯ

Дом, в котором мы живем, давно уже не наш дом, и я уйду, даю вам слово.

ТРОФИМОВ

Если у вас есть ключи от хозяйства, то бросьте их в колодец и уходите. Будьте свободны, как ветер.

АНЯ

(*в восторге*). Как хорошо вы сказали!

ТРОФИМОВ

Верьте мне, Аня, верьте! Мне еще нет тридцати, я молод, я еще студент, но я уже столько вынес! Как зима, так я голоден, болен, встревожен, беден, как нищий, и - куда только судьба не гоняла меня, где я только не был! И все же душа моя всегда, во всякую минуту и днем и ночью, была полна неизъяснимых предчувствий. Я предчувствую счастье, Аня, я уже вижу его..

АНЯ

(*задумчиво*). Восходит луна.

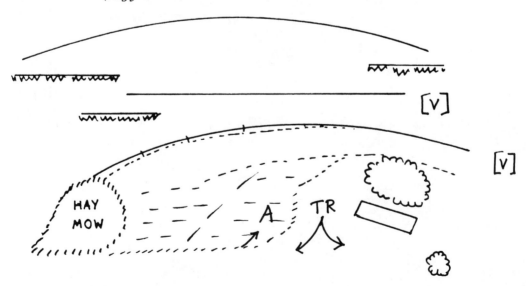

ANYA

The house in which we live has ceased to be our own, and I shall leave it, I give you my word.

TROFIMOV

If you have the keys, fling them into the well and go away. Be as free as the wind.

ANYA

How beautifully you said that!

TROFIMOV

Believe me, Anya, believe me! I'm not yet thirty, I'm young, I'm still a student — but I've known so much suffering already. In winter I'm hungry, sick, harassed, poor as a beggar, pursued and haunted by fate. And still my soul, always, every moment of the day and night, is filled with nebulous visions . . . . visions of happiness, Anya . . . . already I can see it!

ANYA

(*Pensively*.) The moon is rising.

Trofimov inspires Anya with revolutionary feelings. These people were such fine idealists, concerned with only the future, they thought not of themselves at all.

"The majority of [medical students] had in common with [Chekhov] not only the same professional studies, but also the same problems of existence — the everlasting search for odd jobs to pay their rent, to replace a threadbare coat, or to mend a pair of boots so they would not have to go to class wearing only leaky galoshes. . ." [Ernest J. Simmons, **Chekhov: A Biography**.]

Слышно, как Епиходов играет на гитаре все ту же грустную песню. Восходит луна. Где-то около тополей Варя ищет Аню и зовет : "Аня, Аня, где ты?"

ТРОФИМОВ

Да, восходит луна. (*Пауза.*) Вот оно счастье, вот оно идет, подходит все ближе и ближе, я уже слышу его шаги. И если мы не увидим, не узнаем его, то что за беда? Его увидят другие!

ГОЛОС ВАРИ

Аня, где ты?

ТРОФИМОВ

Опять эта Варя! (*Сердито.*) Возмутительно!

АНЯ

Что ж? Пойдемте к реке. Там хорошо.

ТРОФИМОВ

Пойдемте. (*Идут.*)

ГОЛОС ВАРИ

Аня! Аня!

Занавес

Offstage VARYA, looking for ANYA, calls 'Anya' as if far off. After TROFIMOV'S, 'what does it matter', VARYA repeats from offstage, 'yoo-hoo, yoo-hoo'; this is far off. YEPIKHODOV is heard playing the same sad song on the guitar. The moon is rising. Somewhere near the poplars, VARYA is looking for ANYA and calling, 'Anya, where are you?'

TROFIMOV

Yes, the moon's rising. (*Pause*.) Here is happiness, here it comes, it's coming nearer and nearer, and I can already hear it's footsteps. And if we never see it, if we may never know it, what does it matter? Others will see it after us!

VARYA'S VOICE

Anya! Where are you?

TROFIMOV

That Varya again! (*Angrily*.) It's revolting!

ANYA

Never mind, let's go down to the river. It's lovely there.

TROFIMOV

Yes, let's go. (*They go*.)

VARYA'S VOICE

Anya! Anya!

CURTAIN

Anya shares some of Trofimov's convictions; sometimes she gets ecstatic, as in the first act over the memory of going up in a balloon in Paris.

"... If a girl loves anyone, it means she has no morals ..." **Yasha** (Eric Tavares) speaks with **Dunyasha** (Elaine Winters) in Act Two of **Cherry Orchard**.

*"All Russia is our orchard. Our land is vast and beautiful . . . ," Roger Newman as **Trofimov** and Deborah Gordon as **Anya** in Act Two of **Cherry Orchard**.*

ДЕЙСТВИЕ ТРЕТЬЕ

Гостиная, отделенная аркой от залы. Горит люстра. Слышно, как в передней играет еврейский оркестр, тот самый, о котором упоминается во втором акте. Вечер.

В зале танцуют Grand Rond*. Голос Семеонова-Пильщика: *"Promenade a une paire!"*** " Выходят в гостиную: в первой паре Пищик и Шарлотта Ивановна, во второй - Трофимов и Любовь Андреевна, в третьей - Аня с почтовым чиновником, в четвертой - Варя с начальником станции и т.д. Варя тихо плачет и, танцуя, утирает слезы. В последней паре Дуняша. Идут по гостиной, Пищик кричит: *"Grand Rond et balancez!"*** *Les cavaliers a genoux et remercier vos dames! ****.*" Фирс во фраке приносит на подносе сельтерскую воду. Входят в гостиную Пищик и Трофимов.

* Большой круг - одна из фигур танца.
** Прогулка попарно - фигура танца.
*** Большой круг - фигура танца
**** Фигура танца.

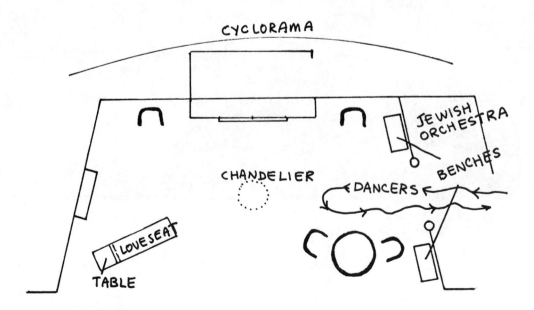

ACT III

A drawing room divided by an arch from the hall. A chandelier is burning. The Jewish orchestra of the second act is playing in the anteroom. It is evening.

In the ballroom, the party is dancing the *Grand Rond*. PISHCHIK calls *"Promenade à une paire."* Enter from the drawing-room in couples: PISHCHIK and CHARLOTTA, TROFIMOV and LYUBOV, ANYA and the POST OFFICE CLERK, VARYA and the STATION-MASTER. VARYA is quietly weeping and wiping away her tears as she dances. PISHCHIK shouts *"Grand Rond et balancez! Les cavaliers à genoux et remerciez vos dames!"* FIRS, in a swallow-tail coat, brings in soda-water on a tray. FIRS listens. As the family dances with their guests, they snake up and down stage left. They enter up stage left again. PISHCHIK and TROFIMOV re-enter.

YZ: At start of reading Act III, I am approaching the play freshly; I haven't thought about it alone in my own room and come to any conclusions. Rather, in reading the play with you, I'm getting ideas; I want you to share with me an appreciation and an awareness of the craft from the beginning. So, I've been thinking of how we should approach our work. We could glue a performance together.

YZ: This is a scene with comedy and comic characters. In Chekhov, you must not aim for surface laughter, but you must get the orchestration of the whole.

*VS: The actors playing the older characters in the present Moscow Arts Theatre production of **Three Sisters** and **Cherry Orchard** were actors who were of the generation of Stanislavski and Chekhov. For young characters, young actors have been introduced into the Chekhov plays.*

ПИЩИК

Я полнокровный, со мной уже два раза удар был, танцевать трудно, но, как говорится, попал в стаю, лай не лай, а хвостом виляй. Здоровье-то у меня лошадиное. Мой покойный родитель, шутник, царство небесное, насчет нашего происхождения говорил так, будто древний род наш Симеоновых-Пищиков происходит будто бы от той самой лошади, которую Калигула посадил в сенате . . . (*Садится.*) Но вот беда: денег нет! Голодная собака верует только в мясо . . . (*Храпит и тотчас же просыпается.*) Так и я . . . могу только про деньги . . .

ТРОФИМОВ

А у вас в фигуре в самом деле есть что-то лошадиное.

ПИЩИК

Что ж . . . лошадь хороший зверь . . . лошадь продать можно . . .

Слышно, как в соседней комнате играют на бильярде. В зале под аркой показывается Варя.

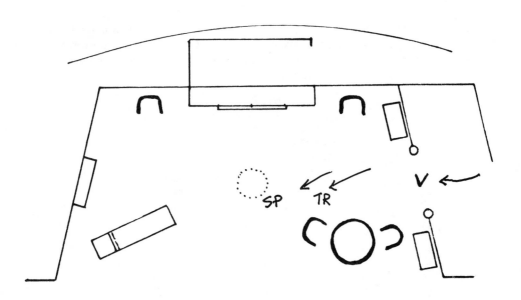

207

PISHCHIK

I am a full-blooded man; I've already had two strokes. Dancing's hard work for me; but as they say, "If you can't bark with the pack you can at least wag your tail." Still, I'm as strong as a horse. My late lamented father, who would have his joke, God rest his soul, used to say this about our origin: the ancient stock of Simeonov-Pishchik was derived from the very horse that Caligula made a member of the Senate. But the trouble is — I have no money. A hungry dog believes in nothing but meat; it's the same with me: I believe in nothing but money.

TROFIMOV

You know, in a funny way, you do remind one of a horse.

PISHCHIK

Well! A horse is a fine beast — one can sell a horse.

Sound of billiards being played in an adjoining room. VARYA appears in the archway.

ТРОФИМОВ

(*дразнит*). Мадам Лопахина! Мадам Лопахина!

ВАРЯ

(*сердито*). Облезлый барин!

ТРОФИМОВ

Да. Я облезлый барин и горжусь этим!

ВАРЯ

(*в горьком раздумье*). Вот наняли музыкантов, а чем платить? (*Уходит.*)

ТРОФИМОВ

(*Пищику*). Если бы эпергия, которую вы в течение всей вашей жизни затратили на поиски денег для уплаты процентов, пошла у вас на что-нибудь другое, то, вероятно, в конце концов, вы могли бы перевернуть землю.

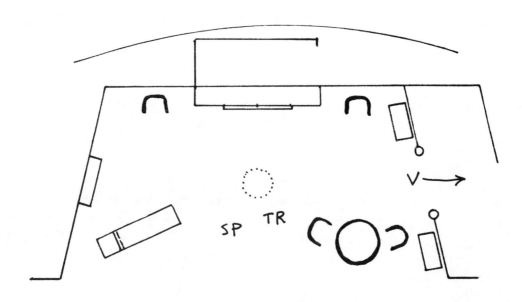

TROFIMOV

(*Teasing her.*) Madame Lopakhin! Madame Lopakhin!

VARYA

(*Angrily.*) Moth-eaten gentleman!

TROFIMOV

Yes, I am a moth-eaten gentleman and I'm proud of it.

VARYA

(*Bitterly.*) Here we've hired musicians! What are we going to pay them with? (*She goes out.*)

TROFIMOV

(*To* PISHCHIK.) You've wasted your whole life finding money to pay your interest — if all that energy had gone into something else, you might have set the world on fire.

YZ: *Varya does not react strongly to Trofimov's remarks; her thoughts are, 'here we've hired musicians.' This is her preoccupation. Therefore her reaction to Trofimov is, 'it's nothing to quarrel about.'*

ПИЩИК

Ницше . . . философ . . . величайший, знаменитейший . . . громадного ума человек, говорит в своих сочинениях, будто фальшивые бумажки делать можно.

ТРОФИМОВ

А вы читали Ницше?

ПИЩИК

Ну . . . Мне Дашенька говорила. А теперь я в таком положении, что хоть фальшивые бумажки делай . . . Послезавтра триста десять рублей платить . . . Сто тридцать уже достал . . . (*Ощупывает карманы, встревоженно.*) Деньги пропали! Потерял деньги! (*Сквозь слезы.*) Где деньги? (*Радостно.*) Вот они, за подкладкой . . . Даже в пот ударило . . .

Входят Любовь Андреевна и Шарлотта Ивановна.

ЛЮБОВЬ АНДРЕЕВНА

(*напевает лезгинку*). Отчего так долго нет Леонида? Что он делает в городе? (*Дуняше.*) Дуняша, предложите музыкантам чаю . . .

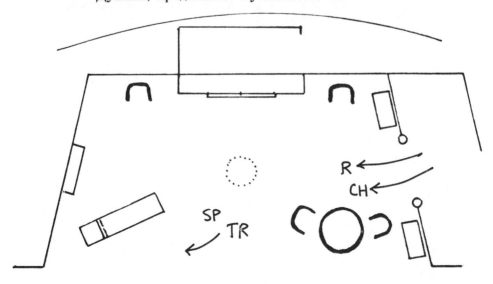

PISHCHIK

Nietzsche, a brilliant and illustrious philosopher —
a man of colossal intellect — says in his works that
it's no crime to commit forgery.

TROFIMOV

Have you read Nietzsche?

PISHCHIK

Nah! Well, Dashenka told me . . . and now I've got to
the point where forgery is about the only way out . .
. the day after tomorrow I have to pay 310 roubles —
I already have 130 . . . (*Sits in right chair. He feels in
his pockets. In alarm.*) The money's gone! (*Jumps up.
Through tears.*) Where's my money? (*Joyfully.*) Here
it is! Inside the lining. (*Laughs.*) I'm sweating all
over . . .

Sits in far left chair. Enter LYUBOV and CHARLOTTA.

LYUBOV

(*Hums the Lezginka*.*) Why is Leonid so long? What
can he be doing in town? Dunyasha, offer the
musicians some tea.

* A courtship dance from the Caucasus mountains.

ТРОФИМОВ

Торги не состоялись, по всей вероятности.

ЛЮБОВЬ АНДРЕЕВНА

И музыканты пришли некстати, и бал мы затеяли некстати . . . Ну, ничего . . . (*Садится и тихо напевает.*)

ШАРЛОТТА

(*Подает Пищику колоду карт*). Вот вам колода карт, задумайте какую-нибудь одну карту.

ПИЩИК

Задумал.

ШАРЛОТТА

Тасуйте теперь колоду. Очень хорошо. Дайте сюда, о мой милый господин Пищик. *Айн, цвай, драй!* Теперь поищите, она у вас в боковом кармане.

ПИЩИК

(*достает из бокового кармана карту*). Восьмерка пик, совершенно верно! (*Удивляясь.*) Вы подумайте!

TROFIMOV

The auction hasn't taken place, most likely.

LYUBOV

It's the wrong time to have the orchestra, and the wrong time to give a dance. Well, never mind. (*Sits down and hums softly.*)

CHARLOTTA

(*Gives* PISHCHIK *a pack of cards.*) Here is a pack of cards. Think of any card you like.

PISHCHIK

I've thought of one.

CHARLOTTA

Shuffle the pack now. That's right. Give it here, my dear Mr. Pishchik. *Ein, zwei, drei!* Now look — it's in your pocket.

PISHCHIK

(*Taking a card out of his pocket.*) The eight of spades! Perfectly right! (*Amazed.*) Just imagine!

ШАРЛОТТА

(*держит на ладони колоду карт, Трофимову*). Говорите скорее, какая карта сверху?

ТРОФИМОВ

Что ж? Ну, дама пик.

ШАРЛОТТА

Есть! (*Пищику.*) Ну? Какая карта сверху?

ПИЩИК

Туз червовый.

ШАРЛОТТА

Есть! (*Бьет по ладони, колода карт изчезает.*) А какая сегодня хорошая погода! (*Ей отвечает таинственный женский голос, точно из под-пола "О да, погода великолепная, сударыня".*) Вы такой хороший мой идеал . . . (*Голос: "Вы, сударыня, мне тоже очень понравился".*)

НАЧАЛЬНИК СТАНЦИИ

(*аплодирует*). Госпожа чревовещательница, браво!

SP

CH

TR

R

CHARLOTTA

(*Holding pack of cards in her hands. To* TROFIMOV.)
Tell me quickly, which is the top card?

TROFIMOV

Well, let's see — the queen of spades.

CHARLOTTA

It is. (*To* PISHCHIK.) Now which is the top card?

PISHCHIK

The ace of hearts.

CHARLOTTA

It is! (*She claps her hands and the pack of cards disappears.*) Ah, what lovely weather it is today! (*A mysterious feminine voice which seems to come out of the floor, answers her.*) "Oh, yes, it's magnificent weather, madame! You are my perfect ideal. And I greatly admire you too, madame."

THE STATION-MASTER

(*Applauding.*) Bravo! The lady ventriloquist!

VS: *There wasn't a good rhythm — there was too much activity. There should be activity and then a pause in order to think of what to do —* **then** *activity, in order to have a satisfying rhythm.*

ПИЩИК

(*удивляясь*). Вы подумайте! Очаровательнейшая Шарлотта Ивановна . . . я просто влюблен . . .

ШАРЛОТТА

Влюблен? (*Пожав плечами.*) Разве вы можете любить? Хороший человек, но плохой музыкант.

ТРОФИМОВ

(*хлопает Пищика по плечу*). Лошадь вы этакая . . .

ШАРЛОТТА

Прошу внимания, еще один фокус. (*берет со стула плед.*) Вот очень хороший плед, я желаю продавать . . . (*встряхивает.*) Не желает ли кто покупать?

ПИЩИК

(*удивляясь*). Вы подумайте!

ШАЛОТТА

Раз, два, три!

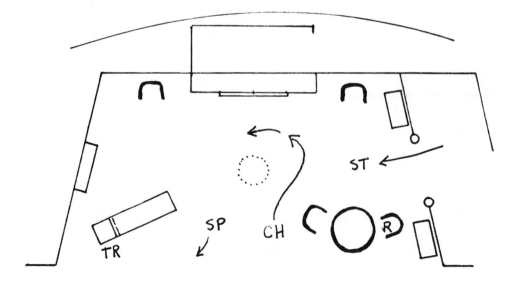

PISHCHIK

(*Amazed.*) Enchanting Charlotta Ivanovna, I'm simply in love with you.

CHARLOTTA

In love? (*Shrugs her shoulders.*) Are you capable of love? *Güter Mensch, aber schlechter Musikant!*

TROFIMOV

(*Slaps* PISHCHIK *on the shoulders.*) You old horse, you!

CHARLOTTA

I beg attention! One more trick! (*Takes a traveling rug from a chair.*) Here is a very good plaid; I want to sell it. (*Shaking it out.*) Does anyone want to buy it?

PISHCHIK

(*Amazed.*) Imagine that!

CHARLOTTA

Ein, zwei, drei!

VS: *I want you to be comfortable in the scene. Do not use heart gestures because it is not appropriate to your feelings. As director, I will not hesitate on occasion to demonstrate to you, if you're a young actor or actress, as to how the scene should be played.*

YZ: *Throughout this scene there is, despite surface gaiety, a mood of calamity. You will develop only by building relationships to one another. We have had a little help in the text to give us clues. The task lies ahead of us. This is just the prelude. We have not yet entered the world of Chekhov.*

Быстро поднимает опущенный плед; за пледом стоит Аня; она делает реверанс, бежит к матери, обнимает ее и убегает назад в залу при общем восторге.

ЛЮБОВЬ АНДРЕЕВНА

(*аплодирует*). Браво, браво! . . .

ШАРЛОТТА

Теперь еще! Раз, два, три. (*Поднимает плед; за пледом стоит Варя и кланяется.*)

ПИЩИК

(*удивляясь*). Вы подумайте!

ШАРЛОТТА

Конец! (*Бросает плед на Пищика, делает реверанс и убегает в залу.*)

ПИЩИК

(*спешит за ней*). Злодейка . . . какова? Какова? (*Уходит.*)

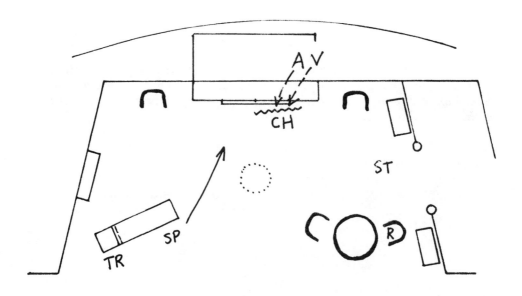

Behind the rug stands ANYA. She quickly raises the rug. She makes a curtsy, runs to her mother, embraces her, and runs back into the larger room, amidst general enthusiasm.

LYUBOV

(*Applauds.*) Bravo! Bravo!

CHARLOTTA

Now again! *Ein, zwei, drei!* (*Behind the rug stands* VARYA, *bowing.*)

PISHCHIK

(*Amazed.*) Imagine that!

CHARLOTTA

That's the end . . .

Throws the plaid at PISHCHIK, makes a curtsy, runs into the larger drawing-room.

PISHCHIK

Mischievous little creature! Imagine that!

PISHCHIK follows CHARLOTTA off stage left. ANYA appears at up left doorway.

ЛЮБОВЬ АНДРЕЕВНА

А Леонида все нет. Что он делает в городе так долго, не понимаю! Ведь все уже кончено там, имение продано или торги не состоялись, зачем же так долго держать в неведении!

ВАРЯ

(*стараясь ее утешить*). Дядечка купил, я в этом уверена.

ТРОФИМОВ

(*насмешливо*). Да.

ВАРЯ

Бабушка прислала ему доверенность, чтобы он купил на ее имя с переводом долга. то она для Ани. И я уверена, бог поможет, дядечка купит.

ЛЮБОВЬ АНДРЕЕВНА

Ярославская бабушка прислала пятнадцать тысяч, чтобы купить имение на ее имя, - нам она не верит, - а этих денег не хватило бы даже проценты заплатить. (*Закрывает лицо руками.*) Сегодня судьба моя решается, судьба . . .

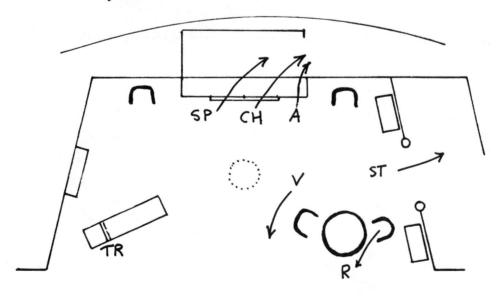

LYUBOV

And still Leonid doesn't come. What can he be doing in town so long? It must be over by now. Either the estate is sold, or the auction hasn't taken place. Why keep us so long in suspense?

VARYA

(*Trying to console her. She crosses up center near couch.*) Uncle's bought it, I feel sure of that.

TROFIMOV

(*Ironically.*) Oh, yes!

VARYA

Great aunt sent him an authorization to buy it in her name, and to transfer the debt. She's doing it for Anya's sake; I'm sure with God's help, dear uncle has bought it. (VARYA, *at back of couch, turns to* MME. RANYEVSKY.)

LYUBOV

My aunt in Yaroslavl sent fifteen thousand to buy the estate in her name, she doesn't trust us — but that's not even enough to pay off the interest. (*Hides her face in her hands.*) Today will decide my fate — my fate.

ТРОФИМОВ

(*дразнит Варю.*) Мадам Лопахина!

ВАРЯ

(*сердито*). Вечный студент! Уже два раза увольняли из университета.

ЛЮБОВЬ АНДРЕЕВНА

Что же ты сердишься, Варя? Он дразнит тебя Лопахиным, ну и что ж? Хочешь - выходи за Лопахина, он хороший, интересный человек. Не хочешь - не выходи; тебя, дуся, никто не неволит . . .

ВАРЯ

Я смотрю на это дело серьезно, мамочка, надо прямо говорить. Он хороший человек, мне нравится.

ЛЮБОВЬ АНДРЕЕВНА

И выходи. Что же ждать, не понимаю!

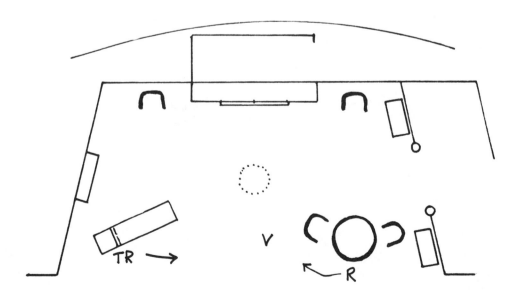

TROFIMOV

(*Teasing* VARYA.) Madame Lopakhin!

VARYA

(*Angrily*.) Eternal student! You've already been turned down twice by the university. (VARYA *turns her back*.)

LYUBOV

What are you so angry about Varya? He's teasing you about Lopakhin. Well, what of that? If you want to marry Lopakhin, do. He's a good man and interesting; if you don't want to, don't! Nobody's compelling you, my pet!

VARYA

Frankly, Mama, I take this thing seriously; he's a good man and I like him.

VARYA steps down to MME. RANYEVSKY.

LYUBOV

All right then, marry him! I can't see what you're waiting for.

ВАРЯ

Мамочка, не могу же я сама делать ему предложение. Вот уже два года все мне говорят про него, все говорят, а он или молчит, или шутит. Я понимаю. Он богатеет, занят делом, ему не до меня. Если бы были деньги, хоть немного, хоть бы сто рублей, бросила бы я все, ушла бы подальше. В монастырь бы ушла.

ТРОФИМОВ

Благолепие!

ВАРЯ

(*Трофимову*). Студенту надо быть умным! (*Мягким тоном, со слезами.*) Какой вы стали некрасивый, Петя, как постарели! (*Любови Андреевне, уже не плача.*) Только вот без дела не могу, мамочка. Мне каждую минуту надо что нибудь делать.

Входит Яша.

ЯША

(*едва удерживаясь от смеха*). Епиходов бильярдный кий сломал! (*Уходит.*)

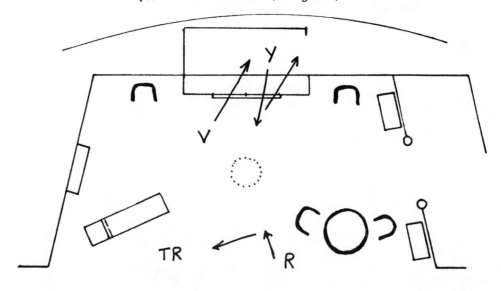

225

VARYA

But Mama, I can't propose to him myself! (VARYA *sits, stage left of* MME. RANYEVSKY.) For the last two years, everyone's been talking to me about him — talking! But he either keeps silent, or else makes a joke. I understand; he's growing rich, he's absorbed in business — he has no time for me. If I had money, were it ever so little, if I had only a hundred roubles, I'd throw everything up and go far away — I'd go into a nunnery.

TROFIMOV

How blessed that would be!

VARYA

(To TROFIMOV.)A student ought to have some sense. (*Softly, with tears.*) How ugly you've grown, Petya! How old you look! (*To* LYUBOV, *without tears.*) I can't live without work, Mamotchka; I must keep busy every minute.

Enter YASHA.

YASHA

(*Hardly restraining his laughter.*) Yepikhodov has broken a billiard cue! (*He goes out.*)

YZ: *Evoke an extreme of sensitivity and an awareness of life, the tragic essence of life.*

ВАРЯ

Зачем же Епиходов здесь? Кто ему позволил на бильярде играть? Не понимаю этих людей . . . (*Уходит.*)

ЛЮБОВЬ АНДРЕЕВНА

Не дразните ее, Петя, вы видите, она и без того в горе.

ТРОФИМОВ

Уж очень она усердная, не в свое дело суется. Все лето не давала покоя ни мне, ни Ане, боялась, как бы у нас романа не вышло. Какое ей дело? И к тому же я вида не подавал, я так далек от пошлости. Мы выше любви!

ЛЮБОВЬ АНДРЕЕВНА

А я вот, должно быть, ниже любви. (*В сильном беспокойстве*). Отчего нет Леонида? Только бы знать: продано имение или нет? Несчастье представляется мне до такой степени невероятным, что даже как-то не знаю, что думать, теряюсь . . . Я могу сейчас крикнуть . . . могу глупость сделать. Спасите меня, Петя. Говорите же что-нибудь, говорите . . .

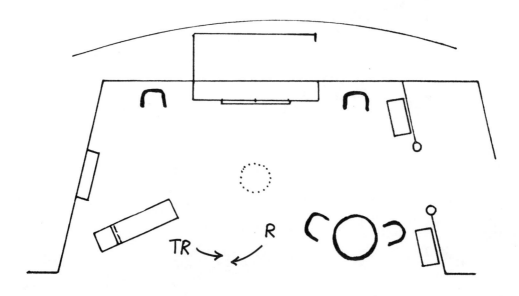

VARYA

Why is Yepikhodov here? Who gave permission to play billiards? I don't understand these people. (*She exits.*)

LYUBOV

Don't tease her, Petya. She's unhappy enough without that.

TROFIMOV

She's so officious — always meddling in other people's business. All summer long she's given Anya and me no peace. She's afraid of a love affair between us. What business is it of hers? Besides I've given no grounds for it — I'm not interested in such banalities. We're above love.

LYUBOV

And I suppose I'm beneath love? (*Very uneasily.*) What can be keeping Leonid? If I only knew whether the estate had been sold or not. This misfortune seems so unbelievable, that I don't even know what to think . . .I feel lost . . . I could scream . . . I could do something stupid . . . save me, Petya, tell me something, talk to me!

Throughout rehearsal, Victor Stanitsyn asked his actors to give a physical indication of change of feeling for characterization. "It's important," he reiterated.

VS: Be free and move about freely. What makes character is one's attitude towards life, one's environment, one's past, and the people one is with.

ТРОФИМОВ

Продано ли сегодня имение или не продано - не все ли равно? С ним давно уже покончено, нет поворота назад, заросла дорожка. Успокойтесь, дорогая. Не надо обманывать себя, надо хоть раз в жизни взглянуть правде прямо в глаза.

ЛЮБОВЬ АНДРЕЕВНА

Какой правде? Вы видите, где правда и где неправда, а я точно потеряла зрение, ничего не вижу. Вы смело решаете все важные вопросы, но скажите, голубчик, не потому ли это, что вы молоды, что вы не успели перестрадать ни одного вашего вопроса? Вы смело смотрите вперед, и не потому ли, что не видите и не ждете ничего страшного, так как жизнь еще скрыта от ваших молодых глаз? Вы смелее, честнее, глубже нас, но вдумайтесь, будьте великодушны хоть на кончике пальца, пощадите меня. Ведь я родилась здесь, здесь жили мои отец и мать, мой дед, я люблю этот дом, без вишневого сада я не понимаю своей жизни, и, если уж так нужно продавать, то продавайте и меня вместе с садом . . . (*Обнимает Трофимова, целует его в лоб.*) Ведь мой сын утонул здесь . . . (*Плачет.*) Пожалейте меня, хороший, добрый человек.

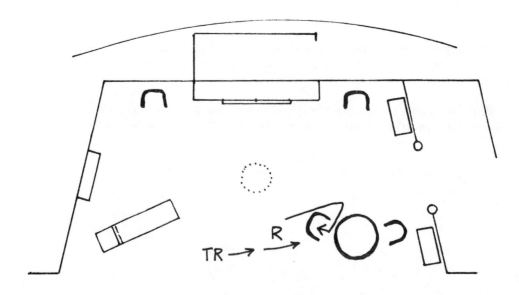

TROFIMOV

Whether the estate is sold today or not makes no
difference. That's all done with long ago — there's no
turning back, the path is overgrown. Calm yourself,
dear Lyubov Andreyevna. You musn't deceive yourself. For once in your life you must face the truth.

LYUBOV

What truth? You can still see the truth — but I seem
to have lost my sight — I see nothing. You settle every
great problem so boldly, but tell me, my dear, isn't
that because you're young? — Because you've never
really suffered? You look ahead fearlessly, but isn't
it that you don't see and don't expect anything dreadful, because life is still hidden from your young eyes?
It's true, you're bolder, more honest, more profound
than we are, but think — be just a little mag-
nanimous — try to have some compassion; after all,
I was born here, my father and mother lived here, my
grandfather lived here, I love this house. I can't
conceive of life without the cherry orchard, and if it
really must be sold, then sell me with the orchard.
(*Embraces* TROFIMOV, *kisses him on the forehead.*) My
son was drowned here. (*Weeps.*) Pity me, my dear,
dear fellow!

VS: *Think about **what** you are playing and not **how** you are playing it.
Reveal contrasting attitudes; meet the need for variety in the scene.*

YZ: *There must be inner monologue; no waiting for cues, for then there is
no life, only reading with gestures. Find this truth in your own mind and
heart. That is a double movement to make the role more and more understandable. This is the most important thing — that I wish to change you
inside. That begins with your feelings, your thoughts.*

ТРОФИМОВ

Вы знаете, я сочувствую всей душой.

ЛЮБОВЬ АНДРЕЕВНА

Но надо иначе, иначе это сказать . . . (*Вынимает платок, на пол падает телеграмма.*) У меня сегодня тяжело на душе, вы не можете себе представить. Здесь мне шумно, дрожит душа от каждого звука, я вся дрожу, а уйти к себе не могу, мне одной в тишине страшно. Не осуждайте меня, Петя . . . Я вас люблю, как родного. Я охотно бы отдала за вас Аню, клянусь вам, только, голубчик, надо же учиться, надо курс кончить. Вы ничего не делаете, только судьба бросает вас с места на место, так это страшно . . . Не правда ли? Да? И надо же что нибудь с бородой сделать, чтобы она росла как-нибудь . . . (*Смеется.*) Смешной вы!

ТРОФИМОВ

(*поднимает телеграмму*). Я не желаю быть красавцем.

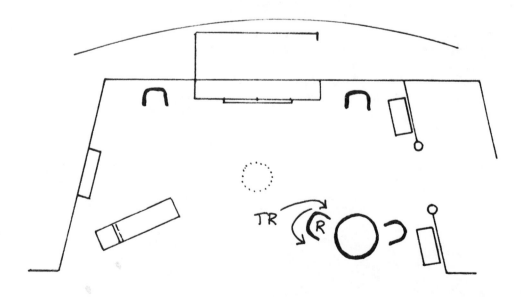

TROFIMOV

You know, I sympathize with all my heart.

LYUBOV

Yes! — But that should have been said differently —
so differently. (*Takes out her handkerchief — a
telegram falls to the floor.*) My heart is so heavy today
— I can't tell you — I'm shaken to my very soul — I
tremble at every sound. And yet I can't go away; I'm
afraid of quiet and solitude. Don't judge me harshly,
Petya . . . I love you as though you were one of us; I
would gladly let you marry Anya — I swear I would
— only, my dear boy, you must study — you must take
your degree — you do nothing — you let yourself be
tossed by fate from place to place — it's so strange. It
is, isn't it? And then, you should do something about
your beard — make it grow somehow! You look so
funny.

TROFIMOV

(*Picks up the telegram.*) I've no wish to be a beauty.

VS: *What do you **think** as the character? The scene must be played simply,
but do not make the mistake of thinking that it is a simple scene. It is a
complex and climatic scene, as are other scenes.*

*There is no need for a re-staging of the Chekhov plays. The present
production is still in an unbroken tradition of original business and interpretations.*

ЛЮБОВЬ АНДРЕЕВНА

Это из Парижа телеграмма. Каждый день получаю. И вчера, и сегодня. тот дикий человек опять заболел, опять с ним нехорошо . . . Он просит прощения, умоляет приехать, и по-настоящему мне следовало бы съездить в Париж, побыть возле него. У вас, Петя, строгое лицо, но что же делать, голубчик мой, что мне делать, он болен, он одинок, несчастлив, а кто там поглядит за ним, кто удержит его от ошибок, кто даст ему во время лекарство? И что тут скрывать или молчать, я люблю его, это ясно. Люблю, люблю . . . то камень на моей шее, я иду с ним на дно, но я люблю этот камень и жить без него не могу. (*Жмет Трофимову руку.*) Не думайте дурно, Петя, не говорите мне ничего, не говорите . . .

ТРОФИМОВ

(*сквозь слезы*). Простите за откровенность бога ради: ведь он обобрал вас!

ЛЮБОВЬ АНДРЕЕВНА

Нет. нет, нет, не надо говорить так . . . (*Закрывает уши.*)

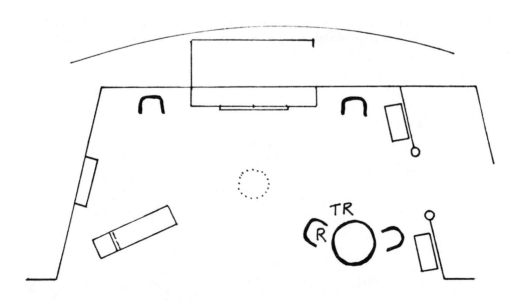

LYUBOV

That's a telegram from Paris. I get one every day.
Yesterday and today. That wild creature is ill again
— he's in trouble again. He begs forgiveness, entreats
me to go to him, and really I ought to go to Paris to
be near him. You looked shocked, Petya; but what is
there to do, my dear? What am I to do? He's ill, he's
alone and unhappy, and who is there to look after
him, who is to keep him from doing the wrong thing,
who is to give him his medicine on time. And why hide
it or be silent — I love him! Isn't that clear? I love
him — love him! He's a millstone round my neck —
he'll drag me to the bottom, but I love that stone — I
can't live without it. (*Presses* TROFIMOV's *hand.*) Don't
think badly of me, Petya — and don't say anything,
don't say . . .

TROFIMOV

(*Through his tears.*) For God's sake, forgive me my
frankness; but after all, he robbed you!

LYUBOV

No, no, no, you musn't say such things! (*Covers her
ears.*)

ТРОФИМОВ

Ведь он негодяй, только вы одна не знаете этого! Он мелкий негодяй, ничтожество . . .

ЛЮБОВЬ АНДРЕЕВНА

(*рассердившись, но сдержанно*). Вам двадцать шесть лет или двадцать семь, а вы еще гимназист второго класса!

ТРОФИМОВ

Пусть!

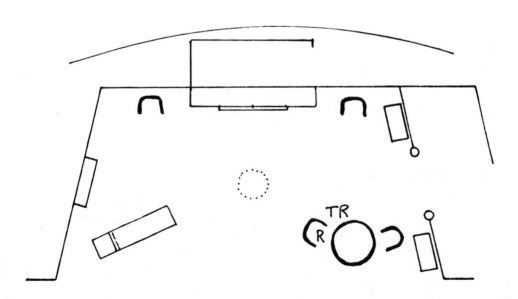

TROFIMOV

He's no good! You're the only one who doesn't know it. He's mean — worthless — beneath contempt.

LYUBOV

(*Angrily, but controlling herself.*) You are twenty-six or twenty-seven years old, but you're still a school-boy.

TROFIMOV

Possibly.

    At times Victor Stanitsyn's direction was as much concerned with technique as with the subjective inner life of the characters. This was one of the occasions when he got up and demonstrated. He warned the young actor not to imitate, but as director he wanted to show how he felt, how he should translate the change of feeling into physical action.

ЛЮБОВЬ АНДРЕЕВНА

Надо быть мужчиной, в ваши годы надо понимать тех, кто любит. И надо самому любить . . . надо влюбляться! (*Сердито.*) Да, да! И у вас нет чистоты, а вы просто чистюлька, смешной чудак, урод . . .

ТРОФИМОВ

(*в ужасе*). Что она говорит!

ЛЮБОВЬ АНДРЕЕВНА

"Я выше любви!" Вы не выше любви, а просто, как вот говорит наш Фирс, вы недотепа. В ваши годы не иметь любовницы! . . .

ТРОФИМОВ

(*в ужасе*). Это ужасно! Что она говорит?! (*Идет быстро в зал, схватив себя за голову.*) Это ужасно . . . Не могу, я уйду . . . (*Уходит, но тотчас же возвращается.*) Между нами все кончено! (*Уходит в переднюю.*)

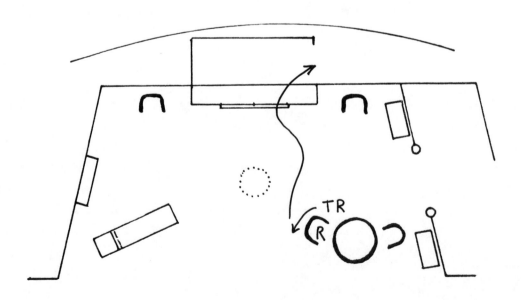

237

LYUBOV

You should be a man at your age. You should understand what love means — and you ought to be in love yourself. You ought to fall in love! (*Angrily.*) Yes, yes! And it's not purity in you, you're simply a puritan, a comic fool, a freak!

TROFIMOV

(*Horrified.*) What is she saying?

LYUBOV

"I'm above love!" You are not above love. You're just a good-for-nothing, as our Firs says. At your age not to have a mistress!

TROFIMOV

This is awful! What is she saying! (*He goes rapidly into the larger drawing-room, clutching his head.*) It's awful — I can't stand it — I'm going! (*Exits but comes right back.*) All is over between us! (*He goes.*)

YZ: *Search for this line of uninterrupted existence: where you are coming from and where you are going. At this point you know more than you can absorb. Every thought must be heard. Chekhovian actors must have a strong sense of rhythm, whether contrasting or the same as the preceding scene. Actors are not to play for audiences. Here you may play for yourselves, it's a reading.*

ЛЮБОВЬ АНДРЕЕВНА

(*кричит вслед*). Петя, погодите! Смешной человек, я пошутила! Петя!

Слышно, как в передней кто-то быстро идет по лестнице и вдруг с грохотом падает вниз. Аня и Варя вскрикиают, но тотчас же слышится смех.

ЛЮБОВЬ АНДРЕЕВНА

Что там такое?

Вбегает Аня.

АНЯ

(*смеясь*). Петя с лестницы упал! (*Убегает.*)

ЛЮБОВЬ АНДРЕЕВНА

Какой чудак этот Петя..

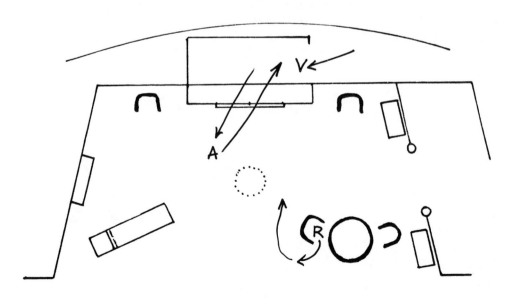

LYUBOV

(*Shouts after him.*) Petya! Wait a minute! You funny creature, I was joking, Petya!

There's a sound of somebody running quickly downstairs and suddenly falling with a crash. ANYA and VARYA scream. But there is a sound of laughter at once.

LYUBOV

What's the matter? What's happened?

ANYA runs in.

ANYA

(*Laughing.*) Petya's fallen downstairs! (*She runs out again.*)

LYUBOV

What a funny creature that Petya is!

Начальник станции останавливается среди залы и читает "Грешницу" А.Толстого. Его слушают, но едва он прочел несколько строк, как из передней доносятся звуки вальса, и чтение обрывается. Все танцуют. Проходят из передней Трофимов, Аня, Варя и Любовь Андреевна.

ЛЮБОВЬ АНДРЕЕВНА

Ну, Петя... ну, чистая душа . . . я прощения прошу . . . Пойдемте танцевать . . . (*Танцует с Петей.*)

Аня и Варя танцуют. Фирс входит, ставит свою палку около боковой двери. Яша тоже вошел из гостиной, смотрит на танцы.

ЯША

Что, дедушка?

ФИРС

Нездоровится. Прежде у нас на балах танцевали генералы, бароны, адмиралы, а теперь посылаем за почтовым чиновником и начальником станции, да и те не в охотку идут. Что-то ослабел я. Барин покойный, дедушка, всех сургучем пользовал, от всех болезней. Я сургуч принимаю каждый день уже лет двадцать, а то и больше; может, я от него и жив.

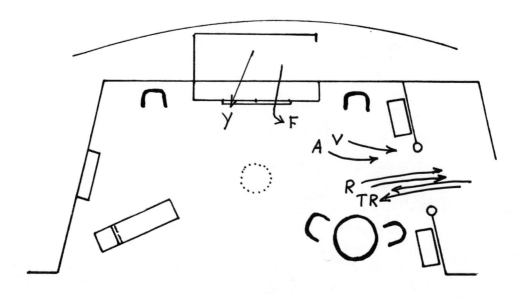

The STATION-MASTER stands in the middle of the ballroom and reads Alexei Tolstoy's **The Sinner**. They listen to him, but he has hardly read a few lines when the sounds of a waltz are heard from the next room. The reading is interrupted. They all dance. TROFIMOV, ANYA and VARYA and LYUBOV come in from the anteroom.

LYUBOV

Petya, Petya, you pure of heart! Please forgive me.
Have a dance. (*She dances with* PETYA.)

ANYA and VARYA dance. FIRS comes in, puts his stick down by the door. YASHA comes in.

YASHA

Well, Grandpa, what's the matter with you?

FIRS

I don't feel well. In the old days we had generals, barons and admirals dancing at our balls, and now we have to send for the post office clerk and the station-master, and even they are none too willing to come. Why do I feel so weak? The late master, the grandfather, used to give us all sealing-wax when we were ill. I've been taking sealing-wax every day for twenty years or more. Perhaps that's what's kept me alive.

VS: *That the attitudes of the individuals be revealed is important. Each actor in the scene reveals his relationships to the other characters.*

YZ: *Different characters have different attitudes towards food. Firs has a delicate stomach and doesn't eat much food; he eats the leftovers off the plates of the family.*

ЯША

Надоел ты, дед. (*Зевает.*) Хоть бы ты поскорее подох.

ФИРС

Эх, ты . . . недотепа! (*Бормочет.*)

Трофимов и Любовь Андреевна танцуют в зале, потом в гостинной.

ЛЮБОВЬ АНДРЕЕВНА

*Мерси.** Я посижу . . . (*Садится.*) Устала.

Входит Аня.

АНЯ

(*взволновано*). А сейчас на кухне какой-то человек говорил, что вишневый сад уже продан сегодня.

* Благодарю

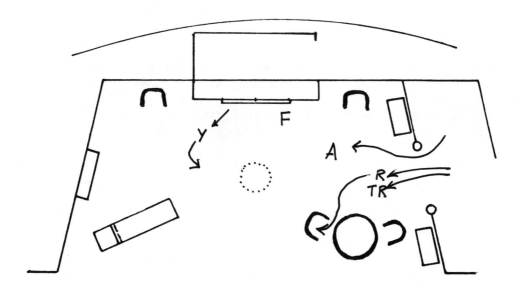

YASHA

(*Yawns.*) You bore me, gramps. It's time you kicked the bucket.

FIRS

Ech, you good-for-nothing. (*Mutters.*)

TROFIMOV and LYUBOV dance in from the Grand Hall to the drawing room.

LYUBOV

Merci. I'll sit down for a little while. I'm tired.

Enter ANYA excitedly.

ANYA

A man was saying in the kitchen just now that the cherry orchard had been sold.

ЛЮБОВЬ АНДРЕЕВНА

Кому продан?

АНЯ

Не сказал, кому. Ушел. (*Танцует с Трофимовым, оба уходят в залу.*)

ЯША

Это там какой-то старик болтал. Чужой.

ФИРС

А Леонида Андреича еще нет, не приехал. Пальто на нем легкое, демисезон, того гляди, простудится. Эх, молодо-зелено!

ЛЮБОВЬ АНДРЕЕВНА

Я сейчас умру. Подите, Яша, узнайте, кому продано.

ЯША

Да он давно ушел, старик-то. (*Смеется.*)

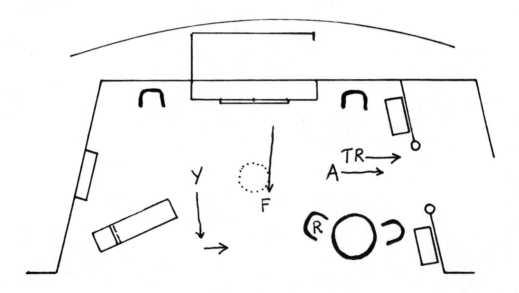

LYUBOV

Sold! To whom?

ANYA

He didn't say. He's gone away.(*She dances off with* TROFIMOV.)

YASHA

There was an old man gossiping there — a stranger.

FIRS

Leonid Andreyevitch isn't here yet, he hasn't come back. He has on his light overcoat; demi-saison; you'll see, he'll catch cold. Ech, foolish young things!

LYUBOV

I shall die — I shall die! Go, Yasha, find out to whom it has been sold.

YASHA

But the old man left long ago. (*He laughs.*)

Victor Stanitsyn was explosive, even sharp with his actors and he is their fellow actor! His actors took direction and only argued sometimes with him, there was at all times an atmosphere of good humor between director and actors. Victor Stanitsyn said to one of his actors: "I want to hear the words, all the words." In life we'll never find a man without thoughts; the only place one will find a human being without thoughts is onstage! That is a bad actor."

ЛЮБОВЬ АНДРЕЕВНА

(*с легкой досадой*). Ну, чему вы смеетесь? Чему рады?

ЯША

Очень уж Епиходов смешной. Пустой челеовек. Двадцать два несчастья.

ЛЮБОВЬ АНДРЕЕВНА

Фирс, если продадут имение, то куда ты пойдешь?

ФИРС

Куда прикажете, туда и пойду.

ЛЮБОВЬ АНДРЕЕВНА

Отчего у тебя лицо такое? Ты не здоров? Шел бы, знаешь, спать..

ФИРС

Да . . . (*С усмешкой.*) Я уйду спать, а без меня тут кто подаст, кто распорядится? Один на весь дом.

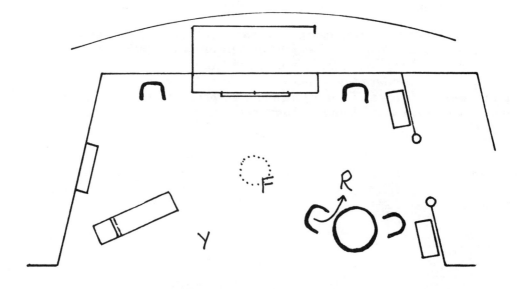

LYUBOV

(*Slightly vexed*.) What are you laughing at? What are you so pleased about?

YASHA

Yepikhodov is so funny. A silly fellow, Twenty-Two Misfortunes!

LYUBOV

Firs, if they sell the estate where will you go?

FIRS

Where you bid me, there I'll go.

LYUBOV

Why do you look like that? Are you ill? You ought to be in bed.

FIRS

(*Ironically*.) Yes! Me go to bed, and who's to serve you? Who's to supervise? I'm the only one in the whole house.

VS: *Lyubov, don't seem to react to the old man Firs, because one doesn't think while reacting.*

ЯША

(*Любови Андреевне*). Любовь Андреевна! Позвольте обратиться к вам с просьбой, будьте так добры! Если опять поедете в Париж, то возьмите меня с собой, сделайте милость. Здесь мне оставаться положительно невозможно. (*Оглядываясь, вполголоса.*) Что ж там говорить, вы сами видите, страна необразованная, народ безнравственный, притом скука, на кухне кормят безобразно, а тут еше Фирс этот ходит, бормочет разные неподходящие слова. Возьмите меня с собой, будьте так добры!

Входит Пищик.

ПИЩИК

Позвольте просить вас . . .на вальсишку, прекраснейшая . . . (*Любовь Андреевна идет с ним.*) Очаровательная , все-таки сто восемьдесят рубликов я возьму у вас . . . Возьму . . .(*Танцует.*) Сто восемьдесят рубликов . . . (*Перешли в залу.*)

ЯША

(*тихо напевает*). " Поймешь ли ты души моей волненье . . ."

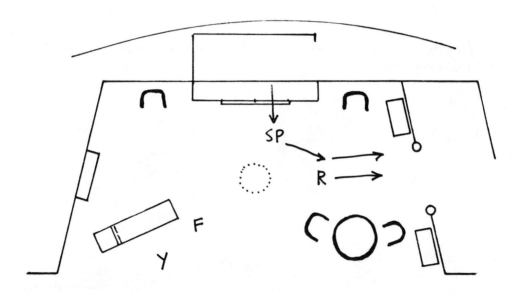

YASHA

(*To* LYUBOV.) Lyubov Andreyevna permit me to make a request of you. If you go back to Paris, take me with you, I implore you. It's positively impossible for me to stay here. (*He looks around and, under his breath, says in a whisper.*) Whatever they may say, you can see for yourself, it's an uncivilized country, the people have no morals, and then the boredom. The food in the kitchen's revolting, and Firs wanders about muttering all sorts of inappropriate remarks. Take me with you — please do!

PISHCHIK enters.

PISHCHIK

Allow me to ask you for a waltz, most beautiful lady. (LYUBOV *goes with him*.) Enchanting lady, you really must let me have 180 roubles. (*They dance.*) Only 180 roubles. (*They pass into the ballroom.*)

YASHA

(*Singing softly.*) "Do you know the trouble in my soul . . ."

В зале фигура в сером цилиндре и в клетчатых панталонах машет руками и прыгает; крики: " Браво, Шарлотта Ивановна!"

ДУНЯША

(*остановилась,   чтобы   попудриться*). Барышня велит мне танцевать - кавалеров много, а дам мало, - а у меня от танцев кружится голова, сердце бьется, Фирс Николаевич, а сейчас чиновник с почты такое мне сказал, что у меня дыханье захватило.

Музыка стихает.

ФИРС

Что же он тебе сказал?

ДУНЯША

Вы, говорит, как цветок.

ЯША

(*зевает*). Невежество . . .(*Уходит.*)

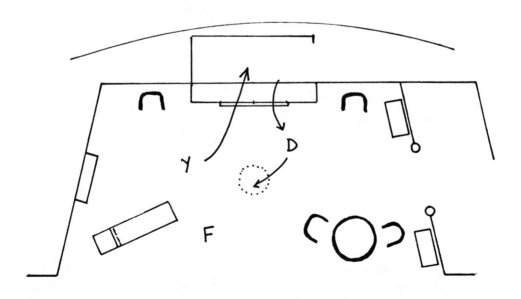

In the ballroom, a figure in a gray top hat and checkered pants waves her hands and leaps. There are cries of: "Bravo, Charlotta Ivanovna!" DUNYASHA enters.

DUNYASHA

(*She powders her face.*) My young mistress has ordered me to dance. There are too many gentlemen and not enough ladies, the dancing makes me dizzy, my heart begins to flutter. Firs, the post office clerk said something to me just now that quite took my breath away.

Music dies down.

FIRS

What did he say?

DUNYASHA

He said I was like a flower.

YASHA

(*Yawns.*) What ignorance. (*He goes out.*)

YZ: *The third act has now reached a pinnacle of festivity, a high point.*

ДУНЯША

Как цветок . . . Я такая деликатная девушка, ужасно люблю нежные слова

ФИРС

Закрутишься ты.

Входит Епиходов.

ЕПИХОДОВ

Вы, Авдотья Федоровна, не желаете меня видеть . . . как будто я какое насекомое. (*Вздыхае*т.) х, жизнь!

ДУНЯША

Что вам угодно?

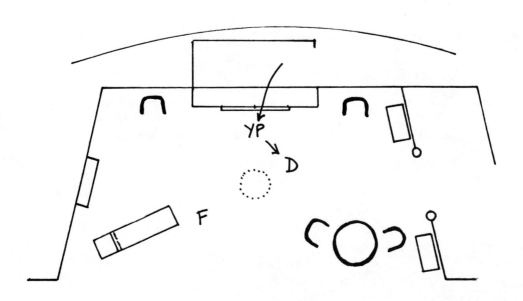

DUNYASHA

Like a flower. I'm such a delicate creature. I simply
adore romantic speeches.

FIRS

You'll get yourself in trouble.

Enter YEPIKHODOV.

YEPIKHODOV

You have no desire to see me, Dunyasha. I might be
some kind of insect. (*Sighs.*) Ah, life!

DUNYASHA

What do you wish?

*YZ: Dunyasha's thoughts at this point are: Everything is going my way.
I'm becoming more and more beautiful. Now, I'm even requested to dance.
I'm very popular. I'm keenly aware, since I'm in love, of my arms, face, hands.
Dunyasha is to concentrate on the act of her being in love. She is thinking,
while in love, of how much she is in love with Yasha.*

VS: Dunyasha, in this scene, has a fan.

ЕПИХОДОВ

Несомненно, может, вы и правы. (*Вздыхает.*) Но, конечно, если взглянуть с точки зрения, то вы, позволю себе так выразиться, извините за откровенность, совершенно привели меня в состояние духа. Я знаю свою фортуну, каждый день со мной случается какое-нибудь несчастье, и к этому я давно уже привык, так что с улыбкой гляжу на свою судьбу. Вы дали мне слово, и хоть я . . .

ДУНЯША

Прошу вас, после поговорим, а теперь оставьте меня в покое. Теперь я мечтаю. (*Играет веером.*)

ЕПИХОДОВ

У меня несчастье каждый день, и я, позволю себе так выразиться, только улыбаюсь, даже смеюсь.

Входит из залы Варя.

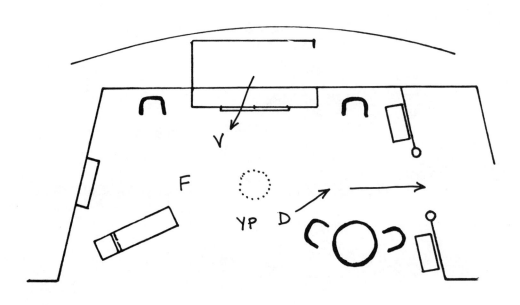

YEPIKHODOV

Undoubtedly you may be right. (*Sighs.*) But of course, if one looks at it from that point of view, you have, if I may allow myself so to express myself, forgive my frankness, completely reduced me to a state of mind. I know my fate. Every day I face some kind of misfortune, and I got used to it long ago, so that now I look at my destiny with a smile. You gave me your word and though I —

DUNYASHA

Let's have a talk later, I entreat you. But now leave me in peace; for I am lost in reverie. (*She plays with her fan.*)

YEPIKHODOV

I have a misfortune every day; and if I may allow myself so to express myself, I merely smile at it, I even laugh.

VARYA enters down left.

VS: *Actors, repeat this short scene without my interruption, then I'll make notes.*

One actor at the rehearsal quipped, "I don't think you'll have enough paper for all the notes you'll probably have to make!" All laughed, and that eased the tension.

ВАРЯ

Ты все еще не ушел, Семен? Какой же ты, право, неуважительный человек. (*Дуняше.*) Ступай отсюда, Дуняша. (*Епиходову.*) То на бильярде играешь и кий сломал, то по гостиной расхаживаешь, как гость.

ЕПИХОДОВ

С меня взыскивать, позвольте вам выразиться, вы не можете.

ВАРЯ

Я не взыскиваю с тебя, а говорю. Только и знаешь, что ходишь с места на место, а делом не занимаешься. Конторщика держим, а неизвестно - для чего.

ЕПИХОДОВ

(*обиженно*). Работаю ли я , хожу ли, кушаю ли, играю ли на бильярде, про то могут рассуждать только люди понимающие и старшие.

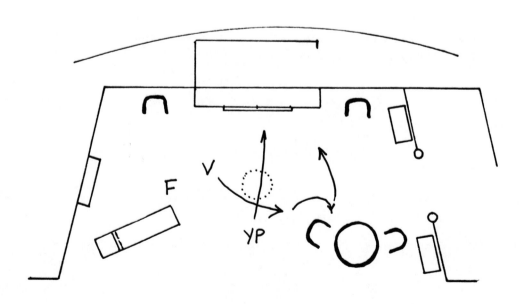

VARYA

Are you still here, Yepikhodov? (VARYA *crosses to the table to get the tray.*) What a disrespectful creature you are really! Go along, Dunyasha. (*To* YEPIK-HODOV.) Either you're playing billiards and breaking the cues, or you're wandering about the drawing room as though you were a guest. (VARYA *crosses right of* YEPIKHODOV.)

YEPIKHODOV

You really cannot, if I may allow myself so to express myself, plague me in this way . . .

VARYA

I'm not plaguing you; (VARYA *crosses back to the table.*) I'm just speaking to you. You merely wander from place to place and don't do your work. We keep you as bookkeeper, but heaven knows what for.

YEPIKHODOV

(*Offended.*) Whether I work or whether I walk, whether I eat or whether I play billiards, is a matter to be discussed only by persons of understanding and of mature judgement.

VS: *Throughout this exchange between Varya and Yepikhodov, Varya's goal is to get things on the table, stage right. When Varya notices Dunyasha, it prompts her line 'Go along Dunyasha'.*

ВАРЯ

Ты смеешь мне говорить это! (*Вспылив.*) Ты смеешь? Значит я ничего не понимаю? Убирайся же вон отсюда! Сию минуту!

ЕПИХОДОВ

(*струсив*). Прошу вас выражаться деликатным способом.

ВАРЯ

(*выйдя из себя*). Сию же минуту вон отсюда! Вон! (*Он идет к двери, она за ним.*) Двадцать два несчастья! Чтобы духу твоего здесь не было! Чтобы глаза мои тебя не видели!

Епиходов вышел; за дверью его голос: " Я на вас буду жаловаться"

ВАРЯ

А, ты назад идешь? (*Хватает палку, поставленную около двери Фирсом.*) Иди . . . Иди . . .Иди, я тебе покажу.. А, ты идешь? Идешь? Так вот же тебе . . . (*Замахивается, в это время входит Лопахин.*)

ЛОПАХИН

Покорнейше благадорю.

VARYA

You dare say that to me — you dare! You mean to say
I've no understanding? Get out of here at once, this
minute!

YEPIKHODOV

(*Intimidated.*) I beg you to express yourself with
delicacy.

VARYA

Out you go this minute! Get out! (YEPIKHODOV *goes
toward the door,* VARYA *following him.*) Twenty-Two
Misfortunes! Take yourself off — don't let me set eyes
on you again!

VARYA puts the tray down. YEPIKHODOV's voice from behind the door: 'I shall
lodge a complaint against you!'

VARYA

You're coming back, are you? (*She snatches up the
stick* FIRS *has put down near the door.*) Well, come on
then . . . come on . . . I'll show you . . . take that! (*She
swings the stick at the very moment that* LOPAKHIN
comes in.)

LOPAKHIN

Very much obliged to you.

ВАРЯ

(*сердито и насмешливо*). Виновата!

ЛОПАХИН

Ничего-с. Покорно благодарю за приятное угощение.

ВАРЯ

Не стоит благодарности. (*Отходит, потом оглядывается и спрашивает мягко.*) Я вас не ушибла?

ЛОПАХИН

Нет, ничего. Шишка, однако, вскочит огромадная.

ГОЛОС В ЗАЛЕ

Лопахин приехал! Ермолай Алексеич!

ПИЩИК

Видом видать, слыхом слыхать . . .(*Целуется с Лопахиным.*) Коньячком от тебя попахивает, милый мой, душа моя. А мы тут тоже веселимся.

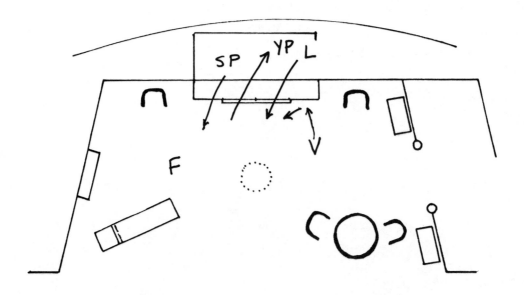

VARYA

(*Angrily and sarcastically.*) I beg your pardon. (VARYA *backs up.*)

LOPAKHIN

Not at all. I humbly thank you for your kind reception.

VARYA

Don't mention it. (*Softly.*) I didn't hurt you, did I? (VARYA *retreats to the door, sits by the door.*)

LOPAKHIN

Oh, no, not at all. There's an enormous bump coming up, though.

VOICE FROM INNER ROOM

Lopakhin has come, Lopakhin!

PISHCHIK

(*Comes in.*) What's this I see and hear? (*Kisses* LOPAKHIN.) There's a little whiff of cognac about you, my dear soul — and we've been celebrating here too.

Входит Любовь Андреевна.

ЛЮБОВЬ АНДРЕЕВНА

Это вы, Ермолай Алексеич? Отчего так долго? Где Леонид?

ЛОПАХИН

Леонид Алексеич со мной приехал, он идет . . .

ЛЮБОВЬ АНДРЕЕВНА

(*волнуясь*). Ну, что? Были торги? Говорите же!

ЛОПАХИН

(*сконфуженно, боясь обнаружить свою радость*). Торги кончились к четырем часам . . . Мы к поезду опоздали, пришлось ждать до половины десятого. (*Тяжело вздохнув.*) Уф! У меня немножко голова кружится . . .

Входит Гаев; в правой руке у него покупки, левой он утирает слезы.

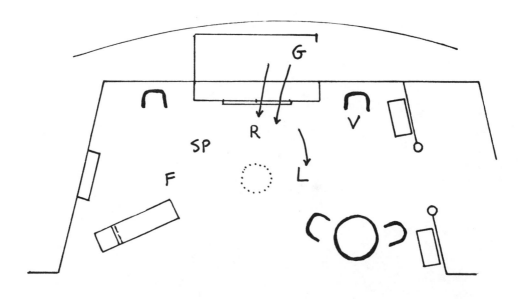

LYUBOV enters.

LYUBOV

Is that you, Yermolay Alexeyevitch? Why have you been so long? Where is Leonid?

LOPAKHIN

Leonid Andreyevitch came with me. He's coming.

LYUBOV

(*Anxiously.*) Well, but what . . .? Well . . . did the sale take place? Tell me, speak!

LOPAKHIN

(*Embarrassed, afraid to show his joy.*) The sale was over at four o'clock. We missed the train — had to wait till half-past nine. (*He sighs heavily.*) Ugh! I feel a little dizzy.

Enter GAYEV. In his right hand he has his purchases, with his left he's drying his tears.

YZ: *Lopakhin has a well organized day and usually has no time to eat. But he eats a big breakfast, and he eats fast.*

ЛЮБОВЬ АНДРЕЕВНА

Леня, что? Леня, ну? (*Нетерпеливо, со слезами.*) Скорей же, бога ради..

ГАЕВ

(*ничего ей не отвечает, только машет рукой; Фирсу, плача*). Вот возьми.. Тут анчоусы, керченские сельди . . . Я сегодня ничего не ел . . . Столько я выстрадал!

Дверь в бильярдную открыта; слышен стук шаров и голос Яши: " Семь и восемнадцать!" У Гаева меняется выражение, он уже не плачет.

ГАЕВ

Устал ужасно. Дашь мне, Фирс, переодеться. (*Уходит к себе через залу, за ним Фирс.*)

ПИЩИК

Что на торгах? Рассказывай же!

ЛЮБОВЬ АНДРЕЕВНА

Продан вишневый сад?

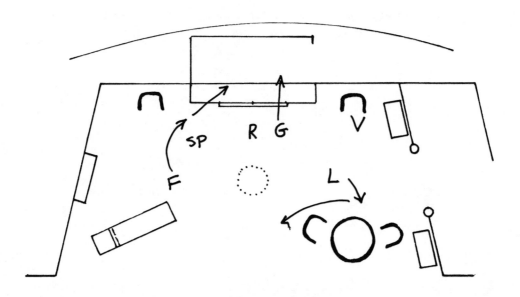

LYUBOV

(*Quickly, with tears.*) Well, dear Leonid, what news?
Quickly, for God's sake!

GAYEV

(*Doesn't answer — simply waves his hand. To* FIRS,
weeping.) Here, take these; anchovies, Kertch herrings . . . I've eaten nothing all day. What I've been
through.

The door to the billiard room is open. We hear the sound of billiard balls
and YASHA's voice calling, 'seven and eighteen!' GAYEV's expression changes.
He no longer is crying.

GAYEV

I'm terribly tired. Firs, help me change my clothes.
(*He exits,* FIRS *following him.*)

PISHCHIK

How about the sale?

LYUBOV

Is the cherry orchard sold?

YZ: *Kertch herrings are from the Black Sea. They are packaged, and they
are very good.*

*Gayev is contradictory. He is not too well physically. Sometimes food
doesn't please him, but at other times he likes certain Russian food. He also
likes flowers.*

ЛОПАХИН

Продан.

ЛЮБОВЬ АНДРЕЕВНА

Кто купил?

ЛОПАХИН

Я купил. (*Пауза.*)

Любовь Андреевна угнетена; она упала бы, если бы не стояла возле кресла и стола. Варя снимает с пояса ключи, бросает их на пол, посреди гостиной, и уходит.

ЛОПАХИН

Я купил! Погодите, господа, сделайте милость, у меня в голове помутилось, говорить не могу . . . (*Смеется.*) Пришли мы на торги, там уже Дериганов. У Леонида Андреича было только пятнадцать тысяч, а Дериганов сверх долга сразу надавал тридцать. Вижу, дело такое, я схватился с ним, надавал сорок. Он сорок пять. Я пятьдесят пять. Он, значит, по пяти надбавляет, я по десяти . . . Ну, кончилось. Сверх долга я надавал девяносто, осталось за мной. Вишневый сад теперь мой! Мой! (*Хохочет.*) Боже мой, господи, вишневый сад мой! Скажите мне, что я пьян, не в своем уме, что все это мне представляетя . . . (*Топочет ногами.*) Не смейтесь надо мной! Если бы отец мой и дед встали из гробов и посмотрели на все происшествие, как их Ермолай, битый, малограмотный Ермолай, который зимой босиком бегал, как тот самый Ермолай купил имение, прекрасней которого ничего нет на свете. Я купил имение, где дед и отец были рабами, где их не пускали даже в кухню.

LOPAKHIN

It is sold.

LYUBOV

Who bought it?

LOPAKHIN

I bought it. (*Pause.*)

MME. RANYEVSKY is absolutely shattered; she would fall if she were not standing near a chair. VARYA, taking the keys from her waist, crosses stage left of LOPAKHIN. She flings the keys to the floor in the middle of the drawing-room and exits down stage left.

LOPAKHIN

I have bought it. Wait a bit, ladies and gentlemen pray, my head's not quite clear — I can't talk. (*Laughs.*)We got to the auction and there was Deriganov. Leonid Andreyevitch had only 15,000 and Deriganov straight off bid 30,000 over and above the interest. I saw what the situation was; I bid against him — bid 40,000. He bid 45,000. I bid 55. And it went on, he's adding five thousands and I adding ten. Well . . . so it ended. I bid ninety and it went to me. Now the cherry orchard's mine — mine! Lord, God, the cherry orchard's mine! Tell me that I'm drunk — out of my mind — that it's all a dream. Don't laugh at me! If my father and grandfather could rise from their graves and see all that has happened — how their Yermolay, ignorant, beaten Yermolay, who used to run about barefoot in winter, how that very Yermolay has bought the finest estate in the world — I have bought the estate where my father and grandfather were slaves, where they weren't even allowed to enter the kitchen.

ЛОПАХИН

Я сплю, это только мерещится мне, это только кажется.. то плод вашего воображения, покрытый мраком неизвестности . . . (*Поднимает ключи, ласково улыбаясь.*) Бросила ключи, хочет показать, что она уже не хозяйка здесь . . . (*Звенит ключами.*) Ну, да все равно. (*Слышно, как настраивается оркестр.*) й, музыканты, играйте, я желаю вас слушать! Приходите все смотреть, как Ермолай Лопахин хватит топором по вишневому саду, как упадут на землю деревья! Настроим мы дач, и наши внуки и правнуки увидят тут новую жизнь . . . Музыка, играй!

Играет музыка. Любовь Андреевна опустилась на стул и горько плачет.

ЛОПАХИН

(*с укором*). Отчего же, отчего вы меня не послушали? Бедная моя, хорошая, не вернешь теперь. (*Со слезами.*) О, скореее бы все это прошло, скорее бы, изменилась как-нибудь наша нескладная, несчастливая жизнь.

ПИЩИК

(*берет его под руку, вполголоса*), Она плачет. Пойдем в залу, пусть она одна . . . Пойдем . . . (*Берет его под руку и уводит в залу.*)

269

(LOPAKHIN)

I am asleep — I'm dreaming — I'm only imagining it. It's not really happening. It's the fruit of your imagination, shrouded in mystery. (*Picks up the keys and smiles tenderly.*) She threw away the keys — wants to show she's no longer the mistress here. Well, what of it? (*Musicians are heard tuning up.*) Hey, musicians! Play! I want to hear you! Come, all of you, and look how Yermolay Lopakhin will take the axe to the cherry orchard and fell the trees to the ground. We will build on it, and our grandsons and great-grandsons will see a new life springing up here. Music! Play up!

Music begins to play. LYUBOV has sunk into a chair and is weeping bitterly.

LOPAKHIN

(*Reproachfully.*) Why, why didn't you listen to me? My dear friend, my poor friend, you can't bring it back now. Oh if only this were over, then our miserable, disjointed lives might somehow soon be changed.)

PISHCHIK

(PISHCHIK *takes him by the arm. Softly.*) She's crying. Let's go into the other room. Let her be alone. Come.(*Starts to lead him out of the room.*)

YZ: *In the third act, Lopakhin is driven by forces; he is talking through the impetus of his forefathers. Of course, just reading it, you can't play that yet, but you* **can** *act it. You just have to dig deep.*

When Lopakhin picks up the keys that have been thrown down by Varya, this becomes a cue, one hears the orchestra in the ballroom tuning up. This is ironic at this moment.

VS: *It may take a long time to get into the character. You may experience the train of thought of the character as strange. Do not worry, with time and work, both the character and his thoughts come.*

ЛОПАХИН

Что ж такое? Музыка, играй отчетливо! Пускай все, как я желаю! (*С иронией.*) Идет новый помещик, владелец вишневого сада! (*Толкнув нечаянно столик, едва не опрокинул канделябры.*) За все могу заплатить! (*Уходит с Пищиком.*)

В зале и гостиной нет никого, кроме Любови Андреевны, которая сидит, сжалась вся и горько плачет. Тихо играет музыка. Быстро входят Аня и Трофимов. Аня подходит к матери и становится перед ней на колони. Трофимов остается у входа в залу.

АНЯ

Мама! . . . Мама, ты плачешь? Милая, добрая, хорошая моя мама, моя прекрасная, я люблю тебя . . . я благославляю тебя. Вишневый сад продан, его уже нет, это правда, правда, но не плачь, мама, у тебя осталась жизнь впереди, осталась твоя хорошая, чистая душа . . . Пойдем со мной, пойдем, милая, отсюда, пойдем! Мы насадим новый сад, роскошнее этого, ты увидишь его, поймешь, и радость, тихая, глубокая радость опустится на твою душу, как солнце в вечерний час, и ты улыбнешься, мама! Пойдем, милая! Пойдем!

Занавес

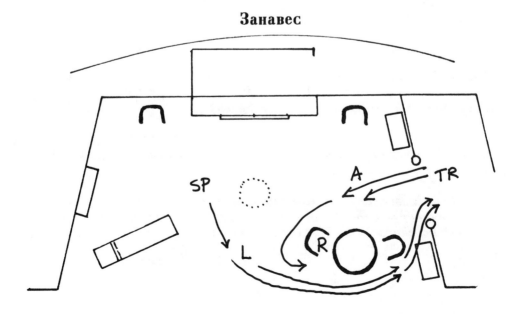

271

LOPAKHIN

What's that? Musicians, play up! All must be as I wish it. Here comes the new master, the owner of the cherry orchard. (*He accidentally tips over a little table, almost upsetting the candelabra.*) I can pay for everything.

Goes out with PISHCHIK. No one is left in the ballroom and dining room except LYUBOV ANDREYEVNA; LYUBOV sits huddled up, weeping bitterly. Music plays softly. ANYA and TROFIMOV come in quickly. ANYA goes to her mother and falls on her knees before her. TROFIMOV stands in the doorway.

ANYA

Mama, Mama you're crying! Dear, kind, good Mama, my precious. I love you; I bless you. The cherry orchard is sold, it's gone, that's true, that's true. But don't cry Mama, life is still before you, you still have your good, pure heart. Let us go, let us go darling, away from here. We will plant a new orchard, even finer than this one. You will see it, you will understand; and joy, quiet, deep joy, will sink into your soul like the sun at evening, and you will smile, Mama. Come, darling, let us go.

CURTAIN

YZ: *In the third act, Lyubov's sorrow is so deep that her crying has no sound.*

ACT THREE: ADDENDUM

VS: *We've finished the reading of the third act. We hardly paused today at all. Today you are reading a little more freely. The question is what to do next. We will try to move on the stage, and if we are not successful, we will go back to working around the table, but without books.*

You don't have to know the lines, but you have to know each scene; e.g. the thought sequences. Because there's very little time, we won't read the other acts as we did the first. I would like you to go off on your own and devote more time than we spend here in rehearsal.

*Left to right: MXAT actress, Stepanova, director Victor Stanitsyn, and John D. Mitchell at a **Cherry Orchard** cast party at the author's home.*

Charlotta *performs her magic trick, revealing* **Anya**, *in Act Three of the Moscow Arts Theatre production of* **Cherry Orchard**.

In Moscow, with Russian actors who are much closer to Chekhov, I would take at least three months to rehearse this play. It is a very difficult play, and the more I listen to it, the more I understand what subtle and exact problems Chekhov presents. The actors have to start from within to develop the external image. The creative process is from within and through yourself.

YZ: With Chekhov, there is constant life and thought. I demand spontaneity without fear. My method of working is that I will gradually take certain things away from you and give you other things. You will get involved and be fascinated by the inner search for the character. The last idea of Stanislavski was the unity of the physical and the spiritual.

Left to right: **Trofimov** *(Roger Stuart Newman),* **Yasha** *(Eric Tavares),* **Yepikhodov** *(Peter Blaxill),* **Dunyasha** *(Elaine Winters),* **Lyubov** *(Muriel Higgins), and* **Gayev** *(Jack Eddleman) in Act Four of IASTA's Denver Festival production of* **Cherry Orchard**.

ACT FOUR

These are some of the things which Yuri Zavadski said to the actors prior to working on the fourth act of **Cherry Orchard:**

Chekhov is very musical and poetic; therefore every word is important. There is difficulty in the translation, since language in Russia is quite colloquial and yet is full of inner poetry.

In Chekhov, to aim at creating an orchestration of performances, the creative process has to be free from within and from yourself.

I shall give you an exercise before we rehearse fully Acts I and IV. This exercise is part of your work, and it gives the possibility of finding the right relationship to your character.

I give you three objects: a book, a flower, a handkerchief, or a pen. You enter a room, sit down in a chair. You write a letter. You re-read the letter. You think about it. You go to the window. You make a gesture, and you leave the room.

You must think about the character, the letter, why you, as the character, write it. Play the same exercise as different characters and with the logic of each character. You have to know what it is for that you enter the room. This is the character's objective. You have to recreate the environment. Thus you change both the inner and outer image in changing the character. Stanislavski spoke of living through the part. Nemirovich-Danchenko said, 'think it through'. In the inner monologue, thoughts are combined with feelings.

Past is everything surrounding all. The actor is not to think, 'this is how I am', but the audience must understand the character, not the actor, and not his subjectivity about himself as an actor.

ДЕЙСТВИЕ ЧЕТВЕРТОЕ

Декорация первого акта. Нет ни занавесей на окнах, ни картин, осталось немного мебели, которая сложена в один угол, точно для продажи. Чувствуется пустота. Около выходной двери и в глубине сцены сложены чемоданы, дорожные узлы и т. п. Налево дверь открыта, оттуда слышны голоса Вари и Ани. Лопахин стоит, ждет. Яша держит поднос со стаканчиками, налитыми шампанским. В передней Епиходов увязывает ящик. За сценой в глубине гул. Это пришли прощаться мужики. Голос Гаева: "Спасибо, братцы, спасибо вам".

ЯША

Простой народ прощаться пришел. Я такого мнения, Ермолай Алексеич: народ добрый, но мало понимает.

Гул стихает. Входят через переднюю Любовь Андреевна и Гаев; она не плачет, но бледна, лицо ее дрожит, она не может говорить.

ГАЕВ

Ты отдала им свой кошелек, Люба. Так нельзя! Так нельзя!

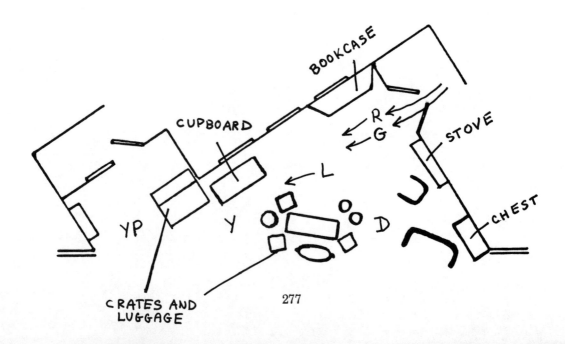

277

ACT IV

Setting is the same as Act I. No curtains or pictures — only a little furniture, piled up as if for sale. A sense of desolation. Packed trunks, traveling bags. A trunk is down stage left. With the door left open, one can hear the voices of VARYA and ANYA calling. LOPAKHIN standing waiting. YASHA holding a tray with glasses full of champagne. YEPIKHODOV tying up a box in the background; YASHA is helping YEPIKHODOV; behind the scene, a hum of talk from the peasants who have come to say good-bye. Voice offstage of GAYEV: "Thanks, brothers, thank-you."

YASHA

The peasants have come to say good-bye. In my opinion, Yermolay Alexeyevitch, the peasants are good, simple people, but they just don't know anything.

The hum of talk dies away. Enter LYUBOV and GAYEV; she is not crying, but is pale. Her face quivers. She is unable to speak.

GAYEV

You gave them your purse, Lyuba. That won't do — that won't do!

Stanislavski once said, 'You want to look for the good and the bad, and the bad and the good. Look for what is not obvious in the writing.'

Yasha is happy to go back to Paris. Dunyasha, down stage left at the opening of this act, remains onstage the whole time, packing mechanically. Yasha is leaving, but Dunyasha doesn't give up hope. 'He is my whole life', thinks Dunyasha.

ЛЮБОВЬ АНДРЕЕВНА

Я не смогла! Я не смогла! (*Оба уходят.*)

ЛОПАХИН

(*в дверь, им вслед*). Пожалуйте, покорнейше прошу! По стаканчику на прощанье. Из города не догадался привезть, а на станции нашел только одну бутылку. Пожалуйте! (*Пауза.*) Что ж, господа! Не желаете? (*Отходит от двери.*) Знал бы - не покупал. Ну, и я пить не стану. (*Яша осторожно ставит поднос на стул.*) Выпей, Яша, хоть ты.

ЯША

С отъезжащими! Счастливо оставаться! (*Пьет.*) Это шампанское не настоящее, могу вас уверить.

ЛОПАХИН

Восемь рублей бутылка. (*Пауза.*) Холодно здесь чертовски.

ЯША

Не топили сегодня, все равно уезжаем. (*Смеется.*)

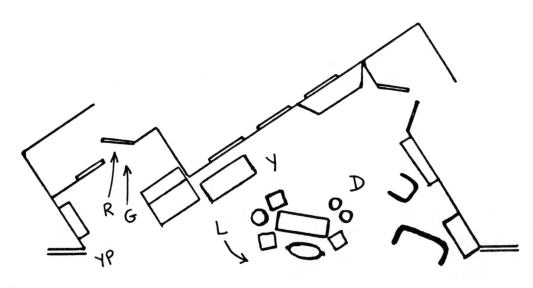

LYUBOV

I couldn't help it — I couldn't! (*Both go out.*)

LOPAKHIN

(*Calls after them.*) Please, I beg of you, a little glass at parting. I didn't think of bringing any from town and at the station I could only find this one bottle. Please — won't you? (*Pause.*) What's the matter? Don't you want any? If I'd known, I wouldn't have bought it. Well, then I won't drink any either. (YASHA *carefully sets the tray down.*) Here, Yasha, at least you have a glass.

YASHA

To the travelers — may they be happy! (*Drinks.*) This champagne isn't the real thing I can assure you.

LOPAKHIN

Eight roubles a bottle. (*A pause.*) It's devilishly cold here.

YASHA

They didn't start the fires today — it wasn't worth it, since we're leaving. (*Laughs.* LOPAKHIN *has crossed up stage; then crossed down stage right; now crosses stage left.*)

Lopakhin wants to relieve his guilt feelings; he offers champagne hoping they'll forgive and that Gayev and Lyubov will forget. Yasha puts down the tray when they refuse the champagne, and then immediately takes it up again.

On Yasha's speech 'to the travelers . . . (he drinks)', a pause is permitted to enable Yasha to fill his glass with more champagne.

Dunyasha's packing continues, as Yasha crosses the stage. She realizes that Yasha will be leaving in about twenty minutes.

ЛОПАХИН

Что ты?

ЯША

От удовольствия.

ЛОПАХИН

На дворе октябрь, а солнечно и тихо, как летом. Строиться хорошо. (*Поглядев на часы, в дверь.*) Господа, имейте в виду, до поезда осталось всего сорок шесть минут! Значит, через двадцать минут на стацию ехать. Поторапливайтесь.

Трофимов в пальто входит со двора.

ТРОФИМОВ

Мне кажется, ехать пора. Лошади поданы. Черт его знает, где мои калоши. Пропали. (*В дверь.*) Аня, нет моих калош! Не нашел!

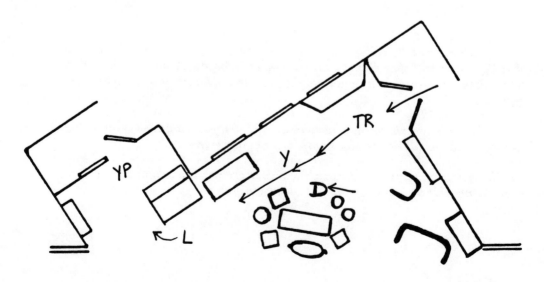

LOPAKHIN

What's the matter with you?

YASHA

I'm just pleased.

LOPAKHIN

It's October, yet it's still and sunny as though it were summer. Good weather for building. (*Looks at his watch. Says in through the doorway.*) Bear in mind, ladies and gentlemen, the train goes in forty-six minutes, so you ought to start for the station in twenty minutes. Better hurry up!

TROFIMOV comes in. Preoccupied, he crosses stage right. DUNYASHA is up stage left.

TROFIMOV

It must be time to start. The horses are ready. The devil only knows what's become of my galoshes; they're lost. (*In the doorway.*) Anya! My galoshes are gone — I can't find them!

I am only proposing to you that you actors get it bit by bit, and then in time all will fuse together, a new transmutation of quantity into quality.

One aspect of the challenge is timing. All the actors should have a greater awareness of time, that it begins slowly to settle in your soul as the character. It is a double process; good as it becomes your own, but it might become complicated. So, you have to find the uniqueness of the moment.

We must have concentrated rehearsals to begin to enter Chekhov's world. Costumes and make-up help.

Chekhov's greatness lies in his placing ordinary people in, for them, extraordinary moments.

ЛОПАХИН

А мне в Харьков надо. Поеду с вами в одном поезде. В Харькове проживу всю зиму. Я все болтался с вами, замучился без дела. Не могу без работы, не знаю, что вот делать с руками; болтаются как-то странно, точно чужие.

ТРОФИМОВ

Сейчас уедем, и вы опять приметесь за свой полезный труд.

ЛОПАХИН

Выпей-ка стаканчик.

ТРОФИМОВ

Не стану.

ЛОПАХИН

Значит, в Москву теперь?

ТРОФИМОВ

Да, провожу их в город, а завтра в Москву.

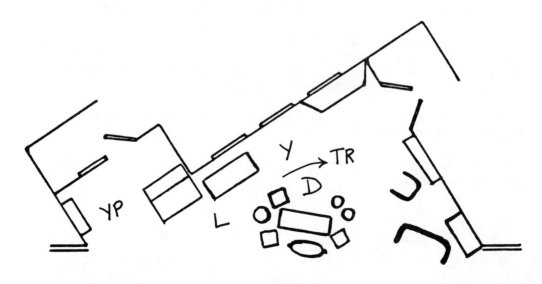

LOPAKHIN

I must to go to Kharkov. I'm going in the same train with you. I'll spend the winter in Kharkov. I've been loafing around here wasting my time with you — going mad with nothing to do. I can't live without work — I don't know what to do with my hands — they flap about as if they didn't belong to me.

TROFIMOV

Well, we'll soon be gone, then you can go on with your profitable labors again.

LOPAKHIN

Have a little glass.

TROFIMOV

No, I won't, thanks.

LOPAKHIN

So you're going to Moscow now? (YEPIKHODOV *is in the doorway.*)

TROFIMOV

Yes. I'll go with them as far as the town, and tomorrow I shall go on to Moscow.

Trofimov is repressing, with difficulty, his anger with Lopakhin.

If an actor says, 'this character is angry or good', and starts acting the way he imagines an angry or a good man would act, it brings him to conventional acting and this is theatrical untruth. That limits theatre art, impoverishes it and acting becomes the external apings of the pseudo-character and serves only to distort truth.

ЛОПАХИН

Да . . . Что ж, профессора не читают лекций, небось, все ждут, когда приедешь!

ТРОФИМОВ

Не твое дело.

ЛОПАХИН

Сколько лет, как ты в университете учишься?

ТРОФИМОВ

Придумай что-нибудь поновее. Это старо и плоско. (*Ищет калоши.*) Знаешь, мы, пожалуй, не увидимся больше, так вот позволь мне дать на прощанье один совет: не размахивай руками! Отвыкни от этой привычки - размахивать. И тоже вот строить дачи, рассчитывать, что из дачников со временем выйдут отдельные хозяева, рассчитывать так - это тоже значит размахивать . . . Как-никак, все-таки я тебя люблю. У тебя тонкие, нежные пальцы, как у артиста, у тебя тонкая, нежная душа . . .

ЛОПАХИН

(*обнимает его*). Прощай, голубчик. Спасибо за все. Ежели нужно, возьми у меня денег на дорогу.

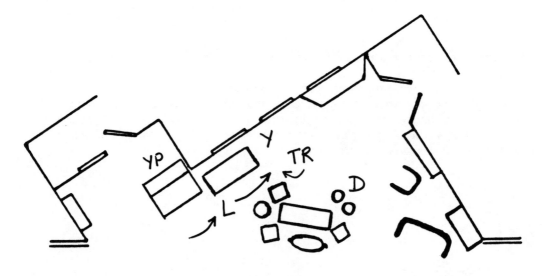

LOPAKHIN

I bet the professors aren't giving any lectures — they're waiting for your arrival. (LOPAKHIN *crosses to cupboard.*)

TROFIMOV

That's none of your business.

LOPAKHIN

Exactly how many years have you been at the university?

TROFIMOV

Can't you think of something newer than that? We shall probably never see each other again, so allow me to give you a piece of advice at parting; don't gesticulate so much with your hands — get out of the habit. And another thing: building dachas, figuring that summer residents will eventually become independent farmers, figuring like that is just another form of gesticulation . . . after all, I'm fond of you; you have fine delicate fingers, like an artist, you have a fine delicate soul.

LOPAKHIN

(*Embraces him.*) Good-bye, my dear fellow. Thank you for everything. Let me give you some money for the journey if you need it.

Every character is different as to his pace. As for gestures: does the character take in the air? Does the character push it away? Characters must know their gestures which come from their feelings in space. Talking goes on while walking, for example.

Lopakhin catches Trofimov by the sleeve; Lopakhin, 'let me give you a little money' is spoken softly, so Yasha will not hear. We must see Lopakhin take money out or make a gesture as if to do it. Lopakhin truly respects Trofimov. He wishes, in some way, to convey that feeling; generally to make amends.

ТРОФИМОВ

Для чего мне? Не нужно.

ЛОПАХИН

Ведь у вас нет!

ТРОФИМОВ

Есть. Благодарю вас. Я за перевод получил. Вот они тут, в кармане. (*Тревожно.*) А калош моих нет!

ВАРЯ

(*из другой комнаты*). Возьмите вашу гадость! (*Выбрасывает на сцену пару резиновых калош.*)

ТРОФИМОВ

Что же вы сердитесь, Варя? Гм . . . Да это не мои калоши!

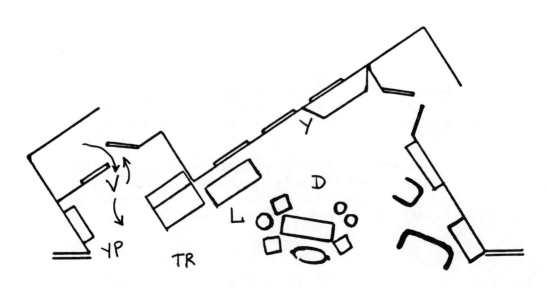

TROFIMOV

What for? I don't need it.

LOPAKHIN

But you haven't any.

TROFIMOV

Yes, I have, thank you. I got some money for a translation. Here it is in my pocket — but where can my galoshes be?

VARYA

(*From the next room.*) Here, take the disgusting things. (*Flings a pair of galoshes onto the stage from the down stage right door.*)

TROFIMOV

What are you so cross about, Varya? Anyway these are not my galoshes.

In the complexity and interweaving of human relationships in this play, Chekhov has said so very much about life. Now you don't have to find the final answer. It will come. In life the human being doesn't know what is going on with him. Only the actors know, all the time. And the truth is they oversimplify everything . . . When a play is well done, the audience becomes talented too. If you play in an oversimplified manner you kill off the work.

All depends upon how well you comprehend what I have been saying. You must think about it at home. I repeat: I dislike actors who say, 'please do anything with me'. I want actors who have their own creativeness, whom I can unite around a single comprehension of the play and the way of working. Vakhtangov used to say: 'I want you to play so that a deaf person would understand by watching, and a blind person by just hearing.'

Varya (off stage) experiences feelings of both sorrow and anger which prompts the manner in which she flings onstage Trofimov's galoshes. When she flings them on, you, Trofimov, see immediately they are not yours.

ЛОПАХИН

Я весной посеял маку тысячу десятин, и теперь заработал сорок тысяч чистого. А когда мой мак цвел, что это была за картина! Так вот я, говорю, заработал сорок тысяч и, значит, предлагаю тебе взаймы, потому что могу. Зачем же нос драть? Я мужик . . . попросту.

ТРОФИМОВ

Твой отец был мужик, мой - аптекарь, и из этого не следует решительно ничего. (*Лопахин вынимает бумажник.*) Оставь, оставь . . . Дай мне хоть двести тысяч, не возьму. Я свободный человек. И все, что так высоко и дорого цените вы все, богатые и нищие, не имеет надо мной ни малейшей власти, вот как пух, который носится по воздуху. Я могу обходиться без вас, я могу проходить мимо вас, я силен и горд. Человечество идет к высшей правде, к высшему счастью, какое только возможно на земле, и я в первых рядах!

ЛОПАХИН

Дойдешь?

ТРОФИМОВ

Дойду. (*Пауза.*) Дойду или укажу другим путь, как дойти.

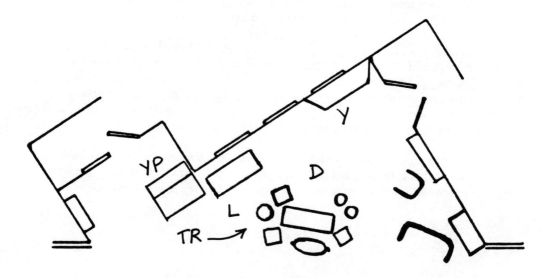

289

LOPAKHIN

I've sowed three thousand acres of poppies in the spring, and now I've cleared 40,000 profit; and when my poppies were in bloom — what a picture! So, as I say, I made 40,000; that means I'm offering you a loan because I can afford it. Why turn up your nose at it? I'm a peasant — I speak bluntly.

TROFIMOV

Your father was a peasant, mine was an apothecary — that proves absolutely nothing whatever. (LOPAKHIN *takes out his pocketbook.*) Stop it — stop that! If you were to offer me two hundred thousand I wouldn't take it — I'm a free man, and everything that all of you, rich and poor alike, prize so highly and hold so dear, hasn't the slightest power over me. It's like so much fluff, floating in the air. I can get on without you, I can pass by you, I'm strong and proud. Humanity is advancing toward the highest truth, the highest happiness which is possible on earth, and I am in the front ranks.

LOPAKHIN

Will you get there?

TROFIMOV

I shall get there. (*Pause.*) I shall get there, or I shall show others the way to get there.

Trofimov, no gestures on 'I'm a free man'. Trofimov's philosophy impresses Lopakhin. Trofimov is not tense or stiff as a free man. Trofimov had been exiled many times to Siberia. Chekhov tells us this in a letter. Trofimov speaks about things that can't be bought. He refuses money. Trofimov must start to look for his galoshes off stage in the same rhythm as onstage.

Lopakhin asks, 'will you get there?' It is important for Lopakhin to know and, he has faith in Trofimov.

Слышно, как вдали стучат топором по дереву.

ЛОПАХИН

Ну, прощай, голубчик. Пора ехать. Мы друг перед другом нос дерем, а жизнь знай себе проходит. Когда я работаю подолгу, без устали, тогда мысли полегче, и кажется, будто мне тоже известно, для чего я существую. А сколько, брат, в России людей, которые существуют неизвестно для чего. Ну, все равно, циркуляция дела не в этом. Леонид Андреич, говорят, принял место, будет в банке, шесть тысяч в год . . . Только ведь не усидит, ленив очень.

АНЯ

(*в дверях*). Мама вас просит: пока она не уехала, чтоб не рубили сада.

ТРОФИМОВ

В самом деле, неужели не хватает такта . . . (*Уходит через переднюю.*)

ЛОПАХИН

Сейчас, сейчас . . . Экие, право . . . (*Уходит за ним.*)

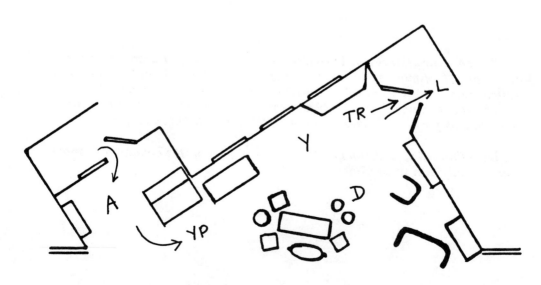

In the distance is heard the stroke of an axe on a tree.

LOPAKHIN

Well, good-bye, my dear fellow, it's time to be off. We may turn up our noses at one another, but life goes on all the while. When I'm working hard, without resting, my spirit grows lighter, and it seems to me that I too know why I exist. But how many people are there in Russia, my dear fellow, who exist, nobody knows what for? Well, it doesn't matter. That's not what makes the world go round. They say Leonid Andreyevitch has taken a position in the bank — 6,000 roubles a year. Only, of course, he won't stay with it — he's too lazy.

ANYA

(*In the doorway.*) Mama begs you not to start chopping down the orchard until she's gone.

TROFIMOV

How can people be so tactless! (*He goes out.*)

LOPAKHIN

I'll see to it — at once! Of all the . . . (*Goes out after him.*)

Chekhov demands full spiritual dedication, spiritual inner fullness. Avoid everything that throws you out of the line of action. For example, very obvious make-up could throw the other actors. A new element introduces an unfamiliar element in the partner's acting; e.g. beards, hairpieces, etc.

АНЯ

Фирса отправили в больницу?

ЯША

Я утром говорил. Отправили, надо думать.

АНЯ

(*Епиходову, который проходит через залу.*) Семен Пантелеич, справьтесь, пожалуйста, отвезли ли Фирса в больницу.

ЯША

(*обиженно*). Утром я говорил Егору. Что ж спрашивать по десяти раз!

ЕПИХОДОВ

Долголетний Фирс по моему окончательному мнению, в починку не годится, ему надо к праотцам. А я могу ему только завидовать. (*Положил чемодан на картонку со шляпой и раздавил.*) Ну, вот, конечно. Так и знал. (*Уходит.*)

ЯША

(*насмешливо*). Двадцать два несчастья . . .

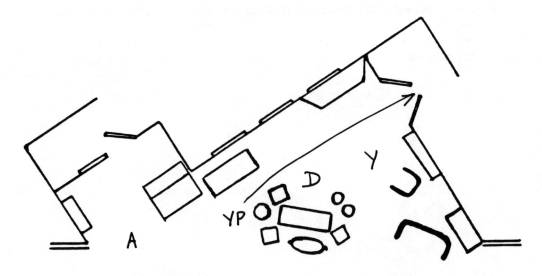

ANYA

Has Firs been taken to the hospital?

YASHA

I told them this morning. They must have taken him.

ANYA

(*To* YEPIKHODOV, *who passes across the room.*) Yepikhodov, please, find out if Firs has been taken to the hospital.

YASHA

(*Offended.*) I told Yegor this morning — why ask a dozen times?

YEPIKHODOV

The aged Firs, in my opinion, is beyond repair. It's time he was gathered to his forefathers — and I can only envy him. (*He puts a trunk down on a cardboard hatbox and crushes it.*) Now there — of course! I might have known it. (*He leaves.*)

YASHA

(*Sarcastically.*) Twenty-Two Misfortunes!

The mood changes radically at Anya's entrance. 'Mama begs you not to start chopping down the orchard until she is gone' prompts you, Lopakhin, to interrupt the nice conversation as you've been having with Trofimov about life. You realize that you are being thought of as senseless and stupid!

Throughout this scene, Dunyasha's thoughts are: 'Yasha is leaving now and I'll have no one', this is her reaction to Yasha's phrase 'I told Yegor this morning'.

Trofimov, the idea of the work is expressed in an oblique way. It is in the framework rather than striking you face on.

ВАРЯ

(*за дверью*). Фирса отвезли в больницу?

АНЯ

Отвезли.

ВАРЯ

Отчего же письмо не взяли к доктору?

АНЯ

Так надо послать вдогонку . . . (*Уходит.*)

ВАРЯ

(*из соседней комнаты*). Где Яша? Скажите, мать его пришла, хочет проститься с ним.

ЯША

(*машет рукой*). Выводят только из терпения.

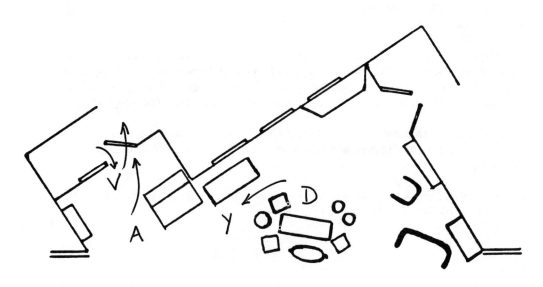

VARYA

(*Through the door.*) Has Firs been taken to the
hospital?

ANYA

Yes.

VARYA

Then why wasn't the note for the doctor taken too?

ANYA

Oh! Then we must send it after them. (ANYA goes out.)

VARYA

(*From the next room.*) Where's Yasha? Tell him his
mother's come and wants to say good-bye.

YASHA

(*Waves his hand.*) I'm losing my patience with her.

*Actors are to concentrate on the subtext for the action. In life, all the time
we do five or six things simultaneously, that is life. It is only on stage that
we do one thing, and then we show it. Concentrate on the continuous line of
experience. Forget **yourselves**. Live the circumstances in the situation. Live
in the environment. Live in the events. You have to believe in the great truth
of Chekhov's art.*

*Varya's line to Dunyasha about Firs being taken to the hospital is in the
nature of a warning to Dunyasha.*

*Act I was arrival; of the feeling of settling down forever. Now is coming
departure much sooner than the family expected. The actors have to imbue
the performance with this inner thought: now you have to live into this and
take away all the stops and pauses and commas where **unnecessary** so that
it should all be like music.*

Дуняша все время хлопочет около вещей; теперь, когда Яша остался один, она подошла к нему.

ДУНЯША

Хоть бы взглянули разочек, Яша. Вы уезжаете . . . меня покидаете . . . (*Плачет и бросается ему на шею.*)

ЯША

Что ж плакать? (*Пьет шампанское.*) Через шесть дней я опять в Париже. Завтра сядем в курьерский поезд и закатим, только нас и видели. Даже как-то не верится. Вив ла Франс! . . . Здесь не по мне, не могу жить . . . ничего не поделаешь. Насмотрелся на невежество - будет с меня. (*Пьет шампанское.*) Что ж плакать? Ведите себя прилично, тогда не будете плакать.

ДУНЯША

(*пудрится, глядясь в зеркальце*). Пришлите из Парижа письмо. Ведь я вас любила, Яша, так любила! Я нежное существо, Яша!

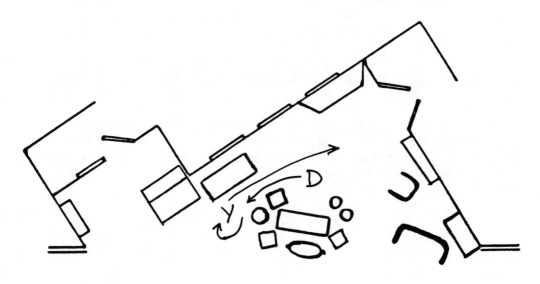

DUNYASHA has been busy with the luggage; she rises. Now that she has been left alone with YASHA, she goes up to him.

DUNYASHA

You might just give me a little look, Yasha. You're going away — you're deserting me — (*Weeps and throws herself on his neck.*)

YASHA

(*Disengages himself; crosses left.*) What's there to cry about? (*Drinks champagne.*) In six days I shall be in Paris again. Tomorrow we shall get into the express train and roll away — that's the last you'll see of us . . . I can scarcely believe it — *vive la France*! It doesn't suit me here — I just can't live here — that's all there is to it. I've had enough of the ignorance here — more than enough. (DUNYASHA *returns and kneels up stage of the luggage.* YASHA *drinks champagne.*) What's there to cry about? Behave yourself properly — then you won't cry.

DUNYASHA

(DUNYASHA *powders her face, looking in a pocket mirror.*) Do send me a letter from Paris. You know how I loved you, Yasha, how I loved you! I'm a tender creature, Yasha.

Since Dunyasha is distracted and emotionally upset, all that she is doing with the luggage is done mechanically.

Dunyasha had been waiting expectantly for Yasha. She knows now that Yasha won't marry her. Even though Dunyasha had hoped to become what Yasha wanted her to be, she had been hoping against hope that Yasha would still want her. Dunyasha, after you've powdered your nose to cover your tears over Yasha's cruelty, you become quieter.

All the things that Yasha are saying and doing give Dunyasha a feeling of rejection. On Yasha's line, 'behave yourself,' Yasha is thinking, 'yes it's my fault, but I did love you.'

ЯША

Идут сюда. (*Хлопочет около чемодана, тихо напевает.*)

Входят Любовь Андреевна, Гаев, Аня и Шарлотта Ивановна.

ГАЕВ

Ехать бы нам. Уже немного осталось. (*Глядя на Яшу.*) От кого это селедкой пахнет.

ЛЮБОВЬ АНДРЕЕВНА

Минут через десять давайте уже в экипажи садиться . . . (*Окидывает взглядом комнату.*) Прощай, милый дом, старый дедушка. Пройдет зима, настанет весна, а там тебя уже не будет, тебя сломают. Сколько видели эти стены! (*Целует горячо дочь.*) Сокровище мое, ты сияешь, твои глазки играют, как два алмаза. Ты довольна? Очень?

АНЯ

Очень! Начинается новая жизнь, мама!

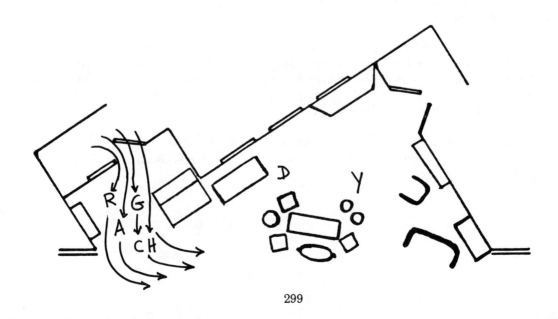

YASHA

Look out! They're coming! (*Busies himself about the trunks.*)

Enter LYUBOV, GAYEV, ANYA and CHARLOTTA.

GAYEV

We ought to be off. There's not much time now. (*He looks at* YASHA.) Who's been eating herring?

LYUBOV

In about ten minutes, we should be getting into the carriages. (*Looks about the room.*) Good-bye old home, dear old home of our fathers. Winter will pass, spring will come, you will no longer be here, they will have torn you down. How much these walls have seen! (*Kisses* ANYA.) My treasure, how radiant you look! Your eyes are sparkling like diamonds. Are you very, very glad?

ANYA

Very glad. A new life is beginning, Mama.

Dunyasha has come to realize she's not pretty. She fears she may have a child by Yasha. All her pride is now gone and she experiences great shame. Dunyasha's not to forget the feelings of shame of having been intimate with Yasha.

On Yasha's speech 'look out,' Yasha is thinking, 'I'm not cruel, and I didn't misbehave.'

ГАЕВ

(*весело*). В самом деле, теперь все хорошо. До продажи вишневого сада мы все волновались, страдали, а потом, когда вопрос был решен окончательно, бесповоротно, все успокоились, повеселели даже . . . Я банковский служака, теперь я финансист . . . желтого в середину, и ты, Люба, как-никак, выглядишь лучше, это несомненно.

ЛЮБОВЬ АНДРЕЕВНА

Да. Нервы мои лучше, это правда. (*Ей подают шляпу и пальто.*) Я сплю хорошо. Выносите мои вещи, Яша. Пора. (Ане.) Девочка моя, скоро мы увидимся . . . Я уезжаю в Париж, буду жить там на те деньги, которые прислала твоя ярославская бабушка на покупку имения - да здравствует бабушка - а денег этих хватит не надолго.

АНЯ

Ты, мама, вернешься скоро, скоро . . . не правда ли? Я подготовлюсь, выдержу экзамен в гимназии и потом буду работать, тебе помогать. Мы, мама, будем вместе читать разные книги . . . Не правда ли? (*Целует матери руки.*) Мы будем читать в осенние вечера, прочтем много книг, и перед нами откроется новый, чудесный мир . . . (*Мечтает.*) Мама, приезжай . . .

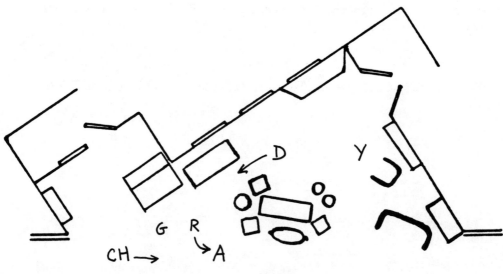

GAYEV

(*Gaily*.) Well, after all, everything is all right now. Before the cherry orchard was sold, we were all worried and wretched; but afterwards, when once the question was settled conclusively, irrevocably, we all calmed down, and even felt quite cheerful. I'm a bank clerk now — a financier — carom off the red! And you. Lyuba, in spite of everything, are looking better, there's no doubt of that.

LYUBOV

Yes, my nerves are better, that's true. (DUNYASHA *hands her her hat and coat*.) I'm sleeping well. Carry out my things, Yasha, it's time. (*To* ANYA.) My little girl, we shall soon see each other again. I'm going to Paris — I can live there on the money your Yaroslavl auntie sent us to buy the estate with — long live Auntie!

ANYA

You'll come back soon — soon, Mama, won't you? Meanwhile I'll study, I'll pass my examination at the high school, and then I'll go to work and be able to help you. We'll read all kinds of books together, Mama, won't we? We'll read in the autumn evenings, we'll read lots of books, and a new wonderful world will open before us. (*Dreamily*.) Mama, come back again.

Mme. Ranyevsky is parting for many years. Denying reality, she wants to think she'll come back to her precious treasures.

The actor wants to play feelings; however, the moment he tries to do so, the real feelings disappear. But, if he makes the thoughts and actions of the character his own, then he awakens the real feeling of the character.

A bad man once said, 'an actor is a man who speaks foreign words not in his own voice'. Our task is to make the audience believe the words are thought of as they are spoken. Chekhov demands this. Any theatricality would be wrong here. We will approach it very slowly. It doesn't mean the whole process is slow. Stanislavski said, 'in our work, to know is to be able to do'.

ЛЮБОВЬ АНДРЕЕВНА

Приеду, мое золото. (*Обнимает дочь.*)

Входит Лопахин. Шарлотта тихо напевает песенку.

ГАЕВ

Счастливая Шарлотта: поет!

ШАРЛОТТА

(*берет узел, похожий на свернутого ребенка*). Мой ребеночек, бай, бай . . . (*Слышится плач ребенка: уа, уа!*) Замолчи, мой хороший, мой милый мальчик. (*Уа! . . . Уа!) Мне тебя так жалко! (Бросает узел на место.*) Так вы, пожалуйста, найдите мне место. Я не могу так.

ЛОПАХИН

Найдем, Шарлотта Ивановна, не беспокойтесь.

ГАЕВ

Все нас бросают, Варя уходит . . . мы стали вдруг не нужны.

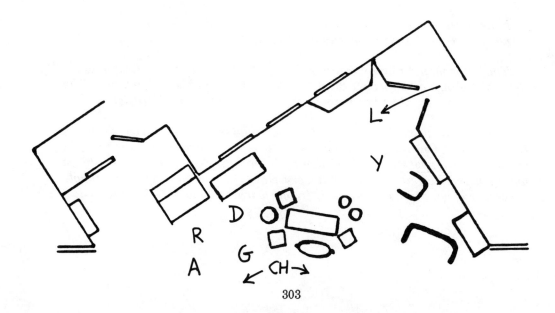

LYUBOV

I shall come back, my precious treasure. (*Embraces her.*)

Enter LOPAKHIN. CHARLOTTA softly hums a song.

GAYEV

Charlotta's happy. She's singing.

CHARLOTTA

(*Picks up a bundle like a swaddled baby.*) Bye-bye, my baby. (*A baby is heard crying 'Ooah! Ooah!'*) Hush, hush, my pretty boy! (*'Ooah! Ooah!'*) Poor little thing! (*Throws the bundle back.*) You must please find me a position — I can't go on like . . .

LOPAKHIN

We'll find you one, Charlotta Ivanovna, don't worry.

GAYEV

Everyone's leaving us. Varya's going away. We're of no use — all of a sudden.

Chekhov says the intelligent actor understands what is underneath, but the character doesn't. So you must understand what Charlotta is doing; why she is doing it. But you, Charlotta, will not know. The actress understands, but Charlotta does not. This playing, this act with the baby — when you say good-bye, this means good-bye to this life. You are, in a way, crying inside, but Charlotta does not know this.

We sometimes act out, from the unconscious, the situation we are in, without knowing what we are doing. And when Charlotta throws the baby — the bundle — she is throwing away what? Her pity, her compassion for herself? This is a very delicate line, very subtle — this double thing that you, the actress as Charlotta, are playing.

ШАРЛОТТА

В городе мне жить негде. Надо уходить . . .
(*Напевает.*) Все равно . . .

Входит Пищик.

ЛОПАХИН

Чудо природы! . . .

ПИЩИК

(*запыхавшись*). Ой, дайте отдышаться . . .
замучился . . . Мои почтеннейшие . . . Воды
дайте . . .

ГАЕВ

За деньгами, небось? Слуга покорный, ухожу от
греха . . . (*Уходит.*)

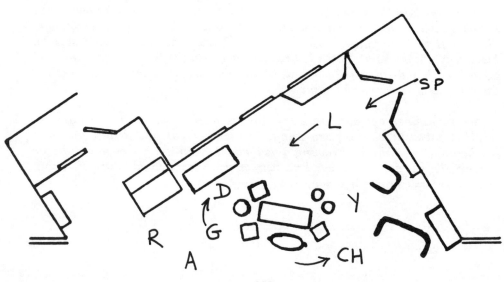

CHARLOTTA

There's no place for me to live in town — I must go
away. (*Hums.*) 'What care I . . . . .'

Enter PISHCHIK.

LOPAKHIN

The freak of nature!

PISHCHIK

(*Gasping.*) Oh . . . let me get my breath . . . I am in
agony . . . my most honored . . . give me some
water . . .

GAYEV

Want some money, I suppose. Your humble servant .
. . I'll go out of the way of temptation. (*Goes out.*)

*Before Pishchik enters, Charlotta, give more energy to the last line 'there's
no place for me to live in town. I must go away. What care I . . . '*

*Balance talent with intellect. There must constantly be an actor's use of
the subtext as to traits of character, reaction of people, thoughts about life.*

*In youth, everyone thinks he is born forever. Thinking, 'everyone will die,
but I won't'. Each person thinks of himself as young, but when he meets
another, he forgets that that person was young, once. In* **Cherry Orchard,**
Firs was always old; Lyubov is ageless.

ПИЩИК

Давненько не был у вас . . . прекраснейшая . . . (*Лопахину*.) Ты здесь . . . рад тебя видеть . . . громаднейшего ума человек . . . возьми . . . получи . . . (*Подает Лопахину деньги*.) Четыреста рублей . . . за мной остается восемьсот сорок. . .

ЛОПАХИН

(*в недоумении пожимает плечами*). Точно во сне . . . Ты где же взял?

ПИЩИК

Постой . . . Жарко... Событие необычайнейшее. Приехали ко мне англичане и нашли в земле какую-то белую глину . . . (*Любови Андреевне*.) И вам четыреста . . . прекрасная, удивительная . . . (*Подает деньги*.) Остальные потом. (*Пьет воду*.) Сейчас один молодой человек рассказывал в вагоне, будто какой-то . . . великий философ советует прыгать с крыш . . . "Прыгай!" - говорит, и в этом вся задача. (*Удивленно*.) Вы подумайте! Воды! . . .

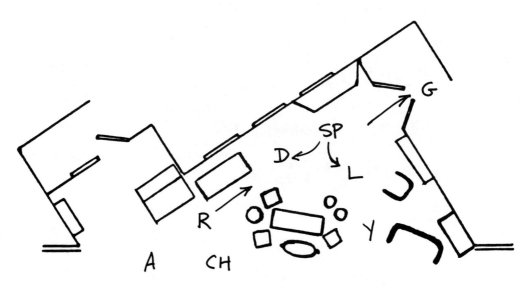

PISHCHIK

It's a long while since I've been to see you, lovely lady. (*To* LOPAKHIN.) You're here . . . glad to see you . . . a man of colossal intellect . . . here . . . take . . . (*Gives* LOPAKHIN *money.*) 400 roubles — that leaves me owing 840.

LOPAKHIN

(*In amazement.*) I must be dreaming — where did you get it?

PISHCHIK

Wait a bit. (*Drinks.*) I'm hot. (*Drinks.*) But most extraordinary occurrence. (*Gives the glass to* DUNYASHA *for more.*) Some Englishmen came along and found on my land some sort of white clay. (*To* LYUBOV.) And 400 for you . . . most lovely . . . most wonderful . . (*Takes a drink. Gives her the money.*) The rest later. (*Sips water.*) A young man on the train was telling me just now that a great philosopher recommends jumping off roof tops. 'Jump!' says he; 'the whole crux of the matter lies in that'. (*In astonishment.*)Just imagine! More water please.

Pishchik is feeling some guilt at what he has borrowed; his paying off debts gives him a feeling of relief. He even has some identification with Lopakhin.

Pishchik comes in a different mood; he wants to get rid of business details as soon as possible in order to tell them about the young man on the train who recommends jumping off the roof! He doesn't know whether to go or to stay; he doesn't feel he has said the right thing. He has an inner conflict.

Pishchik, too long a pause before, 'jump!'

Pishckik pours the second glass water differently from the first; that is, after he has paid his debt to Lyubov.

ЛОПАХИН

Какие же это англичане?

ПИЩИК

Сдал им участок с глиной на двадцать четыре года
. . . А теперь, извините, некогда . . . надо скакать
дальше . . . Поеду к Знойкову . . . к Кардомонову
. . . Всем должен . . . (*Пьет.*) Желаю здравствовать
. . . В четверг заеду . . .

ЛЮБОВЬ АНДРЕЕВНА

Мы сейчас переезжаем в город, а завтра я за
границу . . .

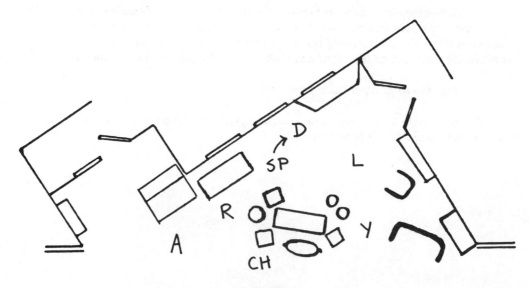

LOPAKHIN

What Englishmen?

PISHCHIK

I've given them the rights to dig the clay for twenty-four years . . . and now, forgive me, I can't stay . . . I must be dashing on . . . I'm going to Znoikovo . . . to Kardamanovo . . . I'm in debt all around. (*Drinks water.*) To your very good health . . . (*Drinks.*) I'll come back on Thursday. (*He hands the water back to* DUNYASHA.)

LYUBOV

We're just off to the town; and tomorrow I leave for abroad.

Art is a selection of means of expression. Chekhov makes precise, calculated choices. Fill it in with overall excitement.

ПИЩИК

Как? (*Встревоженно.*) Почему в город? То-то я гляжу на мебель . . . чемоданы . . . Ну, ничего . . . (*Сквозь слезы.*) Ничего . . . Величайшего ума люди . . . эти англичане . . . Ничего . . . Будьте счастливы . . . Бог поможет вам . . . Ничего . . . Всему на этом свете бывает конец . . . (*Целует руку Любови Андреевне.*) А дойдет до вас слух, что мне конец пришел, вспомните вот эту самую . . . лошадь и скажите: "Был на свете такой, сякой . . . Семеонов-Пищик . . . царство ему небесное "... Замечательнейшая погода . . . Да . . . (*Уходит в сильном смущении, но тотчас же возвращается и говорит в дверях.*) Кланялась вам Дашенька! (*Уходит.*)

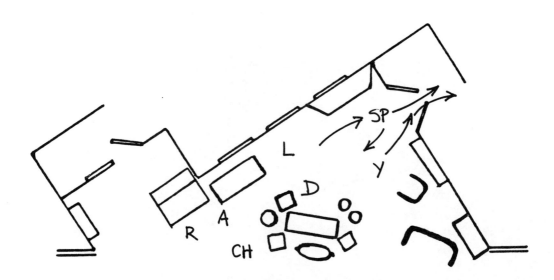

PISHCHIK

What? (*In agitation.*) Why to town? That's why . . . I see. The furniture . . . the suitcases . . . never mind! (*Through his tears.*) Never mind . . . men of colossal intellect, these Englishmen . . . never mind . . . be happy. God will help you . . . never mind . . . Everything in this world must have an end. (*Kisses* LYUBOV's *hand.*) If the rumor reaches you that my end has come, remember this old horse, and say: 'Once upon a time there lived in the world a man . . . Simeonov-Pishchik . . . God rest his soul . . . remarkable weather . . . yes . . . (*Goes out in violent agitation, but at once he returns and speaks from the doorway.*) My little daughter Dashenka sends her regards to you. (*He goes out.* YASHA *escorts him out.*)

Yasha escorts Pishchik from the room when he discovers that Pishchik is a wealthy man. Yasha's attitude toward people depends on their financial status, the opposite of Trofimov.

ЛЮБОВЬ АНДРЕЕВНА

Теперь можно и ехать. Уезжаю я с двумя заботами. Первая - это больной Фирс. (*Взглянув на часы.*) Еще минут пять можно.

АНЯ

Мама, Фирса уже отправили в больницу. Яша отправил утром.

ЛЮБОВЬ АНДРЕЕВНА

Вторая моя печаль - Варя. Она привыкла рано вставать и работать, и теперь без труда она, как рыба без воды. Похудела, побледнела и плачет, бедняжка . . . (*Пауза.*) Вы это очень хорошо знаете, Ермолай Алексеич: я мечтала . . . выдать ее за вас, да и по всему видно было, что вы женитесь. (*Шепчет Ане, та кивает Шарлотте, и обе уходят.*) Она вас любит, вам она по душе, и не знаю , не знаю, почему это вы точно сторонитесь друг друга. Не понимаю!

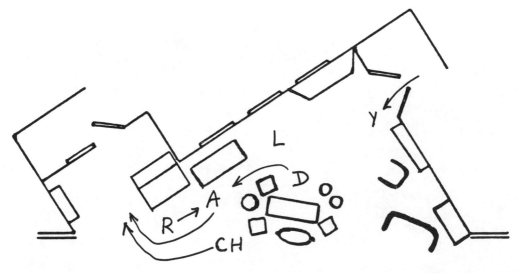

LYUBOV

Now we can go — I leave with two cares in my heart
— the first is leaving Firs ill. (*Looks at her watch.*)
We still have five minutes.

ANYA

Mama, Firs has already been taken to the hospital.
Yasha sent him this morning.

LYUBOV

My other anxiety is Varya. She's used to getting up
early and working; and now, without work, she'll be
like a fish out of water. She has grown thin and pale,
and can't stop crying, poor thing. (*Pause.*) You are
well aware, Yermolay Alexeyevitch, I dreamed of
marrying her to you. Everything seemed to show that
you would get married. (*Whispers to* ANYA *who then
motions to* CHARLOTTA; *they both go out.* YASHA *comes
in quietly.*) She loves you. She suits you. I don't know
— I don't know why it is you seem deliberately to
avoid each other; I can't understand it.

*Make all senses, in varying degrees, responsive to both the external life
and your own inner life.*

*At the end of five hours of rehearsal daily, feel yourselves bursting with
emotion, feelings, yearnings to work, to be part of a performance. Slowly,
slowly, work; go deeply into the inner meanings of each character. Let all the
doors of your inner imagination burst open, fly open.*

ЛОПАХИН

Я сам тоже не понимаю, признаться. Как-то странно все . . . Если есть еще время, то я хоть сейчас готов . . . Покончим сразу - и баста, а без вас я, чувствую, не сделаю предложения.

ЛЮБОВЬ АНДРЕЕВНА

И превосходно. Ведь одна минута нужна, только. Я ее сейчас позову . . .

ЛОПАХИН

Кстати и шампанское есть. (*Поглядев на стаканчики.*) Пустые, кто-то уже выпил. (*Яша кашляет.*) Это называется вылакать.

ЛЮБОВЬ АНДРЕЕВНА

(*оживленно*). Прекрасно. Мы выйдем . . . Яша, *allez*! Я ее позову . . . (*В дверь.*) Варя, оставь все, поди сюда. Иди! (*Уходит с Яшей.*)

ЛОПАХИН

(*поглядев на часы.*) Да . . . (*Пауза.*)

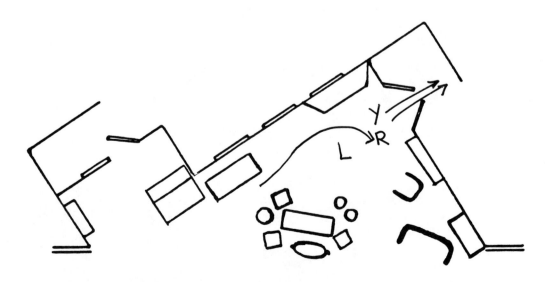

LOPAKHIN

To tell you the truth, I don't understand it myself. It is strange. If there's still time, I'm ready now — at once. Let's settle it straight off, and then — *Basta!* But without you, I feel I'll never be able to propose.

LYUBOV

That's splendid — after all, it will only take a minute. I'll call her at once.

LOPAKHIN

And there's champagne already too. (*Looks at the glasses.*) Empty! Somebody's drunk it all — (YASHA *coughs.*) That's what you might call lapping it up.

LYUBOV

We'll go out. Yasha, *allez!* I'll call her. (*At the door.*) Varya! Leave everything and come here! Come along! (LYUBOV *goes out with* YASHA.)

LOPAKHIN

(*Looking at his watch.*) Yes . . . (*Pause.*)

The actor must be aware of getting into the circumstances and having a mastery over them. A play is what happens between the characters. Feelings are something which are controlled by the mind if the feelings are true. The body will have those strange feelings in the viscera. The actor's thoughts may be wrong if they have nothing to do with the character the actor is playing.

A part is not one; it is all around one. It is also surroundings. The actor must play with all his heart and through the relationships and events a human being thus unfolds.

За дверью сдержанный смех, шепот, наконец, входит Варя.

ВАРЯ

(*долго осматривает вещи*). Странно, никак не найду . . .

ЛОПАХИН

Что вы ищете?

ВАРЯ

Сама уложила и не помню. (*Пауза.*)

ЛОПАХИН

Вы куда же теперь, Варвара Михайловна?

ВАРЯ

Я? К Рагулиным . . . Договорились к ним смотреть за хозяйством . . . в экономки, что ли.

ЛОПАХИН

Это в Яшнево? Верст семьдесят будет. (*Пауза.*) Вот и кончилась жизнь в этом доме . . .

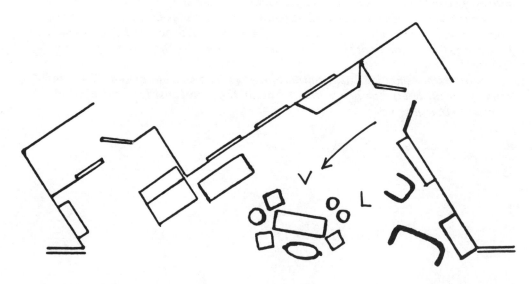

Behind the door, smothered laughter and whispering; at last, enter VARYA.

VARYA

(*Looking over the things.*) How strange — I can't find it . . . (*She kneels by the packing cases; she has mixed feelings, expressing some hostility.*)

LOPAKHIN

What are you looking for?

VARYA

. . . Packed it myself . . . don't remember . . . (*Pause.*)

LOPAKHIN

Where are you going now, Varya?

VARYA

I? To the Ragulins! I've arranged to take charge of their house — as housekeeper.

LOPAKHIN

That's in Yashnovo — about seventy versts away. (*Pause.*) Well, life in this house has ended.

Lopakhin, I do this miming of an action only to hint at the intensity of the intention and the rhythm for the character. What I am interested in, as your director, is for you to have in your mind and your heart, your character. Not literally, but in your heart. Your relationship with people, your future, your past; that is the man. Then you will become, as an actor, another character. You won't be yourself. You will have a new outer and a new inner man, with feelings, with thoughts.

In the Varya-Lopakhin scene, Lopakhin should be full of joy. This gives one a better feeling about having bought the Ranyevsky house.

ВАРЯ

(*оглядывая вещи*). Где же это . . . Или, может, я в сундук уложила . . . Да, Жизнь в этом доме кончилась . . . больше уже не будет . . .

ЛОПАХИН

А я в Харьков уезжаю сейчас . . . вот с этим поездом. Дела много. А тут во дворе оставляю Епиходова . . . Я его нанял.

ВАРЯ

Что ж!

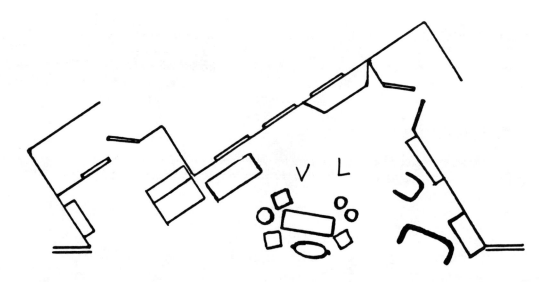

VARYA

(*Looking among the things.*) Where is it? Perhaps I put it in the little trunk. Yes, life in this house has ended . . . there will be no more of it.

LOPAKHIN

I'm just off to Kharkov by this next train. I've a lot of business there. I'm leaving Yepikhodov here — I've taken him on.

VARYA

Oh!

On Varya's speech, 'where is it', Varya is upstage of the packing cases. As she goes on with this speech, 'yes, life in this house' she says this facing out full front to the audience.

Varya, I don't want to only hear your voice. Always, you must speak with your heart and not your voice. Conversations can't go on very long without hope.

Actors should play what happens between each other. There is great anticipation between Varya and Lopakhin in this scene, the proposal scene. You should build on inner monologue and anticipation. This is the process of creation.

ЛОПАХИН

В прошлом году об эту пору уже снег шел, если припомните, а теперь тихо, солнечно. Только что вот холодно . . . Градуса три мороза.

ВАРЯ

Я не поглядела. (*Пауза.*) Да и разбит у нас градусник . . . (*Пауза.*)

ГОЛОС В ДВЕРЬ СО ДВОРА

Ермолай Алексеич!

ЛОПАХИН

(*точно давно ждал этого зова*). Сию минуту! (*Быстро уходит.*)

Варя сидит на полу, положив голову на узел с платьем, тихо рыдает. Отворяется дверь, осторожно входит Любовь Андреевна.

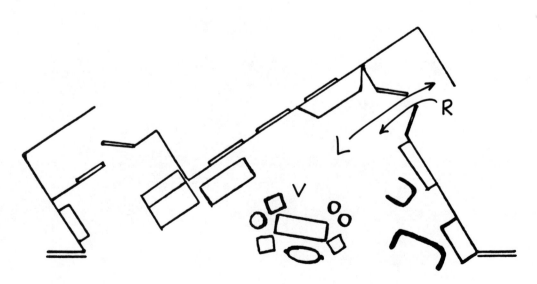

LOPAKHIN

Last year at this time it was snowing, if you remember, but now it's fine and sunny. It's cold, though — three degrees of frost.

VARYA

I didn't look. (*Pause.*) And besides, our thermometer's broken. (*Pause.*)

A VOICE FROM THE YARD

Yermolay Alexeyevitch!

LOPAKHIN

(*Eagerly, having been waiting for this summons.*)
This minute! (*Goes out quickly.*)

VARYA, sitting on the floor, lays her head on the little trunk and sobs quietly. LYUBOV comes in cautiously.

Lyubov must look for Lopakhin after his scene with Varya. She comes back expecting everything is all right; then you see Varya alone and you understand.

My job as director is not only to introduce you to Chekhov's world, but to rebuild your mechanisms so it will be more creative.

ЛЮБОВЬ АНДРЕЕВНА

Что? (*Пауза.*) Надо ехать.

ВАРЯ

(*уже не плачет, вытерла глаза*). Да, пора, мамочка. Я к Рагулиным поспею сегодня, не опоздать бы только к поезду . . .

ЛЮБОВЬ АНДРЕЕВНА

(В дверь). Аня, одевайся!

Входят Аня, потом Гаев, Шарлотта Ивановна. На Гаеве теплое пальто с башлыком. Сходится прислуга, извозчики. Около вещей хлопочет Епиходов.

ЛЮБОВЬ АНДРЕЕВНА

Теперь можно и в дорогу.

АНЯ

(*радостно*). В дорогу!

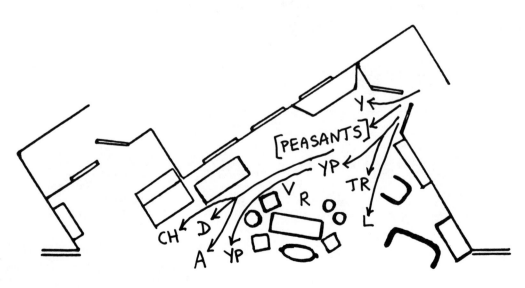

LYUBOV

Well? (*Pause.*) We must be going.

VARYA

(*No longer crying, wiping her eyes.*) Yes, it's time, Mamotchka. I'll be able to get to the Ragulins' today — if only you don't miss the train.

LYUBOV

(*In the doorway.*) Anya, put your things on!

Enter ANYA, followed by GAYEV and CHARLOTTA IVANOVNA. GAYEV is wearing a heavy coat. Suddenly there is a great bustle. The entrance of YEPIKHODOV, TROFIMOV, LOPAKHIN, DUNYASHA, YASHA and several PEASANTS. VARYA assists the moving of packages, as the men remove trunks and large suitcases and packing cases. At the height of the movement, YEPIKHODOV is center stage, ineffectually giving suggestions to all. Making his way stage left with a heavy crate, he bumps into a PEASANT HELPER who relieves him of the crate.

LYUBOV

Now we can start on our journey.

ANYA

(*Joyfully.*) On our journey!

LOPAKHIN, in shirt sleeves, is briskly helping, lifting and carrying the larger crates. DUNYASHA, with cape on, rushes across the stage and out, her arms full of parcels and a hat box.

Anya, on Lyubov's line, 'now we can start on journey', sits down briefly.

ГАЕВ

Друзья мои, милые, дорогие друзья мои! Покидая этот дом навсегда, могу ли я умолчать, могу ли удержаться, чтобы не высказать на прощанье те чувства, которые наполняют теперь все мое существо . . .

АНЯ

(*умоляюще*). Дядя!

ВАРЯ

Дядечка, не нужно!

ГАЕВ

(*уныло*). Дуплетом желтого в середину . . . Молчу . . .

Входит Трофимов, потом Лопахин.

ТРОФИМОВ

Что же, господа, пора ехать!

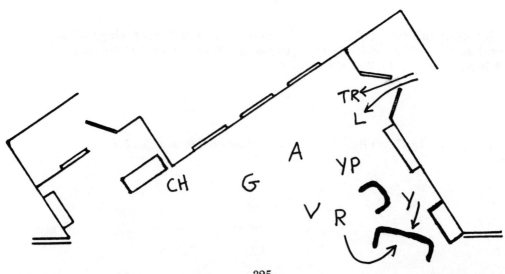

GAYEV

My friends, my dear, my precious friends, leaving this house forever, can I be silent? Can I refrain from giving utterance at leave-taking to those emotions which now flood all my being?

ANYA

(*Imploring*.) Uncle!

VARYA

Uncle, Uncle, don't!

GAYEV

(*Forlornly*.) Carom and into the pocket . . . I'll be silent . . .

Enter TROFIMOV and LOPAKHIN.

TROFIMOV

Well, ladies and gentlemen, it's time to go.

The feeling in this scene is that all are in a hurry to get going. We must all think of the act as music. Have your own rhythm, but within the rhythm of the scene. Sing and shout with joy of work, and art, and life, symbolically.

*The only words we have from the mouth are from Gayev. He chatters. The other characters talk through the eyes, the heart. Each character must listen, not to the words of answers but to the **sense** of answers. That's the inner monologue.*

ЛОПАХИН

Епиходов, мое пальто!

ЛЮБОВЬ АНДРЕЕВНА

Я посижу еще одну минутку. Точно раньше я никогда не видела, какие в этом доме стены, какие потолки, и теперь я гляжу на них с жадностью, с такой нежной любовью . . .

ГАЕВ

Помню, когда мне было шесть лет, в Троицын день я сидел на этом окне и смотрел, как мой отец шел в церковь . . .

ЛЮБОВЬ АНДРЕЕВНА

Все вещи забрали?

ЛОПАХИН

Кажется, все. (*Епиходову, надевая пальто.*) Ты же, Епиходов, смотри, чтобы все было в порядке.

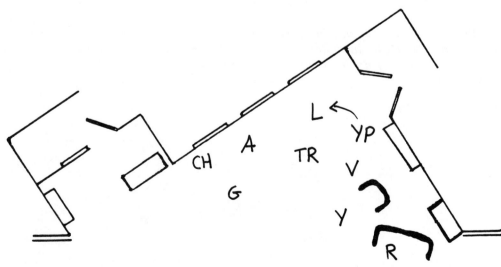

LOPAKHIN

Yepikhodov, my coat.

LYUBOV

I'll sit down just a minute. (YASHA *moves sofa from wall for her to sit.*) It seems as though I've never seen before what the walls in this house were like, the ceilings — and now I look at them hungrily, with such love. (*Sits.**)

GAYEV

I remember when I was six years old, sitting at that window on Whit-Sunday, watching my father go to church.

LYUBOV

Have all the things been taken?

LOPAKHIN

I think so. (*Putting on an overcoat.*) You, Yepikhodov, see that everything's in order.

---

*It's a Russian custom to sit down before leaving. This comes from the old times. When one leaves there is always the chance that one won't see others again.

ЕПИХОДОВ

(*говорит сиплым голосом*). Будьте покойны,
Ермолай Алексеич!

ЛОПАХИН

Что это у тебя голос такой?

ЕПИХОДОВ

Сейчас воду пил, что-то проглотил.

ЯША

(*с презрением*). Невежество . . .

ЛЮБОВЬ АНДРЕЕВНА

Уедем - и здесь не останется ни души . . .

ЛОПАХИН

До самой весны.

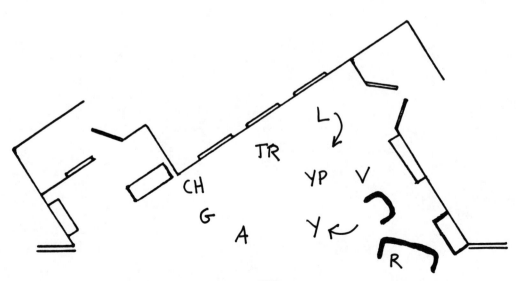

YEPIKHODOV

(*In a husky voice.*) You needn't worry, Yermolay Alexeyevitch.

LOPAKHIN

What sort of voice is that?

YEPIKHODOV

I just had a drink of water. I must have swallowed the wrong way.

YASHA

(*Suspiciously.*) What ignorance!

LYUBOV

We're going, and not a soul will be left here.

LOPAKHIN

Not till the spring.

ВАРЯ

(*выдергивает из угла зонтик, похоже, как будто она замахнулась; Лопахин делает вид, что испугался*). Что вы, что вы . . . Я и не думала.

ТРОФИМОВ

Господа, идемте садиться в экипажи . . . Уже пора! Сейчас поезд придет!

ВАРЯ

Петя, вот они, ваши калоши, возле чемодана. (*Со слезами.*) И какие они у вас грязные, старые . . .

ТРОФИМОВ

(*надевая калоши*). Идем, господа! . .

ГАЕВ

(*сильно смущен, боится заплакать*). Поезд . . . станция . . . Круазе в середину, белого дуплетом в угол . . .

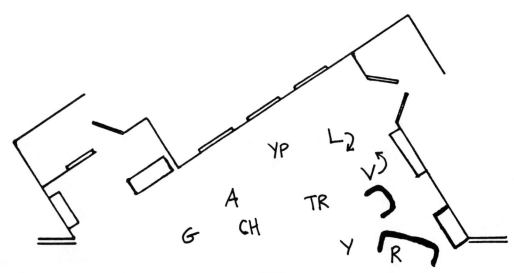

VARYA

(VARYA *pulls out a parasol out of a bundle as though about to hit someone with it.* LOPAKHIN *makes a gesture as though alarmed.*) Now, now, I didn't mean anything!

TROFIMOV

Ladies and gentleman, let's get into the carriage — it's time. The train will be in directly.

VARYA

Petya, here are your galoshes (*With tears in her eyes.*) — and what dirty old things they are!

TROFIMOV

(*Puts on galoshes.*) Let's go, friends.

GAYEV

(*Greatly upset, afraid of weeping.*) The train — the station! Bank shot to the middle.

In interrelationships, you have to find an adjustment, a union of the psychological and the physical.

Stanislavski said the main problem is for the actor to find the key while getting specific details, as well as mastery in everything so as not to lose the most precious, the heart. The actor must make-believe it is all happening.

ЛЮБОВЬ АНДРЕЕВНА

Идем!

ЛОПАХИН

Все здесь? Никого там нет? (*Запирает боковую дверь налево.*) Здесь вещи сложены, надо запереть. Идем!

АНЯ

Прощай, дом! Прощай, старая жизнь!

ТРОФИМОВ

Здравствуй, новая жизнь! (*Уходит с Аней.*)

Варя окидывает взглядом комнату и неспеша уходит. Уходят Яша и Шарлотта с собачкой.

ЛОПАХИН

Значит, до весны. Выходите, господа . . . До свиданция! . . . (*Уходит.*)

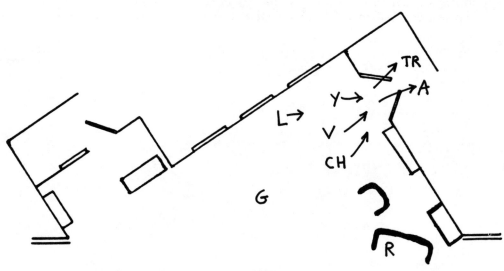

LYUBOV

Let us go.

LOPAKHIN

Are we all here? No one in there? (*Through the door.*)
There are some things stored there — better lock up.
Let us go.

ANYA

Good-bye, home. Good-bye to the old life!

TROFIMOV

Welcome to the new life! (*He goes out with* ANYA.)

VARYA looks round the room then goes out slowly. YASHA and CHARLOTTA,
with her dog, go out.

LOPAKHIN

And so, until the spring. Come, friends, till our next
meeting. (*He exits.*)

*For Anya and Trofimov it is a real flight. They are suddenly free; they
have developed wings.*

Lopakhin feels he has the world before him and that he can change it.

*Lopakhin, on this, your last speech by the door, the whole play unfolds:
the lack of communication between people.*

Любовь Андреевна и Гаев остались вдвоем. Они точно ждали этого, бросаются на шею друг другу и рыдают сдержанно, тихо, боясь, чтобы их не услышали.

ГАЕВ

(*в отчаянии*). Сестра моя, сестра моя . . .

ЛЮБОВЬ АНДРЕЕВНА

О, мой милый, мой нежный, прекрасный сад! . . . Моя жизнь, моя молодость, счастье мое, прощай! . . . Прощай!

ГОЛОС АНИ

(*весело, призывающе*). Мама!..

ГОЛОС ТРОФИМОВА

(*весело, возбужденно*). Ау!..

ЛЮБОВЬ АНДРЕЕВНА

В последний раз взглянуть на стены, на окна . . . По этой комнате любила ходить покойная мать . . .

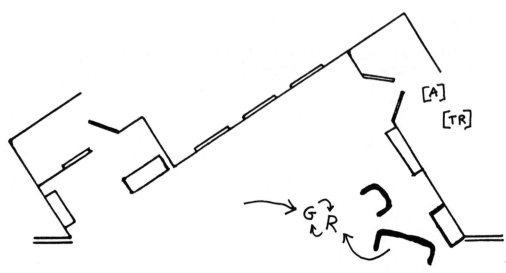

LYUBOV and GAYEV remain alone. As though they'd been waiting for this, they throw themselves on each other's necks, and break into subdued, smothered sobbing, afraid of being overheard.

GAYEV

(*In despair.*) My sister! My sister!

LYUBOV

Oh, my orchard — my sweet, my beautiful orchard! My life, my youth, my happiness — good-bye, good-bye!

VOICE OF ANYA

(*Calling gaily.*) Mama!

VOICE OF TROFIMOV

(*Gaily.*) Ah-oo!

LYUBOV

One last look at the walls, the windows. Our dear mother loved to walk about this room.

Mme. Ranyevsky, in the last moment in the room with Gayev, looks first at the orchard, then at the walls. Lyubov, try to restrain yourself.

If Gayev finds it difficult to reach this character, consider that it took Chekhov five years and a whole lifetime to write this play and to achieve the wisdom to write it.

You move from yesterday to tomorrow. Anya is tomorrow, Varya is yesterday, nothing. It is very necessary that Anya, despite all the pain she had, is quite happy. Dunyasha and Anya believe. Youth, for Chekhov, is faith in life. The above idea is both in Anya and Petya; Chekhov underlines it with the last words of Firs 'ah, these young people'.

ГАЕВ

Сестра моя, сестра моя!..

ГОЛОС АНИ

Мама!..

ГОЛОС ТРОФИМОВА

Ау!..

ЛЮБОВЬ АНДРЕЕВНА

Мы идем! . . . (*Уходят.*)

Сцена пуста. Слышно, как на ключ запирают все двери, как потом отъезжают экипажи. Становится тихо. Среди тишины раздается глухой стук топора по дереву, звучащий одиноко и грустно.

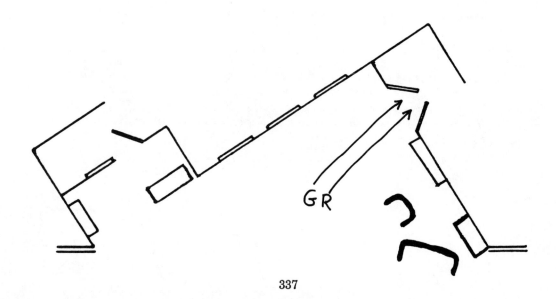

337

GAYEV

My sister, my sister!

VOICE OF ANYA

Mama!

VOICE OF TROFIMOV

Ah-oo!

LYUBOV

We're coming. (*They go out.*)

The stage is empty, sound of doors being locked, of carriages driving away. Then silence. In the stillness there is the dull stroke of an axe on a tree, clanging with a mournful, lonely sound.

The future of all the characters is foreshadowed. Each actor must know his relationship to his belongings. Each of you actors, as the characters, think of the belongings suitable for you, for example, Trofimov would only have a few books and a change of linen.

Слышатся шаги. Из двери, что направо, показывается Фирс. Он одет, как всегда, в пиджаке и белой жилетке, на ногах туфли. Он болен.

ФИРС

(*подходит к двери, трогает за ручку*). Заперто. Уехали . . . (*Садится на диван.*) Про меня забыли . . . Ничего . . . я тут посижу . . . А Леонид Андреич, небось, шубы не надел, в пальто поехал . . . (*Озабоченно вздыхает.*) Я-то не поглядел . . . Молодо-зелено! (*Бормочет что-то, чего понять нельзя.*) Жизнь-то прошла, словно и не жил . . . (*Ложится.*) Я полежу . . . Силушки-то у тебя нету, ничего не осталось, ничего . . . Эх, ты . . . недотепа! . . . (*Лежит неподвижно.*)

Слышится отдаленный звук, точно с неба, звук лопнувшей струны, замирающий печальный. Наступает тишина, и только слышно, как далеко в саду топором стучат по дереву.

ЗАНАВЕС

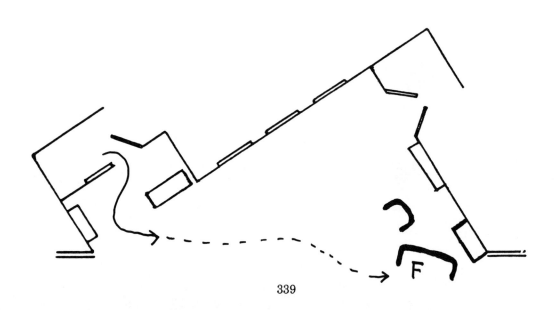

339

Footsteps are heard. FIRS appears in the doorway on the right. He is dressed as usual but with slippers on his feet. He is ill. He goes to the doors and tries the handles.

FIRS

It's locked! They've gone . . . (*He sits down on sofa.*) Why, they've forgotten me . . . never mind . . . I'll sit here a bit . . . I'll be bound Leonid Andreyevitch hasn't put his fur coat on, he's gone off in his light overcoat. (*Sighs anxiously.*) I didn't look after him . . . ah, these young people. (*Mutters something that can't be distinguished.*) Life has gone by as though I had never lived. (*Lies down.*) I'll lie down a bit . . . there's no strength in you, nothing left in you — all gone! Ech! You good for nothing! (*Lies motionless.*)

A sound is heard that seems to come from the sky, like a breaking harp string, dying away mournfully. All is still again. Nothing is heard but the stroke of the axe, far away in the orchard, and the sound of workmen singing.

CURTAIN

Firs, this is what is happening: you are sitting there, an old man, and suddenly you understand you are dying. And for one second, you sit up and, almost with a smile, say 'life has passed me by as though I had never lived' and then you lose your consciousness, gradually you fade out.

Firs should have a small bundle and a shawl over his shoulder. He is ready to leave.

On Firs' line, 'Life has gone by as though I'd never lived', the lights start to dim out one beat after his cane drops.

Firs wanted to say good-bye but it was too late. For one moment he sees his whole life. After his last sentence, there is a pause and then he sighs. Lights fade out softly and the sound of chopping begins.

AFTERWARD

Yuri Zavadski did not believe, in principle, in demonstrating or illustrating to an actor an action. Much as he admired the actor playing Firs, at a rehearsal he sensed that the actor had not understood the detailed meaning of this, his final scene. So Yuri Zavadski, on this rare occasion for his actors, showed us what he was trying to communicate to the actor playing Firs.

*"You might just give me a little look, Yasha . . .", **Dunyasha** (Annette Hunt) laments to **Yasha** (Stephen Daley.)*

Mr. Zavadski, for the actors, became Firs. He reached over to the settee, leaned on it heavily. He wore his thin coat and acted: 'what to do?' To the actors, as he sat on the sofa, it was an extraordinary moment. he had become Firs, dying. Mr. Zavadski sat there and looked out into the dark house, saying absolutely nothing. And the sudden look of astonishment on his face, deep weariness, when he said [in Russian] 'life has gone by as though I had never lived'. It was as if for a moment Firs had come to life and was suddenly a youth with the amazing realization that his life was now at an end. It was a combination of expression of such beauty, yet such weariness that his life was over, that there was a sense of sorrow and poignant and bewildering loss.

When Yuri Zavadski as Firs said [in Russian text] 'I will lie down a bit, there is no strength left in me — all is gone' Mr. Zavadski let himself down on the settee, his hands, his arms falling away from him. As Firs, he was dying. He said [in Russian] 'Ech — you good for nothing'. Firs' right hand touched the floor. In that moment, for the company, Firs died. For all it was an electrifying experience on the stage, in the half dark with only a thin light from the wings on his face.

On the final rehearsal Mr. Zavadski said to the actors:

In the certain way, it is beginning to slightly settle in your souls, actors. It is a double process. In a way it is good, because it becomes your own. At the same time it can also become more common. You have to find the uniqueness of the moment. Chekhov's strength is portraying ordinary people in extraordinary moments.

My goal as director has been to unfold and open up for you the inner life of the play and it's characters. The staging also helps for the internal meaning, the inner life.

The greatest mistake is to judge Chekhov as the bard of gloomy, twilight moods, a pessimist seeing in life only grayness, boredom, vulgarity, petite bourgeoisie. To think this, is not to understand Chekhov.

This is what Stanislavski said of him: 'Actually, Chekhov was the greatest optimist about the future that I ever had the fortune to meet. He painted a cheerful, always lively and confident, picture of future Russian life. It was only that he looked at the present without falsifying it; he was not afraid of the truth. The very people who were labeling him a pessimist were the first to look sourly at times and fulminate against the present, especially in the eighties and nineties when Chekhov lived. 'If one remembers Chekhov's distressing ailment, which caused him so much suffering, his loneliness at Yalta, and the fact that, despite these things, he always had a cheerful expression on his face, was always full of interest in everything about him, then one can scarcely find any traits on which to base the portrait of Chekhov as a pessimist.'

Stanislavski had an expression: 'You have to work so that the difficulties become habit, the habit becomes easy, the easy becomes beautiful.

It's the actors that work through a relationship in the whole play then the fourth act plays by itself. In **Cherry Orchard** *there is true poetry of life. Keep it and develop it. It will remain as important for your future work.*

As a final word, in art you may think that art is happening there only on the stage, but it is really happening in the soul of the spectator. At that time you should have, as actors, no doubts about yourselves. When you are sure of the audio and visual and the inner music of Chekhov's art, all will come through.

* * *

*"We shall probably never see each other again . . .", **Trofimov** (Robert Stattel) takes leave of **Lopakhin** (Bill Berger) as **Yasha** (Stephen Daley) looks on.*

RESIDUUM

A survey of directorial points of view from reading Soviet directors reveals that Yuri Zavadski was much in the mainstream of Russian theatre practice and contemporary Russian interpretations of Stanislavski's "Method."

At the Moscow Art Theatre School, Khedrov stressed that Stanislavski had been concerned and insistent upon the development of the actor's instrument, his body and voice. The Director of the School said, "In Stanislavski's last years this became increasingly a matter of importance to him: the training for period technique, movement, diction." Khedrov stressed, "Technique (practice) and theory are inseparable."

This was reiterated by the Director of the MXAT school saying, "Each year the student actors have some training now in Movement. In all four years they get instruction in voice quality, diction, musical training of the voice, listening to music, and responding to rhythm."

He had the students repeat the opening of the improvisation a good many times, but he was not satisfied with what they were doing. He also said, "You actors were not sufficiently aware of the audience waiting on the other side of the curtain". This teacher seemed to be particularly interested in rhythm.

I asked the teacher, "How much time are students expected to work at home on their assignments. The teacher said, "They are expected to work *all* the time, even on bus, trolley, etc., observing people, etc."

There is an acceptance of the craft aspect of performing. They do not leave this to chance. Even when passionately committed to the Stanislavski method, as is the Moscow Art Theatre; nevertheless, there is a feeling that one must learn the craft of performing: training in voice; continuous work in training the body, through movement, through dance, through gymnastics.

Ruben Simonov, Director of the Vakhtangov Theatre, said he believed that each play must be directed individually; the same style must not be imposed upon each play. In a play of Shakespeare, or in other plays in which the picturesque and "theatrical" are important values, he felt time is wasted by sitting around a table for days or weeks reading and discussing, and that one should put it on its feet immediately and work it onstage.

Simonov continued, "Our theatre is grounded in the idea of reincarnation of the character as developed by Stanislavski. However, in the spirit of its founder, Eugene Vakhtangov, (an early associate and disciple of Stanislavski) I feel that the Vakhtangov has gone beyond Stanislavski, and in addition to the concern with a 'method' is also interested in heightening 'theatrical' values.

"Stanislavski too, was concerned that the artist have the technical skill required for acting. Actors should get more training, begin to work into the company, and have the very palpable experience of performing as a member of a troupe before a paying audience in a public theatre. Methods of training differ and amount of time devoted to training differs.

"What may be deficient is offset by the fact that the young are growing through the rich experiences of working side-by-side with older professional actors."

The Vakhtangov Theatre director, Simonov, informed us, "We have full sets and costumes on stage for about eight rehearsals. Then there are three preview or general rehearsals. The first is for the whole troupe of actors, the second is the "Mama and Papa" general rehearsal, and the third for invited friends. Then the play goes into the repertory for the public to see."

Director for an Arthur Miller play, Alexander Karev, is one of the theatre's directors as well. There are eight staff *regisseurs* (directors). However, MXAT also from time to time, to get new blood into the theatre, invites outside directors to do a production for them.

As Victor Stanitsyn rehearsed, he frequently interrupted with outbursts of trenchant comment, and objections to what the actors were doing. At one point, Stanitsyn turned to me and said, "People often wonder why the Moscow Art Theatre spends many months in rehearsal. As you can see, we keep working on and examining and trying to get behind every word, every phrase, every line. That does take time."

During a break in the rehearsal, we had a chance to talk further with Stanitsyn. He said, "This production had begun rehearsals in January, but while I was away with the troupe on tour in Japan, rehearsals continued with a co-director."

We asked him, "Did you use improvisation early in the rehearsals before the actors had the text of the play to work on, memorize, and rehearse?"

He replied, "There was no need for improvisation ... some directors use improvisation more; some directors less."

Again we return to Stanislavski, who stresses that "knowledge of the system is not enough. It is not enough to know how to live your role on the stage. You must have a strong ... voice ... expressive timbre, perfect diction ... plasticity of movement ..." In examining the methods used by all MXAT directors, Yuri Zavadski and Victor Stanitsyn included, it is clear that remained aware of the fuller aspects of an actor's preparation as he or she creates a role for the stage.

Comparative Chronology to

Chekhov's Life

YEAR	CHEKHOV & THEATRE	DRAMA & LETTERS	MUSIC & OPERA	GRAPHIC & PLASTIC ARTS
1860	(January 17) Anton Chekhov born	Alexander Ostrovski: THE STORM, Russian drama J.M. Barrie, Scottish dramatist, born (died 1937) George Eliot: THE MILL ON THE FLOSS Eugene Labiche: LE VOYAGE DE M. PER-RICHON	Ignace Paderewski, Polish pianist and statesman, born (died 1941) Gustav Mahler, German composer, born (died 1911) First modern Welsh Eisteddfod Hugo Wolf, Austrian composer, born (died 1903)	Jakob Burckhardt: THE CIVILIZATION OF THE RENAISSANCE IN ITALY Degas: "Spartan Boys and Girls Exercising" Manet: "Spanish Guitar Player," painting
1861		Dostoyevski: THE HOUSE OF THE DEAD Elizabeth Barrett Browning dies (born 1806) Rabindranath Tagore, Indian philosopher and poet, born (died 1941) Mrs. Henry Wood: EAST LYNNE	Nellie Melba, Australian operatic soprano, born (died 1931) Royal Academy of Music, London, founded TANNHAUSER, a scandal in Paris	Corot: "Orphee, Le Repos" Charles Garnier designs the Opera, Paris (-1875) Aristide Maillol, French sculptor, born (died 1944)
1862		Ivan Turgenev: FATHERS AND SONS Victor Hugo: LES MISERABLES Gerhart Hauptmann, German dramatist, born (died 1946)	Edith Wharton, American author, born (died 1937) Berlioz: BEATRICE ET BENEDICT, opera, Baden-Baden Claude Debussy, French composer, born (died 1918) Frederick Delius, English composer, born (died 1934)	Verdi: LA FORZA DEL DESTINO, opera, St. Petersburg Manet: "Lola de Valence," painting Manet: "La Musique aux Tuileries" Ingres: "Bain Turque"
1863	Constantin Stanis-lavski, Russian theatrical producer, is born	Gabriele D'Annunzio, Italian poet, born (died 1938) Jakob Grimm, German writer and philologist, dies (born 1785) Friedrich Hebbel, German dramatist, dies (born 1813)	Berlioz: LES TROYENS, opera, Paris Bizet: LES PECHEURS DE PERLES, opera, Paris Pietro Mascagni, Italian composer, born (died 1945)	Manet: "Dejeuner sur l'Herbe" and "Olympia," paintings Edvard Munch, Norwegian painter, born (died 1944) Lucien Pissarro, French painter, born (died 1944) Whistler: "Little White Girl," painting

RUSSIA/USSR AND THE WORLD	MUNDANE EVENTS	CHURCH & THOUGHT	KNOWLEDGE & INVENTION
Founding of Vladivostok The southern part of Sakhalin is acquired from Japan in exchange for the Kuril Islands In the Far East, a Treaty of Peking brings the Russian frontier south to the Amur River coastal regions, south of Vladivostok Abraham Lincoln elected 16th President of the U.S.; South Carolina secedes from the Union in protest	Food and Drugs Act enacted in Britain Christopher L. Sholes, American inventor, devises primitive form of typewriter Beginning of skiing as competitive sport	Russian Orthodox Church establishes monastery in Jerusalem Arthur Schopenhauer dies (born 1788) J. S. Mill: CONSIDERATIONS ON REPRESENTATIVE GOVERNMENT	G. T. Fechner: ELEMENTS OF PSYCHOPHYSICS Lenoir constructs first practical internal-combustion engine Frederick Walton invents cork linoleum
Alexander II (1855-1881) abolishes serfdom Warsaw Massacre - troops fire at demonstrators against Russian rule Charleston, S.C., April 12-outbreak of Civil War; Confederate victory at Bull Run; Union forces later capture Forts Clark and Hatteras Prince Consort Albert dies (born 1819)	Population figures (in millions): Russia, 76; U.S., Great Britain, 23; Italy, 25 First horsedrawn trams appear in London Krupp begins arms production in Essen, Germany		Vladimir Dahl: DICTIONARY OF THE LIVING RUSSIAN TONGUE (-1866) Arthur P. Stanley: HISTORY OF THE EASTERN CHURCH Rudolf Steiner, founder Anthroposophical Society, born (died 1925) William Crookes discovers thallium Pasteur: germ theory of fermentation Semmelweis: CHILDBED FEVER
September 22 - U.S.A.: "Emancipation Proclamation"-effective January 1, 1863 Bismarck becomes Prussian Prime Minister King Otto I of Greece resigns after military revolt Aristide Briand, French statesman, born (died 1932)	Swiss humanist Jean Henri Dunant (1828-1910) proposes the foundation of an international voluntary relief organization- the Red Cross International Exhibition, London English cricket team tours Australia for first time	James Bryce: THE HOLY ROMAN EMPIRE George Rawlinson: THE FIVE GREAT MONARCHIES OF THE ANCIENT EASTERN WORLD (-1867) Herbert Spencer: FIRST PRINCIPLES	Lion Foucault (1819-1868) successfully measures the speed of light R. J. Gatling (1818-1903) constructs 10-barrel gun bearing his name Helmholtz: THE DOCTRINE OF THE SENSATIONS OF TONES Johann von Lamont discovers earth currents
Arizona and Idaho are organized as U. S. territories; West Virginia becomes a state of the U. S. Lincoln's "Gettysburg Address" Mohammed Said Khedive of Egypt, dies; succeeded by Ismail (died 1879) David Lloyd George, British statesman, born (died 1945)	Football Association founded, London Grand Prix de Paris first run at Longchamp Beginning of construction of London Underground railroad U. S. Congress establishes free city mail delivery Roller skating introduced to America	T. H. Huxley: EVIDENCE AS TO MAN'S PLACE IN NATURE J. S. Mill: UTILITARIANISM University of Massachusetts, Amherst, founded as Massachusetts Agricultural College	Henry Ford, American automobile manufacturer, born (died 1947) National Academy of Sciences founded Washington, D.C. Open-hearth steel furnace developed by Martin brothers in France based on Siemens process

YEAR	CHEKHOV & THEATRE	DRAMA & LETTERS	MUSIC & OPERA	GRAPHIC & PLASTIC ARTS
1864		Tolstoy: WAR AND PEACE (-1869) Nathaniel Hawthorne, American novelist, dies (born 1804) Henrik Ibsen: THE CROWN PRETENDERS Frank Wedekind, German dramatist, born (died 1918)	Stephen Foster, American songwriter, dies (born 1826) Giacomo Meyerbeer, German composer, dies (born 1791) Richard Strauss, German composer, born (died 1949)	Leo von Klenze, German architect dies (born 1784) Henri Toulouse-Lautrec, French painter, born (died 1901)
1865		Dimitri Merezhkovshy, Russian author, born (died 1942) Lewis Carroll (C.L. Dodgson, 1832-1898): ALICE'S ADVENTURES IN WONDERLAND Paul Verlaine: POEMES SATURNIENS Walt Whitman: DRUM TAPS	Alexander Glazunov, Russian composer, born (died 1936) Jean Sibelius, Finnish composer, born (died 1957) Wagner: TRISTAN UND ISOLDE, Munich Meyerbeer: L'AFRICAINE posth. opera, Paris	Winslow Homer: "Prisoners from the Front," paintings Hippolyte Taine: LA PHILOSOPHIE DE L'ART (1869) Yale University opens first Department of Fine Arts in U. S.
1866		Dostoyevski: CRIME AND PUNISHMENT Jacinto Benavente, Spanish dramatist, 1922 Nobel Prize, born (died 1954) H.G. Wells, English author, born (died 1946)	Offenbach: LA VIE PARISIENNE, operetta, Paris Smetana: PRODANA NEVESTA (THE BARTERED BRIDE), opera, Prague Ambroise Thomas: MIGNON, opera, Paris	Vassili Kandinsky, Russian painter, born (died 1944) Degas begins to paint his ballet scenes Monet: "Camille," painting
1867	Chekhov enters the Greek parish school	Turgenev: SMOKE Luigi Pirandello, Italian dramatist, 1934 Nobel Prize, born (died 1936) John Galsworthy, English author, born (died 1933) Natsume Soseki, Japanese novelist, born (died 1916)	Gounod: ROMEO ET JULIETTE, opera, Paris Johann Strauss II: The "Blue Danube," waltz Arturo Toscanini, Italian conductor, born (died 1957) Verdi: DON CARLOS, Paris	Paris World's Fair introduces Japanese art to the West Cezanne: "Rape," painting Jean Dominique Ingres, French painter, dies (born 1780)

RUSSIA/USSR AND THE WORLD	MUNDANE EVENTS	CHURCH & THOUGHT	KNOWLEDGE & INVENTION
Russia completes her control of the Caucus Abraham Lincoln re-elected President of the U.S. Massacre of the Cheyenne and Arapahoe Indians at Sand Creek, Colorado First International Workingmen's Association founded by Karl Marx, London and New York	First salmon cannery in U.S. at Washington, California Geneva Convention establishes the neutrality of battlefield medical facilities Knights of Pythias founded, Washington, D.C.	Cesare Lombroso (1836-1909): GENIUS AND MADNESS Cardinal Newman: APOLOGIA PRO VITA SUA Syllabus Errorum issued by Pope Pius IX: condemns Liberalism, Socialism, and Rationalism	Joseph Bertrand: TREATISE ON DIFFERENTIAL AND INTEGRAL CALCULUS (1870) Louis Pasteur invents pasteurization (for wine)
Abraham Lincoln assassinated April 14; succeeded as president by Andrew Johnson U.S. Civil War ends May 26 Thirteenth Amendment to U. S. Constitution abolishes slavery Outbreak of war (1866) between Boers of Orange Free State and Basutos	First carpet sweeper comes into use The first railroad sleeping cars, designed by George M. Pullman, appear in U.S. Union stockyards open at Chicago First woman, Maria Mitchell, appointed as professor of astronomy, Vassar College	J.S. Mill: AUGUSTE COMTE AND POSITIVISM Purdue University, Cornell University, University of Maine, and University of Kentucky founded	Ivan M. Sechenov (1829-1905): REFLEXES OF THE BRAIN on physiological basis of psychic processes Atlantic cable finally completed Massachusetts Institute of Technology founded
Prussia invades Saxony, Hanover, and Hesse 14th Amendment to U.S. Constitution prohibits voting discrimination Revolts in Crete against Turkish rule Sun Yat-sen, Chinese statesman, born (died 1927)	"Black Friday" on London Stock Exchange Dr. T.J. Barnardo (1845-1905) opens his first home for destitute children at Stepney, London	Benedetto Croce, Italian philosopher, born (died 1952) Friedrich Lange: HISTORY OF MATERIALISM	Aeronautical Society of Great Britain founded Alfred Nobel invents dynamite English engineer Robert Whitehead (1823-1905) invents underwater torpedo
Alaska sold to the United States Nebraska becomes a state of the U.S. British North America Act establishes Dominion of Canada Joseph Pilsudski, Polish soldier and statesman, born (died 1935)	"The Queensberry Rules," by John Graham Chambers of the London Amateur Athletic Club Gold discovered in Wyoming Marx: DAS KAPITAL, vol I Walter Bagehot: THE ENGLISH CONSTITUTION E.A. Freeman: HISTORY OF THE NORMAN CONQUEST (1876)		Marie (Sklodowska) Curie, Polish-French scientist, Nobel Prizes, 1903 and 1911, born (died 1934) Joseph F. Monier (1823-1906) patents a reinforced concrete process Railroad completed through Brenner Pass Discovery of South African diamond field

YEAR	CHEKHOV & THEATRE	DRAMA & LETTERS	MUSIC & OPERA	GRAPHIC & PLASTIC ARTS
1868	Chekhov enters the Taganrog School for Boys	Maxim Gorki, Russian author, born (died 1936) Dostoyevski: THE IDIOT Robert Browning: THE RING AND THE BOOK Edmond Rostand, French dramatist, born (died 1918)	Moussorgsky begins work on BORIS GODUNOV (-1874) Tchaikovsky: Symphony No. 1 Brahms: EIN DEUTSCHES REQUIEM, Op. 45 Wagner: DIE MEISTERSINGER VON NURNBERG, Munich	Degas: "l'Orchestre," painting Development of French impressionist style Renoir: "The Skaters"
1869		Flaubert; L'EDUCATION SENTIMENTALE W.S. Gilbert: BAB BALLADS Victor Hugo: L'HOMME QUI RIT Mark Twain: THE INNOCENTS ABROAD	Berlioz dies (born 1803) Karl Loewe, German composer dies (born 1796) R. Wagner: RHEINGOLD, opera, Munich	Henri Matisse, French painter, born (died 1954) Manet: "The Balcony," painting Frank Lloyd Wright, American architect, born (died 1959)
1870		Ivan Bunin, Russian poet, 1933 Nobel Prize, born (died 1953) Ivan Goncharov: THE PRECIPICE, Russian novel Jules Verne: TWENTY THOUSAND LEAGUES UNDER THE SEA Charles Dickens dies (born 1812)	Tchaikovsky: Fantasy-overture ROMEO AND JULIET, Moscow Wagner: DIE WALKURE, Munich Delibes: COPPELIA, ballet, Paris	Ernst Barlach, German sculptor, born (died 1938) Corot: "La Perle," painting Fantin-Latour: "Un Atelier a Batignolles," painting
1871		Ostrovsky: THE FOREST, Russian play Zola: LES ROUGON-MACQUART, series of novels (-1893) George Eliot: MIDDLEMARCH Theodore Dreiser, American novelist, born (died 1945)	Albert Hall, London, opened Saint-Saens: LE ROUET D'OMPHALE, symphonic poem, Op. 31 Verdi: AIDA, Cairo	Rossetti: "The Dream of Dante" Georges Roault, French painter, born (died 1958) Moritz von Schwind, German painter, dies (born 1804)

RUSSIA/USSR AND THE WORLD	MUNDANE EVENTS	CHURCH & THOUGHT	KNOWLEDGE & INVENTION
Russians occupy Samarkand Shogun Kekei of Japan abdicates; shogunate abolished; Meiji dynasty restored King Michael III of Serbia assassinated Ulysses S. Grant elected President of the U.S.	Meat-packing factory of P.D. Armour opens in Chicago The first professional U.S. Baseball Club, The Cincinnati Red Stockings, founded First regular Trades Union Congress held at Manchester, England	Bakunin founds Alliance Internationale de la Democratie Sociale Austrian schools freed from Church control Charles Darwin: "The Variation of Animals and Plants under Domestication"	Robert A. Millikan, U.S. physicist, 1923 Nobel Prize, born (died 1953) T. W. Richards, U.S. chemist, 1914 Nobel Prize, born (died 1928) R.F. Scott, English Antarctic explorer, born (died 1912)
General Grant inaugurated as 18th President of the U.S. Parliamentary system reintroduced in France Opening of Suez Canal by Empress Eugenie Mahatma Gandhi, Indian nationalist leader, born (died 1948)	British debtors' prisons are abolished First Nihilist Congress meets at Basel, Switzerland Dkoda works, Pilsen, Bohemia, open	Matthew Arnold: CULTURE AND ANARCHY Eduard Hartmann: THE PHILOSOPHY OF THE UNCONSCIOUS J.S. Mill: ON THE SUBJECTION OF WOMEN	J.W. Hyatt (1837-1920) invents celluloid Mendeleyev formulates his periodic law for the classification of the elements Gustav Nachtigal (1834-1888) explores the Sudan and the Sahara
Nikolai Lenin, Russian Communist leader, born (died 1924) Franco-Prussian War Western Australia granted representative government Italians enter Rome and name it their capital city	Rosa Luxemburg, German socialist leader, born (murdered 1919) John D. Rockefeller (1839-1937) founds Standard Oil Company DICTIONARY OF AMERICAN BIOGRAPHY is issued for the first time	Alfred Adler, Austrian psychiatrist, born (died 1937) Keble College, Oxford, founded Heinrich Schliemann begins to excavate Troy	T.H. Huxley: THEORY OF BIOGENESIS Adolf Nordenskjold explores the interior of Greenland
Rasputin, Russian monk, born (died 1916) The Commune in Paris rules for two months British Act of Parliament legalizes labor unions William I, King of Prussia, proclaimed German Emperor	P.T. Barnum opens his circus in Brooklyn, N.Y. National Association of Professional Baseball Players founded in New York (dissolved 1876) Stanley meets Livingstone at Ujiji Population figures (in millions): Germany 41; U.S. 39; France 36; Japan 33; Great Britain 26; Ireland 5.4; Italy 26.8	Charles Darwin: THE DESCENT OF MAN Jehovah's Witnesses founded Adolph Wagner: THE SOCIAL QUESTION	Simon Ingersoll (U.S.) invents pneumatic rock drill G.A. Hansen discovers leprosy bacillus Ernest Rutherford, English scientist, 1908 Nobel Prize, born (died 1937)

YEAR	CHEKHOV & THEATRE	DRAMA & LETTERS	MUSIC & OPERA	GRAPHIC & PLASTIC ARTS
1872		Turgenev: A MONTH IN THE COUNTRY Sergei Diaghilev, Russian Ballet impresario, born (died 1929) Jules Verne: AROUND THE WORLD IN 80 DAYS Eleonora Duse's debut at 14 in Verona as Juliet	Alexander Scriabin, Russian composer, born (died 1915) Bizet: incidental music to Daudet's, L'ARLESIENNE	Bocklin: "Battle of the Centaurs," painting Cezanne and Pissarro at Auvers-sur-Oise Whistler: "The Artist's Mother"
1873		Tolstoy: ANNA KARENINA (-1875) Max Reinhardt, German theatrical producer, born (died 1943) Rimbaud: UNE SAISON EN ENFER	Feodor Chaliapin, Russian singer, born (died 1938) Sergei Rachmaninoff, Russian composer and pianist, born (died 1943) Rimsky-Korsakov: IVAN THE TERRIBLE, opera, St. Petersburg Tchaikovsky: Symphony No. 2, Moscow Enrico Caruso, Italian opera singer, born (died 1921)	Cezanne: "The Straw Hat," painting Manet: "Le Bon Bock" Senaper designs the new Burgtheater, Vienna
1874		Robert Frost, American poet, born (died 1963) W. Somerset Maugham, English author, born (died 1965) Verlaine: ROMANCES SANS PAROLES	Moussorgsky BORIS GODUNOV, St. Petersburg Smetana: MA VLAST (MY FATHERLAND), cycle of symphonic poems Johann Strauss II: DIE FLEDERMAUS, operetta, Vienna Verdi: REQUIEM, Milan	First impressionist exhibition, Paris Renoir: "La Loge"
1875	Chekhov in amateur theatricals at Drossi Home Chekhov falls ill from peritonitis	Thomas Mann, German novelist, 1929 Nobel Prize, born (died 1955) Rainer Maria Rilke, Austrian poet, born (died 1926) Mark Twain: THE ADVENTURES OF TOM SAWYER	Tchaikovsky: Piano Concerto No. 1, Op. 23, Boston Bizet: CARMEN, Paris Maurice Ravel, French composer, born (died 1937)	The "Hermes" of Praxiteles found at Olympia, Greece J.F. Millet, French painter, dies (born 1814) Monet: "Boating at Argenteuil," painting

RUSSIA/USSR AND THE WORLD	MUNDANE EVENTS	CHURCH & THOUGHT	KNOWLEDGE & INVENTION
Ballot Act in Britain, voting by secret ballot Three-Emperors League established in Berlin; alliance between Germany, Russia, and Austria-Hungary Compulsory military service introduced in Japan U.S. General Amnesty Act pardons most ex-Confederates	Bakunin expelled from the First International at the Hague conference Building of St. Gotthard Tunnel begins (1881) First U.S. ski club founded at Berlin, New Hampshire	Jesuits expelled from Germany D.F. Strauss: THE OLD FAITH AND THE NEW Bertrand Russell, English philosopher, born (died 1970)	Edison perfects the "duplex" telegraph Brooklyn Bridge opened American engineer George Westinghouse (1846-1916) perfects automatic railroad air brake
Republic proclaimed in Spain Financial panic in Vienna (May) and New York (Sept.) Famine in Bengal	The cities of Buda and Pest are united to form the capital of Hungary Germany adopts the mark as its unit of currency Vienna World Exhibition	John Stuart Mill, English philosopher, dies (born 1806) Walter Pater: STUDIES IN THE HISTORY OF THE RENAISSANCE Herbert Spencer: THE STUDY OF SOCIOLOGY	Jean Charcot: LECONS SUR LES MALADIES DU SYSTEME NERVEUX Color photographs first developed Gunsmith firm of E. Remington and Sons begins to produce typewriters
End of Ashanti war Disraeli becomes prime minister (-1880) Britain annexes Fiji Islands Winston Churchill, British statesman, born (died 1965)	Society for the Prevention of Cruelty to Children founded in New York by E. T. Gerry Civil marriage is made compulsory in Germany First American zoo established in Philadelphia	Ernst Cassirer, German philosopher, born (died 1945) Henry Sidgwick: METHODS OF ETHICS	Guglielmo Marconi, Italian physicist, born (died 1937) A.T. Still (1828-1917) founds osteopathy (Kansas) H. Solomon (U.S.) introduces pressure-cooking methods for canning foods
Kwang Hsu becomes Emperor of China (-1898) Public Health Act is passed in Britain Rebellion in Cuba	Strength of European armies: Russia 3,360,000; Germany 2,800,000; France 412,000; Great Britain 113,000 London's main sewerage system is completed First roller-skating rink opens in London	Theosophical Society founded by Helena Blavatsky in New York Mary Baker Eddy: SCIENCE AND HEALTH C.G. Jung, Swiss psychiatrist and philosopher, born (died 1961) Religious orders abolished in Prussia	London Medical School for Women founded Heinrich Schliemann: TROY AND ITS REMAINS Albert Schweitzer, philosopher, medical missionary, and musician, born (died 1965)

YEAR	CHEKHOV & THEATRE	DRAMA & LETTERS	MUSIC & OPERA	GRAPHIC & PLASTIC ARTS
1876		Henry James: RODERICK HUDSON Jack London, American novelist, born (died 1916) George Sand, French writer, dies (born 1804)	Bayreuth Festspielhaus opens with first complete performance of Wagner's RING DES NIBELUNGEN Brahms: Symphony No. 1, Op. 68 Ponchielli: LA GIOCONDA, opera, Milan	Paula Modersohn-Becker, German painter, born (died 1907) Renoir: "Le Moulin de la Galette," painting
1877		Harley Granville-Barker, English theatrical producer, born (died 1946) Ibsen: THE PILLARS OF SOCIETY Zola: L'ASSOMMOIR	Tchaikovsky: FRANCESCA DA RIMINI, symphonic poem Brahms: Symphony No. 2, Op. 75 Camille Saint-Saens: SAMSON ET DELILA, opera Weimar	Manet: "Nana," painting Building of the Rijksmuseum, Amsterdam Rodin" "The Age of Bronze," sculpture Third impressionist exhibition, Paris
1878		Thomas Hardy: THE RETURN OF THE NATIVE Carl Sandburg, American poet, born (died 1967) Ellen Terry joins Irving's Company at the Lyceum Theatre, London	Gilbert and Sullivan: H.M.S. PINAFORE George Grove begins DICTIONARY OF MUSIC AND MUSICIANS	Garnier designs the Casino at Monte Carlo William Morris: THE DECORATIVE ARTS
1879	Chekhov registers at Moscow University in August	E.M. Forster, English novelist, born (died 1970) Ibsen: A DOLL'S HOUSE Strindberg: THE RED ROOM	Tchaikovsky: EUGEN ONEGIN, opera, Moscow Suppe: BOCCACCIO, operetta, Vienna	Honore Daumier, French painter, dies (born 1808) Renoir: "Mme. Charpentier and her Children," painting Rodin: "John the Baptist," sculpture

RUSSIA/USSR AND THE WORLD	MUNDANE EVENTS	CHURCH & THOUGHT	KNOWLEDGE & INVENTION
Korea becomes an independent nation Massacre of Bulgarians by Turkish troops Colorado becomes a state of the U.S.	Mikhail Bakunin, Russian socialist, politician and writer, dies (born 1814) First Chinese railroad is completed World Exhibition at Philadelphia	Lombroso: THE CRIMINAL G.M. Trevelyan, English historian, born (died 1962)	Alexander Graham Bell invents the telephone Johns Hopkins University, Baltimore opens Heinrich Schliemann excavates Mycenae
Russian invasion of the Balkans Rutherford B. Hayes inaugurated as 19th President of the U.S. Russia declares war on Turkey and invades Rumania; Russians cross Danube and storm Kars; Russians take Plevna, Bulgaria; Bismarck declines to intervene; Serbia declares war on Turkey Satsuma revolt in Japan suppressed	Famine in Bengal First public telephones (U.S.) Frozen meat shipped from Argentina to Europe for the first time	Patent Protection Law enacted in Germany Louis Lucien Rochet, Swiss theologian, founds the "Blue Cross" to fight alcoholism	Edison invents phonograph Robert Koch develops a technique whereby bacteria can be stained and identified Italian astronomer Giovanni V. Schiaparelli (1835-1910) observes Mars' canals
The Congress of Berlin to discuss the Berlin Question ends with Treaty of Berlin; Greece declares war on Turkey Anti-Socialist Law enacted in Germany	Electric street lighting is introduced in London First European crematorium established at Gotha, Germany Paris World Exhibition	Martin Buber, Austrian-Jewish philosopher, born (died 1965) German historian Heinrich Treitschke begins racial anti-Semite movement, and Berlin court preacher Adolf Stoecker founds Christlich-Soziale Arbeiterpartei	David Hughes invents the microphone First use of iodoform as an antiseptic Mannlicher produces repeater rifle
Joseph Stalin, Russian Communist dictator, born (died 1953) Leon Trotsky, Russian Communist leader, born (died 1940) Peace signed with Zulu chiefs	Australian frozen meat on sale in London British churchman W.L. Blackley (1836-1902) proposes a scheme for old-age pensions The public granted unrestricted admission to the British Museum	Anti-Jesuit Laws introduced in France Mary Baker Eddy becomes pastor of Church of Christ Scientist, Boston Henry George: PROGRESS AND POVERTY	Albert Einstein, German physicist, 1921 Nobel Prize, born (died 1955) Fahlberg and Remser discover saccharin London's first telephone exchange established

YEAR	CHEKHOV & THEATRE	DRAMA & LETTERS	MUSIC & OPERA	GRAPHIC & PLASTIC ARTS
1880	Chekhov passes examinations for 1st year: School of Medicine	Dostoyevski: THE BROTHERS KARAMAZOV Lew Wallace: BEN HUR Zola: NANA	Ernest Bloch, Swiss-American composer, born (died 1959) Gilbert and Sullivan: THE PIRATES OF PENZANCE London Guildhall School of Music founded	Cologne Cathedral completed (begun 1248) Renoir: "Place Clichy" Rodin: "The Thinker," sculpture
1881	Chekhov reviews performances of Sarah Bernhardt at the Grand Theatre	Dostoyevski dies (born 1821) The first of all cabarets, "Chat Noir," Paris, founded by Rudolphe Salis	Moussorgsky dies (born 1835) Bela Bartok, Hungarian composer, born (died 1945) Brahms: ACADEMIC FESTIVAL OVERTURE, Op. 80, Breslau	Pablo Picasso born (died 1973) Monet: "Sunshine and Snow," painting
1882	Chekhov finishes 3rd year of medical study	Robert Louis Stevenson: TREASURE ISLAND Becque: LES CORBEAUX Ibsen: AN ENEMY OF THE PEOPLE	Igor Stravinsky, Russian composer, born (died 1971) Tchaikovsky: 1812 OVERTURE Rimsky-Korsakov: THE SNOW MAIDEN, opera, St. Petersburg	Georges Braque, French painter, born (died 1963) Cezanne: "Self-Portrait" Samuel Goldwyn, Hollywood film producer, born (died 1974)
1883	Eugene V. Vakhtangov, Soviet actor and director, is born	Ivan Turgenev, Russian novelist, dies (born 1818) Bjornson: BEYOND HUMAN ENDURANCE	Metropolitan Opera House, New York, opened Delibes: LAKME, opera, Paris Richard Wagner, German opera composer, dies (born 1813)	Walter Gropius, German-American architect, born (died 1969) Edouard Manet, French artist, dies (born 1833)
1884	Chekhov finishes his medical studies on July 25	Mark Twain: HUCKLEBERRY FINN Ibsen THE WILD DUCK Sienkiewicz: WITH FIRE AND SWORD, Polish historical novel	Brahms: Symphony No. 3 in F major, Op. 90 Bruckner: Symphony No. 7, Leipzig Massenet: MANON, opera, Paris	Seurat: "Une Baignade, Asnieres," painting Rodin: "The Burghers of Calais," sculpture Amedeo Modigliani, Italian painter, born (died 1920)
1885	(Summer) Chekhov at Babkino Estate (catalyst for family of THE CHERRY ORCHARD)	Tolstoi: THE POWER OF DARKNESS Richard Burton: THE ARABIAN NIGHTS Zola: GERMINAL	Anna Pavlova, Russian ballet dancer, born (died 1931) Strauss: THE GYPSY BARON, operetta, Vienna Gilbert and Sullivan: THE MIKADO, London	Van Gogh: "The Potato Eaters" Cezanne: "Mont Sainte-Victoire"

RUSSIA/USSR AND THE WORLD	MUNDANE EVENTS	CHURCH & THOUGHT	KNOWLEDGE & INVENTION
France annexes Tahiti Pacific War: Chile against Bolivia and Peru (-1884) J.A. Garfield elected President of the U.S.	Carnegie develops first large steel furnace New York streets are first lit by electricity Railroad mileage in operation: U.S. 87,800; Great Britain 17,900; France 16,400; Russia 12,200	John Claird: PHILOSOPHY OF RELIGION Helen Keller, American deaf and blind educator, born (died 1968) Oswald Spengler, German philosopher, born (died 1936)	T.A. Edison and J.W. Swan independently devise the first practical electric lights Pasteur discovers a chicken cholera vaccine
James A. Garfield inaugurated as 20th President of the U.S.; he is shot and killed in September; succeeded by Vice President Chester Arthur	Freedom of press established in France St. Gotthard Tunnel completed (begun 1872)	Persecution of Jews in Russia Vatican archives opened to scholars	Canadian Pacific Railway Company founded Natural History Museum, South Kensington, London, opened
U.S. bans Chinese immigrants for 10 years The British occupy Cairo	World Exhibition in Moscow London Chamber of Commerce established Bank of Japan founded	Bakunin: GOD AND THE STATE Charles Darwin dies (born 1809)	Edison designs first hydroelectric plant, Appleton, Wisconsin English Engineer Hiram S. Maxim patents recoil-operated machine gun
Reform of U.S. Civil Service begins	Bismarck introduces sickness insurance in Germany The first skyscraper built in Chicago, 10 stories Orient Express, Paris-Istanbul makes its first run	Nietzsche: THUS SPAKE ZARATHUSTRA Fabian society founded in London	Robert Koch describes a method of preventive inoculation against anthrax
Germans occupy South-West Africa Grover Cleveland elected U.S. President Eduard Benes, Czech statesman, born (died 1948)	"Le Matin," Paris, issued Gold discovered in the Transvaal, rise of Johannesburg	Kropotkin: PAROLES D'UN REVOLTE G.B. Shaw becomes a member of the Fabian Society Divorce reestablished in France	Ilya Mechnikov: THEORY OF PHAGOCYTES German physician Arthur Nicolaier (1862-1934) discovers tetanus bacillus Sir Charles Parsons invents first practical steam turbine engine
The Mahdi takes Khartoum; General Gordon killed in the fighting; British evacuate Sudan; death of Mahdi Germany annexes Tanganyika and Zanzibar	First Leipzig Fair First English electrical tram car in Blackpool John M. Fox of Philadelphia introduces golf to America	Karl Marx: DAS KAPITAL VOL. 2 Tolstoy: MY RELIGION Henry Maine: POPULAR GOVERNMENT	George Eastman manufactures coated photographic paper Sir Francis Galton proves the individuality of fingerprints Pasteur devises a rabies vaccine to cure hydrophobia

YEAR	CHEKHOV & THEATRE	DRAMA & LETTERS	MUSIC & OPERA	GRAPHIC & PLASTIC ARTS
1886		Rimbaud: LES IL-LUMINATIONS Henry James: THE BOSTONIANS Alexander Ostrovski, Russian Dramatist, dies, (born 1823)	Franz Liszt, Hungarian composer, dies (born 1811) Wilhelm Furtwangler, German conductor, born (died 1954) Charles Mustel of Paris invents the celesta	Seurat: "Sunday Afternoon on the Grande Jatte," painting Statue of Liberty dedicated Rodin: "The Kiss," sculpture
1887	(November 19) Opening performance: IVANOV, Moscow	Antoine founds the Theatre Libre in Paris Strindberg: THE FATHER, drama Sir Arthur Conan Doyle: A STUDY IN SCAR-LET, the first Sherlock Holmes story	Aleksandr Borodin, Russian composer, dies (born 1834) Verdi: OTELLO, opera, Milan Ignace Paderewski gives his first recital in Vienna	Alexander Archipenko, Russian sculptor, born (died 1964) Marc Chagall, Russian painter who worked in the U.S. and France, born Le Corbusier (C.E. Jeaneret), Swiss architect, born (died 1965)
1888	(February 19) One-act play, SWAN SONG, staged (March) STEPPE, a long story, published (October 28) One-act play, BEAR, staged Chekhov writes one-act farce, PROPOSAL Society of Art and Literature is founded in Moscow	Kipling: PLAIN TALES FROM THE HILLS T.S. Eliot, Anglo-American poet, 1948 Nobel Prize, born (died 1965) Eugene O'Neill, American dramatist, born (died 1953)	Tchaikovsky: Symphony No. 5, St. Petersburg Rimsky-Korsakov: SHEREZADE, Op. 35, symphonic suite, St. Petersburg Irving Berlin , American composer, born	Van Gogh: "The Yellow Chair" Toulouse-Lautrec: "Place Clichy"
1889	(January 31) IVANOV staged, Petersburg Chekhov elected to: Society of Russian Dramatic Writers One-act plays: A TRAGEDIAN IN SPITE OF HIMSELF; WEDDING (December 27) Play, WOOD DEMON, performed: Moscow THE USURPERS OF THE LAW, by Pissemsky is presented by the Society of Art and Literature	Bjornson: IN GOD'S WAY Gerhart Hauptmann: VOR SONNENAUF-GANG, German social drama Charles Chaplin, English-born film actor, born	Cesar Franck: Symphony in D major Richard Strauss: DON JUAN, symphonic poem, Weimar Gilbert and Sullivan: THE GONDOLIERS, London	Van Gogh: "Landscape with Cypress Tree," painting Alexander Gustave Eiffel (1832-1923) designs the 1,056-foot-high Eiffel Tower for the Paris World Exhibition

RUSSIA/USSR AND THE WORLD	MUNDANE EVENTS	CHURCH & THOUGHT	KNOWLEDGE & INVENTION
British Prime Minister W.E. Gladstone introduces bill for Home Rule in Ireland King Louis II of Bavaria dies (born 1845) First Indian National Congress meets	American Federation Labor founded Canadian Pacific Railway completed British School of Archaeology opens at Athens	Karl Marx: DAS KAPITAL, published in English Andrew Carnegie: TRIUMPHANT DEMOCRACY Richard von Krafft-Ebing: PSYCHOPATHIA SEXUALIS	Charles M. Hall (American) and P.L.T. Heroult (French) independently produce aluminum by electrolysis Hydroelectric installations are begun at Niagara Falls Pasteur Institute, Paris founded
Queen Victoria celebrates her Golden Jubilee Union Indo-Chinoise organized by France Chiang Kai-shek, Chinese general and statesman, born	L.L. Zamenhof (1859-1917) devises "Esperanto" Alfred Krupp, German industrialist, dies (born 1812)	Sir Thomas More (1478-1535) beatified by Pope Leo XIII (canonized 1935)	Phenacetin, an analgesic drug, discovered Emil Berliner improves the phonograph's sound quality H.W. Goodwin invents celluloid film
German Emperor William I succeeded by his son William II, the "Kaiser" (1918) Suez Canal convention Benjamin Harrison elected President of the U.S.	"The Financial Times," London, first published Fridtjof Nansen leads an exploring party across Greenland on snowshoes	James Bryce: THE AMERICAN COMMONWEALTH G.J. Romanes: MENTAL EVOLUTION IN MAN	Nikola A. Tesla constructs electric motor (manufactured by George Westinghouse) George Eastman perfects "Kodak" box camera J.B. Dunlop invents pneumatic tire
North Dakota, South Dakota, Montana, and Washington become states of the U.S.; Oklahoma is opened to non-Indian settlement Adolf Hitler, Nazi dictator, born (died 1945)	The first May Day celebration, Paris French Panama Canal Company bankrupt Punch card system created by H. Hollerith	T.H. Huxley: AGNOSTICISM Martin Heidegger, German philosopher, born (died 1969)	Von Mehring and Minkowski prove that the pancreas secretes insulin, preventing diabetes Frederick Abel invents cordite

YEAR	CHEKHOV & THEATRE	DRAMA & LETTERS	MUSIC & OPERA	GRAPHIC & PLASTIC ARTS
1890	Chekhov's trip via Siberia to Sakhalin	Tolstoi: THE KREUTZER SONATA Ibsen: HEDDA GABLER Knut Hamsun: HUNGER	Borodin: PRINCE IGOR, opera, St. Petersburg Tchaikovsky: QUEEN OF SPADES, opera, St. Petersburg Richard Strauss: TOD UND VERKLARUNG	Cézanne: "The Cardplayers," painting Vincent Van Gogh dies (born 1853)
1891	Chekhov sees Duse in Shakespeare's ANTHONY AND CLEOPATRA, Petersburg Stories published: DUEL; DREARY STORY Tommaso Salvini, Italian actor, appears at Imperial Great Theatre in OTHELLO	Ilya Ehrenburg, Russian author, born (died 1967) Shaw: QUINTESSENCE OF IBSENISM J.T. Grein founds Independent Theatre Society, London	Sergei Prokofiev, Russian composer, born (died 1953) Rachmaninoff finishes the first version of his Piano Concerto No. 1 (revised 1917) Gustav Mahler: Symphony No. 1	Henri Toulouse-Lautrec produces his first music hall posters Gauguin settles in Tahiti Van Gogh exhibits at the salon des Independents
1892	GRASSHOPPER appears WARD NO. 6	Walt Whitman dies (born 1819) Ibsen: THE MASTER BUILDER Bernard Shaw: MRS. WARREN'S PROFESSION	Tchaikovsky: THE NUTCRACKER, ballet, St. Petersburg Leoncavallo: I PAGLIACCI, opera, Milan Dvořák becomes director of New York National Conservatory of Music	Monet begins his series of pictures on the Rouen Cathedral Toulouse-Lautrec: "At the Moulin Rouge," painting
1893	TALE OF AN UNKNOWN MAN	Pinero: THE SECOND MRS. TANQUERAY Wilde: A WOMAN OF NO IMPORTANCE Ernst Toller, German dramatist, born (died 1939)	Tchaikovsky dies (born 1840) Tchaikovsky: Symphony No. 6 ("Pathetique"), Op. 74 Verdi: FALSTAFF, opera, Milan	"Art Nouveau" appears in Europe George Grosz, German painter, born (died 1959)
1894	(January) BLACK MONK (June 30) Yuri Alexandrovich Zavadski, Soviet actor and stage director, is born	Edison opens his Kinetoscope Parlor, New York Bernard Shaw: ARMS AND THE MAN George du Maurier: TRILBY, novel	Anton Rubinstein, Russian composer and pianist, dies (born 1829) Sibelius: FINLANDIA Debussy: L'APRESMIDI D'UN FAUNE	Gustave Caillebotte's collection of impressionist paintings rejected by the Musée Luxembourg, Paris Degas: "Femme a sa toilette," painting

363

RUSSIA/USSR AND THE WORLD	MUNDANE EVENTS	CHURCH & THOUGHT	KNOWLEDGE & INVENTION
V.M. Molotov, Russian statesman, born German Social Democrats adopt Marxist program at Erfurt Congress Swiss government introduces social insurance	The first entirely steel-framed building erected in Chicago Global influenza epidemics	J.F. Frazer: THE GOLDEN BOUGH William James: THE PRINCIPLES OF PSYCHOLOGY Heinrich Schliemann, German archaeologist, dies (born 1822)	Rubber gloves are used for the first time in surgery, Johns Hopkins Hospital, Baltimore Emil von Behring announces the discovery of antitoxins
Trans-Siberian Railway was begun Franco-Russian entente Young Turk Movement, hoping to secure liberal reforms, is formed in Geneva Triple Alliance - Germany, Austria, Italy- renewed for 12 years	Widespread famine in Russia In Java, Dutch anthropologist Eugene Dubois discovers Pithecanthropus erectus (Java Man)	R.W. Church: HISTORY OF THE OXFORD MOVEMENT	Beginnings of wireless telegraphy Trans-Siberian railroad construction begins (1917)
Witte is named Russian Minister of Finance Grover Cleveland elected U.S. President Tito, Yugoslav statesman, born	Iron and steel workers strike in U.S. Cape-Johannesburg railroad completed First cans of pineapples	F.J. Romanes: DARWIN AND AFTER DARWIN Emile Faguet: POLITIQUES ET MORALISTES DU DIX-NEUVIEME SIECLE	First automatic telephone switchboard introduced C.F. Cross and E.J. Bevan discover viscose (manufacture of rayon) Diesel patents his internal-combustion engine
Franco-Russian alliance signed Independent Labour Party formed France acquires protectorate over Laos	Imperial Institute, South Kensington, London, founded Manchester Ship Canal completed	F.H. Bradley: APPEARANCE AND REALITY	Karl Benz constructs his four-wheel car J.M. Charcot, French psychiatrist, dies (born 1825) Henry Ford builds his first car
German-Russian commercial treaty Nikita Khrushchev, Russian statesman, born (died 1971) Czar Alexander III dies; succeeded by his son Nicholas II (1917)	Death duties (inheritance tax) introduced in Britain Baron de Coubertin founds committee to organize modern Olympic Games	Benjamin Kidd: SOCIAL REVOLUTION Sidney and Beatrice Webb: HISTORY OF TRADE UNIONISM	Louis Lumière (1862-1948) invents the cinematograph Berliner uses a horizontal gramophone disc instead of a cylinder as a record for sound reproduction Flagstaff Observatory erected, Arizona, U.S.

YEAR	CHEKHOV & THEATRE	DRAMA & LETTERS	MUSIC & OPERA	GRAPHIC & PLASTIC ARTS
1895	A long story: THREE YEARS	Sienkiewicz: QUO VADIS H.G. Wells: THE TIME MACHINE First public film show in Paris, at the Hotel Scribe	Tchaikovsky: SWAN LAKE, ballet, St. Petersburg Richard Strauss: TILL EULENSPIEGEL'S MERRY PRANKS, symphonic poem, Cologne Robert Newman arranges the first Promenade Concerts at Queen's Hall, London; conductor: Henry J. Wood	"Revolt of the Weavers," three prints by Kathe Kollwitz (1898)
1896	Chekhov involved in building new school house in Talezh Chekhov arranges hot meals for poor students A long story: MY LIFE (October) SEAGULL performed: Petersburg	Chekhov: THE SEA GULL, Russian drama John Dos Passos, American novelist, born Harriet Beecher Stowe, American novelist, dies (born 1811)	Richard Strauss: ALSO SPRACH ZARATHUSTRA, symphonic poem, Frankfurt Puccini: LA BOHEME, opera, Turin Giordano: ANDREA CHENIER, opera, Milan	National Portrait Gallery, London, moved from Bethnal Green to Westminster "Die Jugend" and "Simplicissimus," two important German art magazines, appear in Munich
1897	(January) Chekhov meets Stanislavski, who had played in his BEAR Chekhov, a worker for the national census Long story: PEASANTS Stanislavski meets with Nemirovich-Danchenko to discuss possibility of founding MXAT	Joseph Conrad: THE NIGGER OF THE NARCISSUS H.G. Wells: THE INVISIBLE MAN Shaw: CANDIDA	Johannes Brahms dies (born 1833) Gustav Mahler becomes conductor of the Vienna Opera	"Katzenjammer Kids," first American comic strip, begun by Rudolph Dirks Henri "Le Douanier" Rousseau (1844-1910): "Sleeping Gypsy," painting Sir Henry Tate donates Tate Gallery, London to the British people
1898	Chekhov vacations in Nice, France Yalta (1898-1900) Chekhov completes four short stories Rachmaninoff sends Chekhov a composition inspired by his tale, "On the Road" (October 14) Moscow Art Theatre opens (MXAT) (December 17) At MXAT first performance of SEAGULL	Lewis Carroll, author of ALICE IN WONDERLAND dies (born 1832) Bertolt Brecht, German writer, born (died 1956) Shaw: CAESAR AND CLEOPATRA	Paul Robeson, Negro bass singer, born Toscanini appears at La Scala, Milan	Felicien Rops, Belgian painter, dies (born 1833) The Mackintosh School of Art in Glasgow

RUSSIA/USSR AND THE WORLD	MUNDANE EVENTS	CHURCH & THOUGHT	KNOWLEDGE & INVENTION
Cuba fights Spain for its independence Armenians massacred in Turkey Chinese defeated by Japanese at Wei-hai-Wei	King C. Gillette invents the safety razor Kiel Canal, Germany, opened First U.S. Open Golf Championship held	Karl Marx: DAS KAPITAL, VOL. 3 London School of Economics and Political Science founded	Wilhelm Rontgen discovers x-rays Sigmund Freud: STUDIEN UBER HYSTERIE Constantin Isiolkovski formulates the principle of rocket reaction propulsion
The Chinese concede a strip of land for the building of the Trans-Siberian Railroad across Manchuria Czar Nicholas II visits Paris and London Shah of Persia assassinated	First modern Olympics held in Athens Beginning of Klondike gold rush, Bonanza Creek, Canada	Henri Bergson: MATIERE ET MEMOIRE Five annual Nobel Prizes established for those who during the preceding year shall have conferred the greatest benefits on mankind in the fields of physics, physiology and medicine, chemistry, literature, and peace	William Ramsay discovers helium Alfred Nobel dies (born 1833) French physicist A.H. Becquerel discovers radioactivity
Russia occupies Port Arthur William McKinley inaugurated as President of the U.S. Germany occupies Kiaochow, North China	Severe famine in India World Exhibition at Brussels Queen Victoria's Diamond Jubilee	Sidney and Beatrice Webb: INDUSTRIAL DEMOCRACY Havelock Ellis: STUDIES IN THE PSYCHOLOGY OF SEX (-1928)	Ronald Ross discovers malaria bacillus J.J. Thomson discovers electron
China leases Port Arthur in the Yellow Sea, giving Russia a warm water port unimpeded by winter ice. Port Arthur is also connected by railway to the main Trans-Siberian line U.S. declares war on Spain over Cuba "The Boxers," an anti-foreign, anti-Western organization formed in China	Photographs first taken utilizing artificial light Paris Metro opened	Bismarck: REFLECTIONS AND MEMOIRS	The Japanese bacteriologist Shiga discovers dysentery bacillus Pierre and Marie Curie discover radium and polonium German Count Ferdinand von Zeppelin builds his airship

YEAR	CHEKHOV & THEATRE	DRAMA & LETTERS	MUSIC & OPERA	GRAPHIC & PLASTIC ARTS
1899	Gorky and Chekhov meet for first time Olga Knipper visits Chekhov at Yalta (October 26) First performance of UNCLE VANYA (MXAT)	Tolstoi: RESURRECTION Oscar Wilde: THE IMPORTANCE OF BEING EARNEST Pinero: TRELAWNY OF THE WELLS	Elgar: ENIGMA VARIATIONS Sibelius: Symphony No. 1 in E minor Richard Strauss: EIN HELDENLEBEN, symphonic poem, Frankfurt	Giovanni Segantini, Italian painter, dies (born 1858) Alfred Sisley, French painter, dies (born 1839)
1900	IN THE RAVINE, a long story, published For MXAT, Chekhov reads THREE SISTERS October 24, THE ENEMY OF THE PEOPLE (MXAT) Stanislavski makes journey to the Crimea to visit Anton Pavlovich	Maxim Gorky: THREE PEOPLE Tolstoi: THE LIVING CORPSE Anton Chekhov: UNCLE VANYA Theodore Dreiser: SISTER CARRIE	Kurt Weill, German composer, born (died 1950) Gustave Charpentier: LOUISE, opera, Paris Puccini: TOSCA, opera, Rome	Wallace Collection, London, opened Picasso: "Le Moulin de la Galette," painting Film: CINDERELLA, directed by Georges Melies
1901	Chekhov and Olga Knipper marry January 31, THREE SISTERS (MXAT)	Thomas Mann: BUDDENBROOKS	J.M. Barrie : QUALITY STREET, play Frank Norris: THE OCTOPUS, American novel	Gauguin: "The Gold in Their Bodies," painting Walt Disney, film producer, born (died 1966) Apicolysis Blue Period (1905)
1902	Chekhov revises ON THE HARMFULNESS OF TOBACCO, a one-act play November 5, THE POWER OF DARKNESS (MXAT) December 18, THE LOWER DEPTHS (MXAT)	Chekhov: THREE SISTERS Maxim Gorky: THE LOWER DEPTHS, novel Merezhkovski: LEONARDO DA VINCI, biographic novel	Debussy: PELLEAS ET MELISANDE, opera, Paris Sibelius: Symphony No. 2 Enrico Caruso makes his first phonograph recording	Monet: "Waterloo Bridge" Slevogt: portrait of the singer Francesco d'Andrade as Don Giovanni Film: SALOME (Oskar Messter)

RUSSIA/USSR AND THE WORLD	MUNDANE EVENTS	CHURCH & THOUGHT	KNOWLEDGE & INVENTION
First Peace Conference at The Hague Dreyfus pardoned by presidential decree Germany secures Baghdad Railroad contract	London borough councils established	John Dewey: SCHOOL AND SOCIETY H.S. Chamberlain: THE FOUNDATIONS OF THE NINETEENTH CENTURY	Rutherford discovers alpha and beta rays in radioactive atoms First magnetic recording of sound
Boxer risings in China against Europeans The Commonwealth of Australia created William McKinley, 25th President of the U.S., reelected	German Civil Law Code comes in force The Cake Walk becomes the most fashionable dance World Exhibition in Paris	Shintoism reinstated in Japan against Buddhist influence Sigmund Freud: THE INTERPRETATION OF DREAMS Wilhelm Wundt: COMPARATIVE PSYCHOLOGY	F.E. Dorn discovers radon American scientist R.A. Fessenden transmits human speech via radio waves Arthur Evans's excavations in Crete: discovery of Minoan culture (1908)
Cuba Convention makes the country a U.S. protectorate Prince Ito of Japan in St. Petersburg seeking concessions in Korea; negotiations end without agreement Social Revolutionary Party founded in Russia	Trans-Siberian Railroad reaches Port Arthur Oil drilling begins in Persia First British submarine launched	Rudolf Steiner founds anthroposophy Rabindranath Tagore founds his Santiniketan school (Bengal)	Max Planck: LAWS OF RADIATION The hormone adrenalin first isolated Enrico Fermi, Italian physicist, 1938 Nobel Prize, born (died 1954)
Leon Trotsky escapes from a Siberian prison and settles in London Coal strike in U.S., May-October U.S. acquires perpetual control over Panama Canal	Aswan Dam opened Casualties in Boer War: 5,774 British and 4,000 Boers killed	William James: THE VARIETIES OF RELIGIOUS EXPERIENCE Benedetto Croce: PHILOSOPHY OF THE SPIRIT Werner Sombart: MODERN CAPITALISM	American neurological surgeon H.W. Cushing begins study of pituitary body Adolf Miethe invents panchromatic plate

YEAR	CHEKHOV & THEATRE	DRAMA & LETTERS	MUSIC & OPERA	GRAPHIC & PLASTIC ARTS
1903	Chekhov completes short story, BETROTHED Chekhov tells Stanislavski title of new play: THE CHERRY ORCHARD Chekhov returns to Yalta to complete THE CHERRY ORCHARD (September) Chekhov finishes first draft of THE CHERRY ORCHARD February 24, THE PILLARS OF SOCIETY (MXAT) October 2, JULIUS CAESAR (MXAT)	Shaw: MAN AND SUPERMAN Nobel Prize for Literature: Bjornsterne Bjornson (Norwegian) Jack London: THE CALL OF THE WILD, novel	Delius: SEA DRIFT Oscar Hammerstein builds the Manhattan Opera House, New York First recording of an opera: Verdi's ERNANI	James Whistler, Anglo-American painter dies (born 1834) Film: THE GREAT TRAIN ROBBERY (longest film to date: 12 minutes) Camille Pissarro, French painter, dies (born 1830)
1904	(January 17) Premier, at MXAT, of THE CHERRY ORCHARD October 19, IVANOV (MXAT) (July 2) Anton Chekhov dies (born 1860)	James Barrie: PETER PAN Abbey Theatre, Dublin, founded	Puccini: MADAME BUTTERFLY, opera, Milan Victor Herbert: MLLE. MODISTE, operetta, New York Leos Janacek: JENUFA, opera, Brno	Picasso: "The Two Sisters," painting Henri Rousseau: "The Wedding"

RUSSIA/USSR AND THE WORLD	MUNDANE EVENTS	CHURCH & THOUGHT	KNOWLEDGE & INVENTION
Alaskan frontier is settled At its London Congress the Russian Social Democratic Party splits into Mensheviks (led by Plechanoff) and Bolsheviks (led by Lenin and Trotsky)	Motor-car regulations in Britain set a 20 mile-per-hour speed limit Emmeline Pankhurst founds National Women's Social and Political Union Henry Ford, with capital of $100,000 founds the Ford Motor Company	G.E. Moore: PRINCIPIA ETHICA Anti-Jewish pogroms in Russia Henri Poincare: SCIENCE AND HYPOTHESIS	Orville and Wilbur Wright successfully fly a powered airplane R.A. Zsignondy invents the ultramicroscope Wilhelm Einthoven invents the electrocardiograph
Japan began hostilities directed against Russia Theodore Roosevelt wins U.S. presidential election	10-hour work day established in France Paris Conference on white slave trade Broadway subway opened in New York First trenches used in Russo-Japanese war	Church and state separated in France Lafcadio Hearn (1850-1904): JAPAN: AN ATTEMPT AT INTERPRETATION Freud: THE PSYCHOPATHOLOGY OF EVERYDAY LIFE	W.C. Gorgas eradicates yellow fever in Panama Canal Zone Work begins on the Panama Canal Marie Curie: RECHERCHES SUR LES SUBSTANCES RADIOACTIVES

Original 1904 Cast of Cherry Orchard Director: C. Stanislavski

Lyubov Ranyevsky - Olga Knipper-Chekhova[1]

Anya - M. Lilina

Gayev - K. Stanislavski

Varya - Savitskya

Lopakhin - L. Leonidov

Trofimov - V. Kachalov

Simeonov-Pischik - Gribuniro

Charlotta - Muratova

Yepikhodov - Ivan Moskvin

Dunyasha - Kahlutina

Firs - A. Artem

Yasha - Alexandrov

Cast directed by Yuri Zavadski in Acts One and Four

Lyubov Ranyevsky - Margaret Draper

Anya - Patricia Peardon

Gayev - Frederick Rolf

Varya - Joy Dillingham

Lopakhin - Bill Berger

Trofimov - Robert Stattel

Simeonov-Pischik - Graham Jarvis

Charlotta Ivanovna - Elena Karam

Yepikhodov - Niels Miller

Dunyasha - Annette Hunt

Firs - Eugene Wood

Yasha - Stephen A. Daley

---

[1]   On a late MXAT Recording, Chekhov's widow is re-creating her role as the first Lyubov.

Cast of IASTA's Denver Festival Production
Director: John D. Mitchell

Lyubov Ranyevsky - Muriel Higgins

Anya - Deborah Gordon

Gayev - Jack Eddleman

Varya - Miriam Mitchell

Lopakhin - Michael Durrell

Trofimov - Roger Stuart Newman

Simeonov-Pischik - Stephen A. Daley

Charlotta Ivanovna - Miriam Porter

Yepikhodov - Peter Blaxill

Dunyasha - Elaine Winters

Firs - William Whedbee

Yasha - Eric Tavares

Cast for recording by the Moscow Art Theatre

Lyubov Ranyevsky - Olga Knipper-Chekhova

Anya - Angelina Stepanova[2]

Gayev - V. Ershov

Varya - L. Koreneva

Lopakhin - S. Blinnikov

Trofimov - V. Orlov

Simeonov-Pischik - M. Kedrov

Charlotta Ivanovna - S. Khalyutnia

Yepikhodov - V. Topokov

Dunyasha - O. Androvskaya

Firs - Vladimir Popov

Yasha - Alexei Gribov

---

2   As is characteristic of repertory theatre as an institution with continuity, as an actor ages, he or she moves into appropriate roles: e.g., in 1965, in New York City, Stepanova played the role of Charlotta.

Cast of Cherry Orchard - 1965 Production, New York City Center

Lyubov Ranyevsky - Alla Tarassova

Anya - Larissa Kachanova

Gayev - Pavel Massalsky

Varya - Tatiana Lennikova

Lopakhin - Mikhail Zimin

Trofimov - Leonid Gubanov

Simeonov-Pischik - Mikhail Yanshin

Charlotta Ivanovna - Angelina Stepanova

Yepikhodov - Alexander Lomissarov

Dunyasha - Klementia Rostovtseva

Firs - Alexei Gribov

Yasha - Yuri Leonidov

Selected Bibliography

Barraclough, Geoffrey, editor, **The Times Atlas Of World History (Revised Edition)**. Maplewood, New Jersey: Hammond, Incorporated, 1983.

Chekhov, A. P., **Plays 1887-1903** (Text in Russian.) Moscow: 1962.

Emeljanow, Victor, editor, **Chekhov: The Critical Heritage**. London: Routledge & Kegan Paul, 1981.

Gorchakov, Nikolai M., **Stanislavsky Directs**, Foreword by Norris Houghton, translated by Miriam Golina. New York: Limelight Editions, 1985.

Houghton, Norris, **Moscow Rehearsals**. New York: Harcourt, Brace and Company, 1936.

Houghton, Norris, **Return Engagement**. New York: Holt Reinhart and Winston, 1962.

Mitchell, John D., **Theatre: The Search For Style.** Midland, Michigan: Northwood Institute Press, 1982.

Mitchell, John D., **1959 Theatre Research: England, Germany, France, Sweden, USSR, Japan**, 4 Vols. (Available to scholars at the Institute for the Advanced Studies in Theatrical Arts, 12 West End Avenue, New York City, New York, 10023; Northwestern University, School of Speech, Evanston, Illinois.)

Nemirovitch-Dantcheko, **My Life in the Russian Theatre**, translated by John Cournos. London: Geoffrey Bles, 1937.

Preobrazhensky, A. G., **Etymological Dictionary of the Russian Language.** New York: Columbia University Press, 1964.

Pritchett, V. S., **Chekhov: A Spirit Set Free**. New York: Random House, 1988.

Simmons, Ernest J., **Chekhov: A Biography**. Boston: Little, Brown and Company, 1962.

Stanislavaki, Constantin, **Creating A Role**, translated by Elizabeth Reynolds Hapgood. New York: Theatre Arts Books, 1961.

Stanislavski, Constantin, **My Life In Art**, translated by J. J. Robbins. London: Eyre Methuen, 1980.

Styan, J. L., **Chekhov In Performance: A Commentary On The Plays**. Cambridge University Press, 1988.

Troyat, Henri, **Chekhov**, translated by Michael Henry Heim. London: Hamish Hamilton Paperback, 1988.

Walsh, Warren Bartlett, **Russia and the Soviet Union: A Modern History**. Ann Arbor: University of Michigan Press 1958.

Worrall, Nickolas, **Modernism to Realism on the Soviet Stage: Tairov, Vakhtangov-Oklopkhov.** London: Cambridge University Press.

OTHER MATERIALS AVAILABLE FROM IASTA

Films - Videocassettes - Books

FILMS

All films are in 16mm and are available on VHS or Beta videocassette.

ASPECTS OF THE CLASSIC GREEK THEATRE, 13 minutes.

EURIPIDES' LIFE AND TIMES: THE TROJAN WOMEN, 38 minutes.

ROMAN COMEDY, PT.I, 22 minutes. Scenes from Plautus' **Amphitryon** and Shakespeare's **A Comedy of Errors**.

ROMAN COMEDY, PT.II, 24 minutes. Scenes from Terence's **Phormio** and Molière's **Scapin**.

ITALY: ORGINS OF THE THEATRE TO PIRANDELLO, 20 minutes.

MEDIEVAL THEATRE, 16 minutes.

ASPECTS OF THE COMMEDIA DELL'ARTE, 14 minutes.

THE GREEN BIRD, 35 minutes. Carlo Gozzi's *commedia dell'arte* classic.

SHAKESPEARE'S THEATRE AND MACBETH, 16 minutes.

SHAKESPEARE'S KING LEAR AND THE MIDDLE AGES, 31 minutes.

SHAKESPEARE AND WEBSTER: JACOBEAN ENGLAND, 33 minutes.

PARABLES OF POWER, PT. I: SHAKESPEARE'S HENRY VIII, 40 minutes.

PARABLES OF POWER, PT. II: MARLOWE'S EDWARD II, 45 minutes.

PARABLES OF POWER, PT. III: MARLOWE'S TAMBURLAINE AND DR. FAUSTUS, 50 minutes.

THE SPANISH GOLDEN AGE OF THEATRE, PT. I, 38 minutes. Scenes from Lopé de Vega's **Knight from Olmedo**.

THE SPANISH GOLDEN AGE OF THEATRE, PT. II, 26 minutes. Scenes from Calderón de la Barca's **Phantom Lady**.

MOLIÈRE AND THE COMEDIE FRANÇAISE, 17 minutes.

ASPECTS OF THE NEO-CLASSIC THEATRE, 13 minutes. Scenes from Racine's **Phèdre**.

SHERIDAN'S 18TH CENTURY ENGLAND, PT. I, 33 minutes. Scenes from **The Rivals**.

SHERIDAN'S 18TH CENTURY ENGLAND, PT. II, 36 minutes. Scenes from **The School for Scandal**.

ASPECTS OF THE 18TH CENTURY COMEDY, 12 minutes.Congreve and Marivaux.

PARIS AND THE 19TH CENTURY NOVELISTS, 26 minutes. Balzac, Flaubert, Dumas, Stendhal, Hugo, George Sands, Zola.

IBSEN'S LIFE AND TIMES, PT. I: YOUTH AND SELF-IMPOSED EXILE, 28 mintues.

IBSEN'S LIFE AND TIMES, PT. II: THE LATER YEARS, 24 minutes.

ENGLAND'S WRITERS OF THE 19TH CENTURY, 36 minutes. (Wordsworth, Byron, the Brownings, Keats, Shelley, Wilde, Tennyson.)
GEORGE BERNARD SHAW AND HIS TIMES, 35 mintues.
IRISH THEATRE & JUNO AND THE PAYCOCK, 16 minutes.
CHEKHOV AND THE MOSCOW ART THEATRE, 13 minutes.

ASIAN THEATRE FILMS

SANSKRIT DRAMA, 14 minutes.
THE STYLE OF THE CLASSIC JAPANESE NOH THEATRE, 17 minutes.
ASPECTS OF THE KABUKI THEATRE OF JAPAN, 12 minutes.
ASPECTS OF THE PEKING OPERA, 15 minutes.
MARTIAL ARTS OF PEKING OPERA, 12 minutes. (B&W)

FOREIGN LANGUAGE FILMS

GERMAN THEATRE: BRECHT & SCHILLER, 16 minutes. (German soundtrack.)
PARIS AND THE 19TH CENTURY NOVELISTS, 26 minutes. (French soundtrack.)
THE SPANISH GOLDEN AGE OF THEATRE, 13 minutes. (Spanish soundtrack.)

OTHER BOOKS BY THE AUTHOR
Published by Northwood Press

THEATRE: THE SEARCH FOR STYLE
ACTORS TALK: ABOUT STYLES OF ACTING
THE GREEN BIRD
THE FOX CAT (Substituted for the Crown Prince)
MACBETH UNJINXED
JEAN RACINE'S PHÈDRE ON STAGE
MAKING A BROADWAY MUSICAL, MAKING IT RUN: An Anatomy of Entrepreneurship
STAGING A SPANISH CLASSIC: THE HOUSE OF FOOLS

ORDERS AND INQUIRIES

The Institute for Advanced Studies in the Theatre Arts (IASTA)
12 West End Avenue, Room 304
New York, NY 10023 (212) 581-3133
Toll Free Number (Outside New York)
1-800-843-8334

Photo Credits

Cover photo - courtesy of Frederick Rolf
p. ix - courtesy of Frederick Rolf
p. xiii - courtesy of Frederick Rolf
pp. 121, 122 - Alix Jeffry
p. 123, Alix Jeffry, courtesy of Margaret Draper
p.124, top and bottom - University of Denver, Richard W. Purdie
pp.125, 126 - courtesy of the Moscow Arts Theatre
pp. 203, 204 - University of Denver, Richard W. Purdie
p. 273 - courtesy of the author
p. 274 - courtesy of the Moscow Arts Theatre
p. 341 - University of Denver, Richard W. Purdie
p. 343 - Alix Jeffry, courtesy of Margaret Draper
p. 344 - Alix Jeffry
Back cover - Martha Swope